PASS THE BAR!

Library of Congress Cataloging-in-Publication Data

Riebe, Denise.
Pass the bar / by Denise Riebe, Michael Hunter Schwartz.
   p. cm.
Includes bibliographical references and index.
   ISBN 1-59460-165-8 (alk. paper)
1. Bar examinations--United States.   I. Schwartz, Michael Hunter. II. Title.
   KF303.R54 2006
   340.076--dc22   2005034209

CAROLINA ACADEMIC PRESS
700 Kent Street
Durham, North Carolina 27701
Telephone (919) 489-7486
Fax (919) 493-5668
www.cap-press.com

Printed in the United States of America
Cover Illustration: Bruno Budrovic © images.com/Veer

PASS THE BAR!

Denise Riebe

DUKE UNIVERSITY SCHOOL OF LAW

Michael Hunter Schwartz

CHARLESTON SCHOOL OF LAW

CAROLINA ACADEMIC PRESS
Durham, North Carolina

CONTENTS

APPENDICES

ACKNOWLEDGEMENTS

This text reflects a forty-year journey, between the two of us, in the legal profession: becoming lawyers, practicing law, teaching at law schools, and working with law students. We feel grateful that we've had such interesting and fulfilling career experiences, and that our paths intersected (by coincidence, over the Internet) to produce this text as collaborators. We would like to thank the numerous individuals and institutions that have supported us as individuals as well as the publication of this text.

Professor Riebe

It's fascinating to witness a variety of professional and life experiences merge to produce a text such as *Pass the Bar!* I'm grateful for the widespread support I've received for this project, and I'd like to thank everyone who has supported my efforts.

Thanks first to my family: my husband, Mike, and our wonderful daughters, Elizabeth and Hannah. It's my hope that Elizabeth and Hannah will both become engaged learners whose lives are enriched by life-long learning, and that they'll find in their careers the level of satisfaction I've experienced coaching students.

Second, thanks to my extended family: my mother and father, Duane and Ruth Daggett; my second set of parents, Ken and Elaine Riebe; my siblings, Dave Daggett, Dawn Brackmann, Danielle Shealy, and Darci Grady, and their families; and Ann Robertson, Coleen Miller, and Chris McLeod, three amazing women who have had a significant impact on my life.

Third, I wish to thank my professional mentors and colleagues. I am fortunate to live in an area with several excellent law schools, and especially fortunate to have the opportunity to teach at two of them: Duke University School of Law in Durham, North Carolina, and the University of North Carolina School of Law ("UNC") in Chapel Hill, North Carolina.

I would like to thank my Duke colleagues for their encouragement and support: Professor Sara Beale, Professor Tom Metzloff, Dean Theresa Newman, Dean Jill Miller, Dean Bruce Elvin, Professor Diane Dimond, Professor Hans Linnartz, Professor Sarah Ludington, Professor Joan Magat, Professor JoAnn Ragazzo, and my assistant, Eileen Wojciechowski.

Also, thanks to my UNC colleagues. Professor Ruth Ann McKinney at UNC is the person who first recommended that I write a book about the bar exam. She is an immensely wise woman, was my first and most influential mentor, and is a wonderful colleague and friend. I also thank my other colleagues at UNC who have supported my professional efforts: Dean Gail Agrawal, Dean Slyvia Novinsky, and Professor Bobbi Boyd.

Next, I thank my coauthor, Michael Schwartz, an incredibly caring and talented professional who is deeply committed to academic success and who has a positive effect on all those with whom he interacts. I feel fortunate that I met you, am grateful that you were willing to be my collaborator, and thank you for teaching me so much about educational theory.

Finally, I thank my students—the reason I teach. I'm grateful to have worked with many bright, enthusiastic, and energetic students who I am confident will make significant contributions during their legal careers. Special thanks to my students who have taken the time to read and edit the manuscript for our text: Brian Berman, Jeff Goldman, Chris Hart, Heather Howard, Matt Leerberg, Alyssa Rower, and Britt Whitesell. I'm confident they'll pass the bar as well as set new ones in their legal careers.

Professor Schwartz

The opportunity to write a set of acknowledgements daunts me because of the difficulty of including everyone who has influenced my life and work. But I also enjoy the process because it gives me perspective. So, here goes.

Thanks to my wife Stacey, who is not only the best editor I know but is also the best advisor, wife, friend, and person I know. Every time I have listened to you, good things have happened. I hope I keep paying attention. Thanks also to my daughters, Kendra and Samantha; you inspire me in every way—to try to be the best father, teacher, and man I can be.

I thank my mom, Alice Gokkes, for teaching me to care so much about the people who mean something to me and my father, Albert Schwartz, whose model of how to be a spouse, a father, and a man I have adopted without reserve. I also thank my siblings, Jackie, Terry, Gail, and Steve and my stepfather, Harry, for supporting me and my career, even when my career caused me to move 3,000 miles away.

Thanks also go in many professional directions. Thanks to my former colleagues at Western State University School of Law; I know of no faculty that is more committed to the success of its students. In particular, I thank Susan Keller, whom I still regard as a mentor and the legal thinker I hope someday to be. Her insights into legal learning in general and about the bar exam in particular influence me in ways so numerous and varied that I can no longer trace all of them.

Thanks also to my new colleagues at Charleston School of Law. I feel lucky to be joining a group I admire so much. Thanks also to three deans, Dennis Honabach, one of the smartest people I have ever met, Maryann Jones, one of the most dedicated and hardest-working people in legal education, and Richard Gershon, for whom I'd gladly work at any job.

Professional (and personal) thanks also are due Professor Jan Heck, who started me on the path that has given me a career I never anticipated. I also wish to acknowledge the professional and personal inspiration of Professors Gerry Hess, Vernellia Randall, Paula Lustbader, Alice Thomas, Ruth Ann McKinney, Barbara Glesner-Fines, Sophie Sparrow, Carole Buckner, Roy Stuckey, Laura Rovner, Larry Krieger, and Justine Dunlap.

Thanks also to my many students over my thirteen years in teaching. I remain amazed to be paid to have the opportunity to teach and learn from you.

Finally, thanks to my coauthor and friend, Denise Riebe. I greatly admire your insight, intelligence, thoughtfulness, and diligence, and I greatly value your kindness, sense of humor, patience, and wonderful listening skills.

Professors Riebe and Schwartz

We thank all of the professors working in academic success programs at law schools across the nation, an incredibly dedicated group of professionals who have a positive impact in the lives of thousands of law students. Since we undertook writing this text, we've had widespread support from academic success professionals—including colleagues we've met at conferences and others we've never met in person who have sent us e-mails congratulating us on our publication contract and expressing their interest in our work.

We extend special thanks to two of these professional colleagues who volunteered to review our text before publication: Nancy Luebbert, Director of the Academic Support Program at the University of Idaho College of Law in Moscow, Idaho, and Emmeline Reeves, Associate Professor for Academic Success at the University of Richmond School of Law in Richmond, Virginia.

We also thank our publisher, Carolina Academic Press, our primary contact, Robert Conrow, Jennifer Gilchrist, and Erin Ehman for making the publication of our text a reality.

Further, we thank the Law School Admissions Council ("LSAC") and the American Bar Association ("ABA"). As organizations, both the LSAC and the ABA have recognized the obligation that legal educators have to assist students in passing their bar exams and becoming practicing lawyers, and the link between bar passage efforts and student recruitment, retention, placement, and increasing the diversity of our profession. We especially thank Kent Lollis, Associate Executive Director and Assistant to the President for Minority Affairs at the LSAC, a committed professional who spearheads numerous projects to increase the effectiveness of legal education and to increase the diversity of the profession.

—Denise Riebe
—Michael Hunter Schwartz
August 2005

FOREWORD

Once in awhile, the perfect book comes along at the perfect time. *Pass the Bar!* is just such a book, arriving at an ideal time to help law students and legal educators get a grip on how to maximize each student's chance for success on the bar exam in the jurisdiction of his or her choice.

In their Introduction, the authors accurately refer to the bar exam as the "last hurdle" in a student's quest to become a licensed attorney. The approach the authors take to help a student clear this hurdle is both logical and powerful, and would immediately enhance any bar taker's chances of success. Beginning with critical background information about the application and examination process, the book moves to foundational educational principles that will increase the student's ability to learn effectively, and then to concrete strategies each student can use profitably to approach multiple-choice, essay, and performance questions with confidence. While this book would be useful at any point in a student's legal education, it would be particularly valuable to rising third-year law students who are facing the reality of a bar exam within a year.

Each chapter contains core concepts that are followed by reflection questions and hands-on exercises that pull the reader into the subject at hand. These questions and exercises turn what might otherwise be an overwhelming sea of information into useful knowledge that is personally meaningful to each reader. Rooted in active learning principles, the book could easily be used as a self-instructional guide by individual students seeking answers to their bar exam questions.

And while the book is an empowering self-instructional tool, it lends itself equally well to use in a group or classroom setting. For many learning styles, there is strength in numbers. The synergy created by a group of students who choose to go through the chapters together, or in a classroom led by an experienced law professor, would enhance the learning of each group participant. In any case, the tone of the book is so congenial and the information so accessible that each reader—whether working in a group or working alone—will develop a sense of personal engagement with the authors throughout the book.

The powerful impact of this book's logical structure should come as no surprise. The authors are experienced legal educators with shared expertise in bar preparation and legal learning. After graduating with honors and law review credentials from Wake Forest University School of Law, Professor Denise Riebe began her career practicing in an international law firm and then became the regional director for a commercial bar review company. Later, she moved into legal education, earning high student praise as an adjunct professor here at the University of North Carolina School of Law before moving to a position at Duke University School of Law. Professor Michael Hunter Schwartz has been a law professor for over thirteen years and has specific expertise in law student learning and law school teaching. Recently, he published *Expert Learning for*

Law Students, a book that has its roots in self-regulated learning theory and in his practical expertise as director of the STELLAR™ law student program at Western State University College of Law in Fullerton, California, a highly successful academic support and bar preparation program.

Pass the Bar! gives every law student—and every legal educator working with students—a tool that can be used to help students clear the last hurdle in the race they began when they started law school. Rather than facing that hurdle uncertain and alone, any student can now approach this challenge with confidence and with a coach by his or her side. It is a book I will recommend happily to generations of students as they gather their energy to cross the finish line in this important and challenging race.

—Professor Ruth Ann McKinney

Director, The Writing & Learning Resources Center

The University of North Carolina School of Law

Chapel Hill, North Carolina

PREFACE

The time for your bar exam—the final hurdle for obtaining your law license and becoming a licensed attorney—is drawing near. If you're like most students, you're feeling some apprehension about, and aren't looking forward to, the bar exam—and for good reason: there's a lot at stake! The good news is that by understanding the bar review and bar exam process, making strategic studying decisions, and following a smart study plan, you can pass the bar. That's what this book will help you do.

So, what do we know? And why should you believe that we can help you pass the bar?

Professor Riebe's first contact with a bar exam was taking—and passing!—the Virginia bar exam in 1986. After practicing for two years with a large, international firm, she moved to North Carolina and sat for—and passed!—the North Carolina bar exam. Then she became the North Carolina Director for Bar/Bri, a national bar review company.

In her role as the North Carolina Director of Bar/Bri, she inevitably met students who were unsuccessful on their bar exams. (We've yet to see a one hundred percent passage rate in any state.) Her heart went out to these students. After thousands of dollars and years of time invested in becoming attorneys, these students were devastated by their failure to pass their final hurdle to becoming licensed. Perhaps even more painful, it was a public failure—fellow students, friends, families, and employers all knew that these students, consistently high achievers, had "failed."

Professor Riebe wanted to know what differentiated passers and "repeaters" (those failing their exams who would need to take the exams again), and she felt a personal obligation to help those who used her company's products.

In 1994, she started informally meeting and talking with repeaters, debriefing them about their bar exam experiences, and trying to diagnose why they weren't successful in passing their bar exams. She also started helping repeaters prepare to take the bar a second time—explaining the process and helping them with study plans and essay writing. And it worked. Despite the low passage rates that repeaters face,[1] a high percentage of the repeaters with whom she worked passed the bar on their next attempt.

Professor Riebe eventually left her job with Bar/Bri to teach at the University of North Carolina School of Law in Chapel Hill, North Carolina ("UNC"). At UNC, she had another opportunity to work with repeaters when the Director of the law school's

---

1. Students repeating bar exams have significantly lower passage rates than first-time takers. *See* National Conference of Bar Examiners, *2004 Statistics*, THE BAR EXAMINER 10–12 (May 2005), *available at* www.ncbex.org/pubs/pdf/740205_2004statistics.pdf. For example, here are a few comparisons of passage rates for first-time takers and repeaters for the July 2004 bar exam: Alabama, 86% compared to 17%; Georgia, 87% compared to 29%; Michigan, 76% compared to 28%; and Maryland, 73% compared to 23%. *Id.* at 10–11.

Writing and Learning Resources Center invited her to help coach a group of students who were repeating their bar exams. At the same time, she started a consulting and coaching company, Pass the Bar!®, to provide individualized services to students preparing for bar exams.

Through her experiences with bar review courses, bar exams, consulting, and coaching students, Professor Riebe has developed a good sense of what separates passers from repeaters, and consequently what it takes to pass the bar. Since bar examiners keep most test results confidential, and usually only repeaters have a right to review their exams, her perspective is necessarily based on her first-hand experience. Her personal experience has been that, in most cases, not much separates passers and repeaters— just a little more work, information, or focus. What a shame, she thought, not to provide an early heads-up to save students the pain and price of failing.

Fortunately, the law schools where she teaches—she's now a Senior Lecturing Fellow at Duke University School of Law in Durham, North Carolina, and still an adjunct professor at UNC's School of Law—allow her to teach bar exam workshops to third-year students so they can start preparing themselves for the bar exam before their bar review courses begin.

Professor Schwartz also passed a bar exam on the first try—the dreaded California bar exam. He then practiced law for four years before becoming a law professor. He has taught law for thirteen years now, teaching many subjects that appear on bar exams (agency, contracts, corporations, criminal law, and remedies).

Six years ago, Professor Schwartz assumed responsibility for the academic support and bar passage programs at Western State University College of Law in Fullerton, California ("Western State"). He was drawn to this work by his interest in learning and his heartfelt belief that law school and bar passage failures are the result of curable problems, not lack of ability. Some of the curable problems include inappropriate study strategies, insufficient persistence, inadequate time management, inadequate stress management, insufficient motivation, and lack of self-confidence.

Accordingly, Professor Schwartz designed and implemented programs at Western State aimed at increasing his law school's bar passage rate while reducing its academic attrition ("flunk-out") rate. These programs have proven successful: even though student-entrance credentials did not change, and the first-year attrition rate decreased by 67.5%, approximately 35% more students passed their bar exams on their first attempts than had done so in the past.[2]

Professor Schwartz has also written extensively in the areas of law school teaching and learning methodology.[3] His book, *Expert Learning for Law Students*, is designed to

---

2. When Professor Schwartz took over Western State's academic support and bar passage programs, the law school's bar passage rate was hovering around 34% (29% at its lowest point). Since then, the law school's passage rate has steadily climbed (with the exception of some February bar exam deviations) as follows: 34% (July 2001), 43% (Feb. 2002), 44% (July 2002), 41% (Feb. 2003), 46% (July 2003), 40% (Feb. 2004), and 49% (July 2004).

3. *See, e.g.*, Michael Hunter Schwartz, Expert Learning For Law Students (2005); Michael Hunter Schwartz, *Teaching Law Students to Be Self-Regulated Learners*, 2003 Mich. St. D.C.L. L. Rev. 447; Michael Hunter Schwartz, *Teaching Law By Design: How Learning Theory and Instructional Design Can Inform and Reform Law Teaching*, 38 San Diego L. Rev. 347 (2001). Professor Schwartz is also a member of the Steering Committee for the Clinical Legal Education Association's monograph on legal education, *The Best Practices of Law Schools for Preparing Students to Practice Law* (forthcoming 2006).

teach first-year law students to learn successfully.[4] In recent years, he has also given presentations about teaching and learning research to law faculties and at conferences across the country.

By sharing our expertise relating to research about how students learn and the bar exam process, we hope this book will help you maximize your chances of passing your bar exam. Specifically, our intent is to help you understand the bar review and bar exam process, develop realistic expectations about the process, and develop an individualized plan for success.

Although we designed this book to help you maximize your chances of success on your bar exam, passing your exam is up to you. It requires your own personal commitment to making your bar review and exam a priority. It's up to you to take on and tackle this process, and your level of motivation will be a primary factor in your success.

In addition to your level of motivation, your success will be determined by both your aptitude and level of optimism.[5] Research demonstrates that aptitude is an imperfect predictor of success; pessimists drop below their potential and optimists exceed theirs.[6] Thus, your level of optimism will be a key factor determining your success. Fortunately, as chapter 3 explains, optimism is a factor that you can completely control.

If you're committed to doing the best you can to succeed on your bar exam, where do you start and where do you go? Here's how we recommend you use this book: first, skim through the table of contents to obtain an understanding of its structure and topics covered. Then, read chapter 1 and look over the action plan checklists in chapter 2. Note which time frame you're in, and do the checklist items for that time frame. (Make sure to refer to the corresponding chapters because the checklists are just shorthand lists of items you need to accomplish).

Then, continue to proceed through the book. You'll notice that we've included many checklists and exercises throughout. We urge you to use them to integrate the information you've read. Educational research demonstrates that you'll be a more successful learner if you take the time to integrate information with active learning techniques like the ones we've provided throughout this text.[7]

Note that, as you work through this book, you'll likely find that many of the points made seem elementary. That's great, but please do not disregard them. Many students who are unsuccessful on their bar exams realize, in hindsight, that they've failed to understand fundamental points. One of our goals is to ensure that you understand the bar review and exam process on the front end—so that you don't miss any of the fundamental points that many students who fail their bar exams overlook.

Finally, remember: if you can get into and graduate from law school, you, too, can pass the bar! Whether you will is up to you.

GOOD LUCK!

---

4. Professor Schwartz's self-regulated learning book and articles have been required readings at law schools across the country, including Cleveland-Marshall College of Law in Cleveland, Ohio; Michigan State University College of Law in East Lansing, Michigan; University of Dayton School of Law in Dayton, Ohio; University of the District of Columbia David A. Clarke School of Law in Washington, D.C.; and Western State.

5. Martin E.P. Seligman, Learned Optimism 137, 154 (2d ed. 1998).

6. *Id.*

7. *E.g.*, Alan K. Lerner, *Law & Lawyering in the Work Place: Building Better Lawyers by Teaching Students to Exercise Critical Judgment as Creative Problem Solvers*, 32 Akron L. Rev. 107, 116 (1999).

PASS THE BAR!

PART ONE

BAR EXAM
PRELIMINARIES

CHAPTER 1

WHAT ARE "BAR EXAMS" AND WHY ARE THEY SO HARD?

Bar Exams

What is a "bar exam"? The short answer is: a test you have to take and pass in order to get licensed to practice law.[1] That answer raises another question: What is the "practice of law"? The "practice of law" means providing clients legal advice—in other words, advising clients how the law will apply to their specific factual situations.

Just like other professions—for example, medicine, dentistry, and architecture—if you want to practice law, you must obtain a license to do so. Practicing law without a license constitutes the unauthorized practice of law and is unlawful.

What kind of test is a bar exam? Some people say, "a test is a test is a test"—and, yes, that's true to an extent. But, the bar exam is also unique and unlike other tests you've taken so far in your academic career. You don't take a bar exam to achieve an academic credential. Rather, the purpose of taking a bar exam is to obtain a license to practice law. Thus, the good news is that, if you don't want to practice law, you don't need to put yourself through the time and expense of taking a bar exam unless you have another personal reason for doing so.[2]

In addition, unlike other academic tests you've taken, the bar exam is a rite of passage.[3] The experience is also a test of endurance and perseverance.

Bar exams are the vehicle bar examiners use to guarantee a minimum level of competence in the legal profession. Bar examiners are not trying to exclude you or anyone

---

1. The term "bar exam" originated in English legal practice. In England, a barrister is "called to the bar." Richard Cabrera, *Working to Improve: A Plan of Action for Improving the Bar Exam Pass Rate*, 27 Wm. Mitchell L. Rev. 1169, 1169 n.1 (2000). Written bar exams in the United States date back to 1855 when Massachusetts became the first state to have a written exam. Robert M. Jarvis, *An Anecdotal History of the Bar Exam*, 9 Geo. J. Legal Ethics 359, 374 (1996).

2. For example, some students decide to take a bar exam because they want a sense of closure or to have flexible career options.

3. *See, e.g.*, Jarvis, *supra* note 1, at 381; Loretta Walder, Pass This Bar: A Readiness Guide For Bar Exam Preparation 3 (1982).

else from the profession; they only want to uphold their duty to the public to ensure that those holding licenses to practice law are competent to do so.[4]

Accordingly, when you take a bar exam your goal is to demonstrate to your audience—the examiners—that you're competent to practice law (unlike law school exams where your goal is to show your audience—your professors—that you've mastered the law that they've taught you over the course of a semester).

Because law licenses and bar exams are state-specific, each state's bar exam is unique. Despite their differences, though, bar exams are remarkably similar. As chapter 5 explains, almost all states' exams include the National Conference of Bar Examiners ("NCBE") Multistate Bar Exam ("MBE")[5] and Multistate Professional Responsibility Exam ("MPRE").[6] All states use essay questions (either state-created essays or the Multistate Essay Exam ("MEE")),[7] and many include performance tests that require exam takers to perform fundamental lawyering skills such as writing memoranda, writing persuasive briefs, drafting contract terms, preparing pleadings, and drafting discovery.[8]

Why Bar Exams Are Hard

We're sure you've heard many stories about bar exams—including that bar exams are "hard." Accordingly, most students have some level of apprehension about studying for and taking their bar exams. Typical responses range from "this is the last way in the world I want to spend my summer" to fear, dread, anxiety, and panic attacks.

It's true; bar exams are hard. Successful bar takers usually devote more than six hundred hours to bar preparation, memorizing countless rules of law, practicing thousands of multiple-choice questions, and writing practice essays.

So, why do professional students with long records of academic success find the bar exam hard? Bar exam questions aren't really any more difficult than the questions used on law school exams. Indeed, many students believe the questions on bar exams are easier than those on law school exams because they tend to be more concrete and less theoretical than law school exam questions.[9]

---

4. *See, e.g.*, Cabrera, *supra* note 1, at 1172; Society of American Law Teachers, *Society of American Law Teachers Statement on the Bar Exam*, 52 J. Legal Educ. 446, 447 (2002); State Board of Bar Examiners, *How the Bar Exam is Written and Graded*, 9 Nev. Lawyer 26, 26 (2001).

5. *See* NCBE, The Multistate Bar Exam 2005 Information Booklet, *available at* www.ncbex.org/tests/Test%20Booklets/MBE_IB2005.pdf. The MBE is a nationally designed two-hundred question, multiple-choice test encompassing six doctrinal areas: contracts (including sales), torts, real property, evidence, criminal law and procedure, and constitutional law. *Id.* at 11.

6. *See* NCBE, The Multistate Professional Responsibility Exam 2005 Information Booklet, *available at* www.ncbex.org/tests/Test%20Booklets/MPRE_IB2005.pdf. The MPRE is a nationally designed sixty-question, multiple-choice test focusing on professional responsibility law. *Id.* at 31–32.

7. *See* NCBE, The Multistate Essay Exam 2005 Information Booklet, *available at* www.ncbex.org/tests/Test%20Booklets/MEE_IB2005.pdf.

8. The NCBE Multistate Performance Test ("MPT") is an example of a performance test. *See* Ncbe, The Multistate Performance Test 2005 Information Booklet, *available at* www.ncbex.org/tests/Test%20Booklets/MPT_IB2005.pdf.

9. For example, see the sample essay questions in chapter 15 and on the NCBE Web site, www.ncbex.org (last visited May 7, 2005).

Moreover, most law students have a "reading week" before their exams at the end of each semester during which they must master three to five subjects they just started learning from scratch fourteen weeks earlier at the beginning of their semester. In contrast, bar exam takers have approximately ten weeks after graduation to master subjects that, for the most part, they've already been exposed to while in law school.

There are three primary reasons that bar exams are hard:[10]

1. **The stakes:** Your license to practice law and your legal career are at stake. You've put a lot of time, money, and energy into law school, making this final hurdle a crucial one. Additionally, friends, loved ones, and employers are expecting you to pass the bar exam. That said, please remember that bar exams are not "do or die"; there are plenty of attorneys who didn't initially pass their bar exams, have taken the exams again, and have gone on to have outstanding legal careers.[11]

2. **The time pressure:** You'll likely feel time pressure while studying for the bar exam and taking the exam itself. While studying for the bar, you need to review your entire law school career—and, for many students, review some courses you haven't taken in law school, too. Bar review courses move at a pace of approximately one semester's course per day! During the exam itself, most students also feel time pressure. For example, for the MBE, you need to pace yourself at 1.8 minutes per multiple-choice question for two hundred questions in a single day.

3. **The amount of material covered:** Many students find themselves squeezed by the quantity of material they must master. Depending on how you count and the number of subjects on your state's bar exam, you'll likely need to review at least twenty subjects. Many of the subjects will be tested during a two- or three-day bar exam period. You're used to studying for and then taking a test for one subject at a time—for example, studying evidence and then taking an evidence exam. Your evidence final exam came with a label ("Evidence Final") so the scope of possible issues was confined. Bar exams are more like the practice of law. You're expected to know all the subjects, and any given question may require your answer to address several subjects you've studied.

In sum, yes, bar exams are hard! But, remember: you're an experienced test taker. You've successfully taken exams throughout your entire academic career. Also, bar exam questions are often analytically less complex than those on law school exams and test subjects that, for the most part, you already know. In short, the fact that you got into and graduated from law school means that you have the ability to pass the bar.

---

10. *See* WALDER, *supra* note 3, at 55.

11. *See, e.g.,* Jarvis, *supra* note 1, at 387 (Charles Evans Hughes, who ran for President in 1916 and served as Chief Justice of the United States Supreme Court from 1930–41, failed the New York bar exam seven times).

Reflection Questions

1. What is your greatest concern about taking the bar exam, and how will you deal with that concern?

2. What aspects of the bar exam seem similar to what you've been doing in law school, and what aspects seem different? Do the differences concern you? Why?

3. In what ways are bar exams easier than law school exams?

CHAPTER 2

ACTION PLAN CHECKLISTS

Introduction

Planning is a key to success in any learning context—and critical in the context of the bar exam. Studies across educational disciplines show that students who plan consistently outperform those who fail to plan.[1]

On the next several pages, you'll find a collection of checklists that include the most important things you should do before and during your bar preparation period and your bar exam. The checklists are succinct; for more detailed information, see the referenced chapters.

As you look over these checklists, notice that there are things you should probably be doing right now and possibly even some things you should have already done. Don't let either of these possibilities discourage you. Most of the early tasks can be completed fairly rapidly if you put your mind to it. The key is to start now and take control over your bar exam process. Learning research demonstrates that the more control you assert over your preparation process, the more successful you'll be.[2]

Also notice that each checklist leaves space for you to add items that you want to take care of during each time frame. Before your bar review begins, use this extra space to add any additional tasks you need to complete. After your bar review course begins, any additional tasks you add should be related to preparing for your bar exam.

---

1 *See* Barbara K. Hofer et al., *Teaching College Students to be Self-Regulated Learners, in* SELF-REGULATED LEARNING: FROM TEACHING TO SELF-REFLECTIVE PRACTICE 57, 68 (D.H. Schunk & B. Zimmerman eds., 1998).

2. Barry J. Zimmerman & Andrew S. Paulson, *Self-Monitoring During Collegiate Studying: An Invaluable Tool for Academic Self-Regulation, in* NEW DIRECTIONS IN COLLEGE TEACHING AND LEARNING: UNDERSTANDING SELF-REGULATED LEARNING 65, at 13–14 (Paul R. Pintrich ed., 1995).

Checklist 2-1: Six to Twelve Months Before Your Bar Review Starts

To Do / Notes

❒ Understand the bar review and bar exam process so you can develop realistic expectations and a plan for success (chapters 1–12, 17, 19).

❒ Ask yourself if you want to practice law:
  ○ If not, consider whether you need to take a bar exam (chapter 1).
  ○ If yes, continue.

❒ Decide where you want to practice law (chapter 6):
  ○ If you don't know, consider deferring taking the bar until you know the state in which you'll be practicing.
  ○ If you know where you want to practice, continue.

❒ Find the name and contact information for the licensing entity in your chosen state (chapter 7; appendix B).

❒ Contact the licensing entity and obtain the following information (chapter 7):
  ○ Your state's licensing requirements.
  ○ Registration requirements for the bar exam.
  ○ Deadlines for registering for the bar exam.
  ○ Registration fees for the bar exam.
  ○ Dates and location of the bar exam.
  ○ Format and subjects tested on the bar exam.
  ○ Whether your state requires the Multistate Professional Responsibility Exam ("MPRE"), and, if so, by when you must pass it (chapter 5).
  ○ Rules that govern your state's licensing process.

❒ Mark your calendar to allow plenty of time to fill out your bar exam application and submit it with your application fee, giving yourself at least two weeks more than you think you will need (many students spend forty or more hours!).

❒ If your state requires the MPRE exam, submit an MPRE application with your registration fee six to twelve weeks before you want to take the MPRE (chapter 5).*

❒ If necessary, make hotel arrangements for your bar exam.

---

* You can register for the MPRE online at National Conference of Bar Examiners, *MPRE Registration*, www.ncbex.org/mpre.htm, or The Multistate Professional Responsibility Exam, www.actrs19.act.org/app3/mpre/mpre (last visited May 7, 2005).

❐ Additional plans:

1. _____
2. _____
3. _____
4. _____
5. _____
6. _____

Checklist 2-2: Four to Six Months Before Your Bar Review Starts

| | *To Do / Notes* |

❐ Read your state's licensing rules.

❐ Plan for your bar review period:

○ Assess the degree to which you're at risk for not passing the bar exam (chapter 9).

○ Decide what you need to do to pass the bar exam, including whether you need to do some remedial studying or take a long-term bar review course. *

❐ Make sure you have a winning game plan (chapter 10):

○ Do a time check: review and plan to minimize your commitments (*e.g.*, work, volunteer groups, religious groups, childcare) during your bar review period.

○ Do a financial check: make sure you have enough money set aside to pay your living expenses during your bar review period; if necessary, borrow the money.

○ Do an academic check: review your law school history and the subjects tested in your state to see if there are any subject areas in which you should do remedial studying before your bar review period begins.

○ Transition your writing skills for bar exam essays, developing your own essay writing process and "template" (chapter 15).

○ If your state has a performance test, familiarize yourself with the types of legal documents you may be required to create and adapt your writing skills for those documents (chapter 16).

○ Do a stress/attitude check: think about how you'll stay fresh, positive, and focused during your bar review period (chapter 3).

○ Ask recently licensed attorneys in the state where you're going to take the bar exam for advice about the bar review companies in your state (chapter 8).

❐ Register for a bar review course.

❐ Enjoy your life/last semester of law school!

---

* Most bar review courses are scheduled to begin after students graduate from law school. In some states, bar review companies now offer long-term bar reviews that students begin before graduating from law school.

❏ Additional plans:

1. _____
2. _____
3. _____
4. _____
5. _____
6. _____

Checklist 2-3: One Month Before Your Bar Review Starts

To Do / Notes

❐ Develop a written bar preparation schedule (chapters 11–17) that includes:

   ○ Time to read your bar review outlines.

   ○ Time to attend your bar review classes.

   ○ Time to master the substantive law.

   ○ Time to do practice test questions.

   ○ Time for sleep, exercise, and relaxation.

❐ Contact all the people who are significant to you, explain to them the importance of passing the bar exam and the study time needed (at least fifty hours per week) (chapter 4).

❐ Do at least one thing that you enjoy that you won't have time to do while you're studying for the bar exam.

❐ Remind yourself why you believe you'll pass the bar exam.

❐ Additional plans:

1. _____

2. _____

3. _____

4. _____

5. _____

6. _____

Checklist 2-4: First Eight Weeks of Your Bar Review Period

To Do / Notes

❐ Get into a routine right away, including attending class, studying your bar review outlines, reviewing the material covered in class for reinforcement, and doing practice test questions (chapters 11–17). Strive to at least:

　　○ Do thirty-four Multistate Bar Exam ("MBE") questions every day.

　　○ Do two essay questions per week.

　　○ Do one performance question per week if your state uses the Multistate Performance Test ("MPT") or administers its own performance test.

　　○ Master the doctrine for three subject areas per week.

　　○ Refresh your learning of at least two subjects per week.

❐ Take a scheduled ten-minute break every hour and reward yourself at the end of every day and every week.

❐ Remind yourself why you believe you'll pass the bar exam.

❐ Additional plans:

　　1. _____

　　2. _____

　　3. _____

　　4. _____

　　5. _____

　　6. _____

Checklist 2-5: Last Two Weeks of Your Bar Review Period

To Do / Notes

❒ Confirm that you know where your exam will be administered, how you'll get there, and where you'll park.

❒ Confirm any hotel reservations.

❒ Pack what you need to take with you to the bar exam (*e.g.*, exam admission ticket, photo identification, pens, pencils, watch, tissues, ear plugs).

❒ Plan what you'll eat (go out to lunch or pack a lunch?).

❒ Plan to take layers of clothing along so you can adjust if the exam-room temperature is uncomfortable.

❒ Test your memory of every subject as often as possible and restudy areas of law you cannot recall (chapter 13).

❒ Do just enough practice questions to stay in the flow:

  ○ Thirty-four MBE questions per day in mixed-subject sets.

  ○ Two essay questions each week.

  ○ If your state uses the MPT or administers its own performance test, one practice question per week.

❒ Take care of yourself so that you'll feel fresh for the bar exam:

  ○ Take a scheduled ten-minute break every hour and reward yourself at the end of every day and every week.

  ○ Get some exercise every day.

  ○ Start going to bed early enough to wake up at the time you'll need to wake up for the bar exam.

❒ Do your studying primarily during the same hours you'll be taking the exam so you'll feel comfortable on your exam days.

❒ Plan how you'll manage your stress on your exam days (chapter 3).

❒ Plan how you'll celebrate the end of all your hard work after the bar exam is over.

❒ Remind yourself why you believe you'll pass the bar exam.

❒ Additional plans:

  1. _____

  2. _____

  3. _____

  4. _____

  5. _____

  6. _____

Checklist 2-6: During Your Bar Exam
(Chapter 19)

To Do / Notes

❏ Get plenty of sleep the night before each day of the bar exam.

❏ Arrive early, but be prepared to wait.

❏ Avoid talking with other students about the exam or comparing notes.

❏ Stay focused, use your stress management strategies, and be mentally tough (chapter 3).

❏ Listen to and follow the exam administrators' instructions.

❏ Use your time wisely.

❏ Force yourself to forget each question after you finish each answer; treat each question, as well as each day, as an opportunity to do well.

❏ Remind yourself why you believe you'll pass the bar exam.

❏ Additional plans:

1. _____

2. _____

3. _____

4. _____

5. _____

6. _____

Reflection Questions

1. Have you ever taken a similarly intentional and detailed approach to managing your workload? How did such an approach work for you?

2. Why are students who take control over their workload more successful than those who don't?

3. Does anything on the checklists in this chapter surprise you? Why?

CHAPTER 3

STAYING POSITIVE: INCREASING YOUR LIKELIHOOD OF PASSING YOUR BAR EXAM BY MANAGING YOUR MOOD, ATTITUDE, AND STRESS

Introduction

We have yet to meet or work with a student who hasn't felt some level of anxiety or stress while preparing for and taking a bar exam. In other words, feeling some level of anxiety or stress is "normal."[1]

Looking on the bright side, feeling some level of anxiety or stress can be beneficial! It can serve as motivation to do the hard work that you will need to do. Some days will be worse than others, but as long as you generally are able to keep up with your study schedule, you're likely doing fine. Likewise, most students perform well on their exams despite some level of anxiety or stress.[2]

Common sources of anxiety and stress include the amount of information you need to review, the feeling that you're falling behind with your studying, and knowing what's at stake—your law license. While anxiety and stress are normal, excessive anxiety and stress can cause various symptoms, including difficulty concentrating, fatigue, irritability, depression,[3] fear, interpersonal problems, and moodiness.

---

1. *See, e.g.,* Richard Cabrera, *Working to Improve: A Plan of Action for Improving the Bar Exam Pass Rate,* 27 Wm. Mitchell L. Rev. 1169, 1170 (2000); Robert M. Jarvis, *An Anecdotal History of the Bar Exam,* 9 Geo. J. Legal Ethics 359, 388 (1996) (students suffer considerable stress while preparing for and taking their exams, and then waiting for the results).

2. *See* Loretta Walder, Pass This Bar: A Readiness Guide For Bar Exam Preparation 55 (1982).

3. We're using the term depression as a lay term for feeling down or blue. If you believe you have clinical symptoms of depression, and certainly if you have any thoughts of suicide, see a medical professional immediately. Martin Seligman's book, Learned Optimism (2d ed. 1998), includes a depression test that might be helpful to assess your mood, as well as practical information for treating depression. *Id.* at 59–62, 71–91.

Just because some level of anxiety or stress is "normal," however, doesn't mean that you should endure it. Below is a list of techniques you can use to control your attitude and mood, thereby ensuring you're fresh and at your best as you study and when you sit for your bar exam.

How You Can Control Your Mood, Attitude, and Stress

There are many techniques you can use to manage your mood, attitude, and stress. Read the list below and think about which techniques you've used in the past. Also, make notes about which techniques you think would work well for you.

1. **Take care of yourself.** Eat right, get adequate sleep, exercise, limit your intake of alcohol and caffeine, and refresh yourself in between the hard hours of preparation you're putting in. All of these activities promote self-worth and increase your energy level and stamina.

2. **Vary your routine to avoid boredom and stay fresh.** For example, if you usually study in a library, try going to a different library or a coffee shop for a change of pace. Or, instead of exercising at the end of the day, try exercising during the middle of the day.

3. **Define "success" as doing your personal best.** Avoid focusing on the black/white result of passing or failing the bar exam.[4]

4. **Set mastery-learning goals.** Focus on mastery (for example, "I'll be able to paraphrase all the contract law rules") as opposed to results (for example, "I will get an 'A'" or "I will pass"). An irony of focusing on mastery instead of results is that it'll actually help you do better on the bar exam. A series of educational studies have found that students who set mastery-learning goals get higher grades than those who set results-oriented goals.[5]

5. **Connect with others.** Research shows that social support is a factor that can boost personal well-being.[6] Be aware, though, that seeking support from fellow "sufferers" may be counter-productive—they may be too stressed and irritable to provide beneficial support. If so, seek support from and connection with friends who aren't studying for the bar (but don't expect too much from them: unless they've been through a bar exam, they're unlikely to fully understand or relate to what you're going through).

---

4. *See, e.g.,* John Wooden With Steve Jamison, Wooden: A Lifetime Of Observations And Reflections On And Off The Court 52 (1997). Coach Wooden is the former coach of the record-setting UCLA basketball team, winning ten national championships in twelve years. Coach Wooden stresses that, although there are many factors we cannot control, we can control the effort we give toward doing our best. Accordingly, Coach Wooden defines success as working your hardest to do your personal best. *Id.*

5. *See* Michael Hunter Schwartz, *Teaching Law Students to Be Self-Regulated Learners*, 2003 Mich. St. D.C.L. L. Rev. 447, 479.

6. Martin E.P. Seligman, Learned Optimism 174 (2d ed. 1998).

6. **Take action.** Both planning and studying are ways you can take constructive action to ward off or minimize anxiety and stress.

7. **Take time to relax.** There are many ways to relax; pick something that works for you. We recommend following the guidelines of Dr. Herbert Benson in his best-selling book, *The Relaxation Response.*[7]

Dr. Benson is a researcher and clinical cardiologist at Harvard Medical School who studied what he called the "Relaxation Response," an inducible, physiological state of quietude.[8] Dr. Benson studied how regular elicitation of the Relaxation Response, by focusing one's mind through repetitive mental activities, can prevent—and compensate for damage caused by—anxiety, stress, tension, and nervous reactions.[9]

Two essential components are required to elicit the Relaxation Response: (1) repeating a sound, word, phrase, prayer, or muscular activity; and (2) disregarding everyday thoughts that inevitably come to mind and returning to the repetition.[10] The Relaxation Response can be elicited in a number of different ways—active or still, sitting or standing, silent or singing or chanting.[11] For example, the Relaxation Response can be elicited while doing yoga, swimming, running, biking, meditating, praying, or knitting.[12] The beneficial effects of the Relaxation Response can be achieved by practicing it just once or twice daily for about ten minutes per session.[13]

8. **Think like an optimist.** We use the term "optimist" in the way that Martin Seligman, a leading researcher in the area of positive psychology, uses it in his book, *Learned Optimism.*[14] In short, optimists have a specific explanatory style: they explain failures or setbacks as temporary, affecting just one part of their life, and not as their fault (not permanent, not pervasive, and

---

7. Herbert Benson, The Relaxation Response (2001).

8. *Id.* at xvii.

9. *Id.* Dr. Benson's findings are evidence-based and meet the strict standards of Western scientific medicine—measurability, predictability, and reproducibility. *Id.* at xxxiii. Data incontrovertibly demonstrates that the Relaxation Response technique brings about a set of measurable, reproducible, and predictable physiological changes in the body: a drop in heart rate, metabolic rate, breathing rate, and blood pressure (if elevated to begin with). *Id.* at xvi, xxviii. Further research establishes that the Relaxation Response is effective in treating headaches, cardiac irregularities, premenstrual syndrome, anxiety, depression, allergic skin reactions, asthma, coughs, insomnia, nausea, and side effects of cancer. *Id.* at xix, xli–xlii.

10. *Id.* at xx–xxi.

11. *Id.* at xviii–xxii.

12. *Id.* at xxi–xxii.

13. Note that self-care through use of the Relaxation Response is not a replacement for a balanced approach to medicine, including discussing medical complaints with your personal physician and taking medicine and undergoing medical procedures when warranted. *Id.* at xliii, xlvi. Dr. Benson describes a "sturdy" approach to medicine as a three-legged stool consisting of medications, medical procedures, and self-care. *See id.* at xii. For more information about the Relaxation Response, see other books by Dr. Benson: Beyond The Relaxation Response (1984); Timeless Healing: The Power And Biology Of Belief (1996); and, together with Eileen M. Stuart, The Wellness Book (1992). *See also* Steven Keeva, Transforming Practices: Finding Joy And Satisfaction In The Legal Life (1999) (encouraging relaxation techniques for practicing attorneys).

14. Seligman, *supra* note 6, at 5. Positive psychology is *not* about merely mouthing positive-sounding platitudes (such as "Every day, in every way, I'm getting better and better."). Rather, it focuses on people's explanations of the events in their lives. *Id.*

not personal).[15] Accordingly, optimists are unfazed by setbacks; they view them as challenges and try harder.[16] They stay active and "chipper."[17]

Pessimists, on the other hand, tend to believe bad events will last a long time, will undermine everything they do, and are their own fault (permanent, pervasive, and personal). Not surprisingly, this view leads pessimists to give up more easily, accomplish less, become passive, and get sick and depressed more often.[18]

Seligman asserts that anyone can learn to be optimistic by learning a new explanatory style—specifically, explaining bad events as temporary, impersonal, and only relating to a single aspect of one's life.[19] And, even better, learning this skill takes little time (one hour per week for three months) and can be permanent.[20] Seligman explains his techniques and provides exercises for changing your explanatory style in *Learned Optimism*. In a nutshell, his cognitive approach uses five tactics:[21]

a. Recognize automatic negative thoughts (such as "I can't do it" or "I'm not smart enough") that go through your mind when you feel your worst;

b. Dispute those automatic thoughts by marshalling contrary evidence (such as "I've learned much harder things like future interests");

c. Learn to make different explanations for bad events (bad events are not permanent, not pervasive, and not personal);

d. Distract yourself from negative and obsessive thoughts; and,

e. Learn to recognize and question negative assumptions governing what you do.

In sum, optimists are more likely to succeed with difficult tasks. So, develop the skill of optimism to maximize your chances for success with your bar exam.

9. **Invoke self-efficacy to enhance your likelihood of success.** "Self-efficacy" is the personal belief that you can attain a desired goal (like passing the bar exam!).[22] Having high self-efficacy is empowering. Empirical studies show

---

15. *See id.* at 4–5. Seligman asserts that it's what you think when you fail, not when things go well, that is the central skill of optimism. In addition, optimists use an opposite explanatory style for good events: they are due to their own personal qualities, pervade their lives, and will last a long time (personal, pervasive, permanent). *Id.* at 5.

16. *Id.* at 5.

17. *Id.* at 67.

18. *Id.* at 4–7.

19. *Id.* at 40–51.

20. *Id.* at 75, 90.

21. *Id.* at 89–91.

22. Ruth Ann McKinney, *Depression and Anxiety in Law Students: Are We Part of the Problem and Can We Be Part of the Solution?* 2002 J. Legal Writing Inst. 229, 233 (citing Self-Efficacy, Adaptation, And Adjustment: Theory, Research, And Application 7 (James E. Maddux ed., 1995) [hereinafter Maddux]). The term "self-efficacy" was coined by Albert Bandura in his landmark article, *Self-Efficacy: Toward a Unifying Theory of Behavioral Change*, 84 Psychol. Rev. 191 (1983). Bandura's concept of self-efficacy has become a widely recognized and highly developed construct of human behavior in the field of social psychology. McKinney, *supra*, at 232. As McKinney notes, the literature in the field of social psychology is replete with literally thousands of studies based on Bandura's landmark work in the area of self-efficacy. *Id.* at n.16.

Diagram 3-1: Self-Efficacy

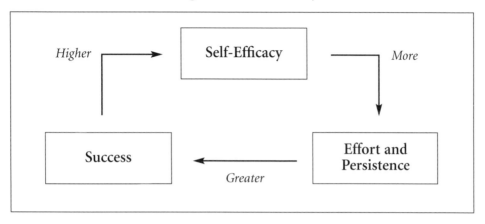

that individuals with high self-efficacy for a task are more likely to engage in behavior necessary to succeed with that task, and to persist when the going gets tough.[23] For example, students with high self-efficacy about their ability to master a subject are far more likely to study efficiently and longer than their less confident peers.[24] In fact, in studies in which researchers induced self-efficacy simply by telling experimental groups of students that they were going to do well, the experimental groups of students significantly outperformed the students in control groups who weren't told anything about how well they'd perform.[25]

Self-efficacy has a powerful influence on your success because it operates cyclically as depicted in diagram 3-1. The higher your level of self-efficacy, the more likely you are to persist when you encounter a learning difficulty. The more you persist, and the more effort you expend, the more likely you are to succeed. Each success in learning will increase your self-efficacy further, which leads to more persistence and effort, and brings even more success.

Developing high self-efficacy about your ability to pass the bar exam will have the same rewarding benefit for you. People develop self-efficacy beliefs through five types of experiences. Use these five types of experiences, listed below, to develop high self-efficacy for passing your bar.[26]

a. **Personal experience.** Recall your success learning a difficult task—it could be something you learned in law school or anything else—for

---

23. McKinney, *supra* note 22, at 234 (citing Maddux, *supra* note 22, at 12–13).

24. *Id.*

25. *See* Martin M. Chemers et al., *Academic Self-Efficacy and First-Year College Student Performance and Adjustment*, 93 J. Educ. Psychol. 55, 55–56 (2001). In contrast, low self-efficacy in relation to specific tasks creates a spiraling effect that significantly reduces students' chances to reach their full potential. Low self-efficacy reduces students' ability to make wise choices about how to achieve goals and their commitment to behaviors that would lead to the successful attainment of the goals. Thus, *regardless of ability level*, students who don't believe they can achieve a goal are far less likely to do so than their peers who believe they can. McKinney, *supra* note 22, at 236 (citing Bandura, *supra* note 22, at 214).

26. McKinney, *supra* note 22, at 237–40.

example, how to play a musical instrument, do calculus, or windsurf. Also, build success by doing practice bar exam questions.

b. **Imagined experience.** Imagine yourself passing the bar exam. Professional athletes frequently use this technique as they're engaged in their sports.

c. **Vicarious experience (modeling).** Identify with previous students you know who've succeeded with the bar exam.

d. **Social feedback.** Get encouragement from someone who knows you and your strengths. It's especially effective to get encouragement from a person with expertise whom you trust—for example, a professor, administrator, or friend who has passed the bar.

e. **Physical and emotional reactions.** If you simply focus on feeling good about your chances on the bar exam, you'll activate thoughts of past accomplishments and increase your belief that you're able to reach your goal of passing. To feel good, attend to details you can control in your study environment—temperature, noise, and privacy—and study when you are relaxed, not pressed for time, and not hungry or tired.[27]

10. **Consider professional help to manage your stress and anxiety.** How do you know if professional help would be appropriate? If you think professional help would be a benefit, then it probably would. In addition, consider seeing a counselor at regular intervals during your bar preparation if you have a history of exam anxiety or current, persistent symptoms of anxiety, stress, or depression.

11. **Reframe negative thoughts into positive ones.** Turn negative thoughts such as, "There's no way I'll ever pass the bar exam," into positive ones such as, "I've aced many exams throughout my academic history; this is just one more."

12. **Use positive reinforcement to your advantage.** Reward yourself every day after you complete your study plan for the day and at the end of every week. Rewards don't have to be big, time-consuming, or expensive. Anything you find pleasant can serve as a reward (for example, a bubble bath, watching a movie, or a half-hour break to read a book).[28] Rewarding yourself routinely will keep your energy high.

13. **Take it one step at a time.** Break overwhelming tasks (passing the bar exam) into manageable chunks (daily and weekly study schedules). Ideal goals are specific, measurable, challenging, and short-term.[29]

14. **Take time to play.** Ten weeks is a long time to work. Adults need time to "play" from time to time to keep their spirits up. Think about the things you do for fun and include some of them each week of this challenging

---

27. *Id.* at 253.

28. Be cautious about using food as a reward. Although it may be effective for some students, it may also induce eating problems. Also, some students feel negative (regretful, depressed) after eating more than they believe they should have.

29. Michael Hunter Schwartz, Expert Learning For Law Students 42–44 (2005).

time. Avoid the use of drugs or excessive alcohol, though, because recuperating from them takes time and energy that you will need to be able to study effectively.

Caution

If you get ill during your preparation period, don't assume that it's caused by bar exam stress. You may actually have a medical problem. See your doctor to rule out a medical problem rather than just trying to push through significant symptoms that are atypical for you.

Be careful taking any medication you haven't taken before — either by self-medicating (not recommended!) or with a professional's prescription. Some medications can cause a hangover effect and others could interfere with your mental processing. Unless you're experiencing extreme symptoms, you're likely better off using techniques like those listed in this chapter to manage your stress and anxiety.

Additional Resources to Help You Stay Positive

Here are some of Professor Riebe's favorite books for boosting your attitude and relieving stress:

- Herbert Benson, *The Relaxation Response* (2001) (also see the Web site for Dr. Benson's Mind/Body Institute at Harvard, www.mbmi.org/default.asp).

- Joel and Michelle Levey, *Living in Balance* (1998).

- Rebecca Merrill, *Living in Yes* (2003) (also see Merrill's Web site, www.lifestructuring.com).

- Martin E.P. Seligman, *Learned Optimism* (2d ed.1998).

- Martin E.P. Seligman, *Authentic Happiness* (2002) (also see Seligman's Web site, www.authentichappiness.com).

Exercise 3-1: Mental State Plan of Action

Recommendation	Implementation Plan
❏ Take care of yourself: eat right, exercise, limit the use of caffeine and alcohol, and get adequate sleep.	I will _____ _____ _____
❏ Vary your routines to avoid boredom and stay fresh.	I will _____ _____ _____
❏ Define "success" as your personal best.	I will _____ _____ _____
❏ Set mastery goals.	I will _____ _____
❏ Connect with others.	I will seek support from _____ _____ _____ _____
❏ Take action—plan and do your studying.	I will _____ _____
❏ Take time to relax.	I will relax by _____ _____ _____
❏ Think like an optimist.	I will _____ _____
❏ Invoke and maintain self-efficacy.	I will remind myself that I'll succeed on the bar exam by _____ _____ _____ _____
❏ Consider professional help.	I will _____ _____
❏ Reframe negative thoughts into positives.	I will _____ _____
❏ Use positive reinforcement.	I will reward myself by _____ _____ _____
❏ Take one step at a time.	I will _____ _____
❏ Take time to play.	I will _____ _____

Exercise 3-2: Self-Refreshment Plan

Take a few minutes to think about what activities are refreshing to you. These activities are ones you should build into your bar preparation plan so that you'll stay fresh and avoid burning out before your bar exam. Check each item that you like to do below, and add your own ideas, too. Then, when you create your individualized study schedule (*see* chapter 17), make sure to integrate a variety of those activities.

- ❐ Going to the movies.

- ❐ Coffee with friends.

- ❐ Shopping.

- ❐ Napping.

- ❐ Exercising.

- ❐ Meditating.

- ❐ Getting outdoors.

- ❐ Hiking.

Fill in more ideas of your own below:

- ❐ _____

- ❐ _____

- ❐ _____

- ❐ _____

- ❐ _____

- ❐ _____

Exercise 3-3: Self-Care Commitment

Take a few minutes to review the techniques examined in this chapter. Think about what techniques would work best for you. Then, make a commitment to use three of the techniques every week to enhance your attitude and mood and manage stress. After each technique you list, provide specific information about when and how you'll integrate the technique into your life.

Example:

Technique: Invoke self-efficacy.

Specifics: I will call Sally (who passed the bar last summer) and see if she'll meet me for coffee and describe to me what she did that helped her pass.

1. Technique: _____

Specifics:

2. Technique: _____

Specifics:

3. Technique: _____

Specifics:

Reflection Questions

1. Why will the recommendations in this chapter about staying positive help you perform better?

2. Which of the recommendations in this chapter have you used before?

3. Why are the recommendations in this chapter (focusing on your mood and attitude) so crucial to your success (given the fact that bar exams test knowledge and skills)?

CHAPTER 4

PREPARING YOUR SIGNIFICANT OTHERS FOR THE BAR EXAM

Introduction

Your significant others play an important role in your efforts to pass the bar exam. They can be a source of support, providing encouragement and a sympathetic ear to help you cope with the stress and workload involved in preparing for the exam. They also can help you study for the bar exam—for example, by running interference with other people who make demands on your time and by helping you memorize the law. Relationship problems with significant others, however, can be a risk factor for *not* passing the bar exam.

We believe that personal relationships are the most important things in our lives and yours. For this reason, we've written this chapter with the hope that you make plans and choices that maximize not merely your chance of passing the bar exam, but also of maintaining your important relationships.

Throughout this text, we emphasize the importance of strategic planning to ensure that you study effectively, meet the licensing requirements necessary to become a member of the state bar, arrive at your bar exam ready to take the exam, manage your stress as you prepare for and take the bar exam, and pass your bar exam.

Similarly, preparing the important people in your life for your bar exam takes strategic planning. As early as possible, inform your significant others about the amount of time and effort required to prepare for the bar exam, why passing the bar is important to you, the amount of stress you'll be under, and your needs while you're studying for the bar exam.

At the end of this chapter you'll find the *PASS THE BAR! Handout for Significant Others*, which we recommend you copy and give to your significant others. The handout is written for people who may not be familiar with the bar review and bar exam process. Taking the time before you start your bar preparation to make sure everyone knows what you'll be doing, why you'll be doing it, and what help you'll need will minimize conflicts later when you are unavailable, tense, and anxious.

The significant others in your life will appreciate that you've taken the time to think through the effect of your actions on them, to explain to them what they should expect from you, and to describe what they can do to help. They'll also be touched that you care about their feelings and your relationships with them. And you'll feel more comfortable and less guilty doing the things you need to be doing.

Although you will likely try to be a "good" spouse, child, parent, sibling, or friend to your significant others, you need to accept the fact that you probably won't be as effective in these roles as you usually are. Most people will understand. Some won't. The key for you will be both accepting your limitations while you're studying for the bar exam and accepting that some people might be unhappy with you.

It's helpful to identify the significant others who are most likely to make unreasonable demands on you during your bar review and exam. Some significant others may ask a lot of you and may have a hard time taking "no" for an answer. Make sure you know who these people are, make sure you carefully explain your time, energy, and emotional constraints to them, and make sure you've thought through how you'll avoid letting them interfere with your bar study. Before you start your bar review, consider giving these people extra time as a sort of send-off. Most of all, give yourself permission to say "no" and to be imperfect.

Things to Explain to Your Significant Others

An important place to start with your significant others is sharing why passing the bar exam is important to you. Unless your significant others have some experience with the licensing process, they may not know that you must pass a bar exam to be able to practice law. Explain the costs of not passing: the cost of taking the exam, the cost of a bar review course, and the income you'll lose if you have to study for the bar exam again instead of working as a lawyer. If you have a job lined up, explain that your new employer expects you to pass the exam and start working as soon as possible. Also explain any additional reasons why passing the bar exam is important to you.

Another issue that often comes up is that the significant others in your life may doubt your need to study hard. Nonlawyers often assume that the point of law school is to prepare you for the bar exam and that additional study between the end of law school and the bar exam is overkill. They may also expect you to have more time for them once you graduate. Explain that the bar exam tests some subjects you didn't study in law school and that law school tests are very different from the bar exam.[1] Consider showing them all your subject outlines and explaining that you need to memorize everything in them. Explain that many successful bar takers have made and memorized thousands of flashcards as part of their bar preparation process.

Also explain that many very smart people don't pass. To help them understand this point, consider sharing your state's bar passage rates.[2] This information will help them understand that graduation from law school doesn't translate to an automatic bar pass and that you'll need to do more hard work.

---

1. For example, many law schools do not use multiple-choice tests whereas the multiple-choice portion of the bar exam is crucial.

2. *See* National Conference of Bar Examiners ("NCBE"), *2004 Statistics*, THE BAR EXAMINER 6–7 (May 2005), *available at* www.ncbex.org/pubs/pdf/740205_2004statistics.pdf. Note that the NCBE Web site contains detailed information about the most recent passage rates in all states. *See id.* at 6–16.

These explanations will help your significant others understand why people who pass the bar work incredibly hard, usually studying for at least six hundred hours for their bar exams. In other words, bar exam study requires more work than a full-time job.

It's also helpful to include your significant others in your planning process. Ask them what you can do so they feel connected to you and what they'd most like you to do to remain connected to them. Then, plan your calendar, including time for your significant others, and share it with them. Let them see how much time you've scheduled for study and when you can spend time with them.

While you're studying for and taking the bar exam, your significant others are likely to notice not only your absence (because you'll be studying a lot), but also the fact that you seem stressed. Having explained to them the time required, the risk of not passing, and the consequences if you don't, they won't be surprised you're stressed. Consider apologizing in advance if you're likely to be grouchier than normal. Also make sure that your significant others understand that you'll try to be your usual self, but you may simply be unable to be as present, helpful, and thoughtful as you usually are.

How Significant Others Can Help

One tool for helping you to avoid personal demands while maintaining personal relationships during your bar preparation is to ask someone to serve as a "point person" for you. A significant other can work well in this role; in fact, you'd be wise to ask the person who deserves the largest amount of your time and attention to be your point person.

The point person's job is to serve as a liaison between you and the other significant people in your life. He or she can run interference with respect to the demands on you that can be postponed, bring to your attention the rare emergency that only you can address, and keep you up to date on what you need to know about what's going on in everyone else's life. Similarly, he or she can keep everyone informed about how you are, how your bar study is going, and everything else that's going on in your life.

Let everyone know who the liaison is and what he or she will be doing. While it is doubtful everyone will like the fact that you've asked someone (and not them, in some cases) to be your liaison, they're likely to prefer that form of contact to being ignored by you altogether.

Your significant others can also help you prepare for the bar examination—for example, by helping you rehearse your memorization of the law. As we explain in chapter 13, one key strategy in passing the bar exam is overlearning the law so that your recall during the bar exam is automatic. For instance, there should be no perceptible delay between the moment you ask yourself what the test for personal jurisdiction is and the moment you recall the minimum contacts test. One way to develop such automatic recall is to "rehearse," which means to practice remembering. Your significant others can help you by testing you with flashcards. By inviting your significant others into your studying process in this way, you can connect with them, make them feel involved and important, and, at the same time, add companionship and variety to your studying process.

Significant others also can help out by taking on tasks of day-to-day living like cooking meals, shopping for groceries, washing dishes, doing laundry, cleaning house, taking care of pets, and paying bills.

In sum, the bar exam doesn't have to do any harm to your important relationships. Most people, once informed, will respect your need for concentrated study. The keys are planning and communication. If you have a good plan and communicate it to your significant others, they can be an important resource during your bar preparation process.

Exercise 4-1: To-Do List to Prepare Your Significant Others

❒ Get together with your significant others and explain:

    ○ Why passing the bar is important to you;

    ○ Why you're at risk for not passing the bar;

    ○ The amount of time and effort required; and

    ○ The stress you'll be experiencing and your likely reactions to it.

❒ Give your significant others this text to skim and the *PASS THE BAR! Handout for Significant Others* to read so that they gain an understanding of what your bar exam is all about and what's involved.

❒ Ask your significant others what they need from you during your bar preparation process so that they can remain connected to and supportive of you.

❒ Develop a bar study calendar, including time for significant others.

❒ Find ways to involve significant others in your bar study, such as by having them test your memorization.

❒ Identify the people in your life who are most likely to interfere with your bar study; make sure you address any possible concerns, and plan how you'll avoid letting such people interfere.

❒ Appoint a point person to run interference, keep in touch, and otherwise serve as a liaison between you and others.

The PASS THE BAR! Handout for Significant Others[*]

If you know someone who will soon be taking the bar exam, this document is for you. This document has been created by two experts on passing the bar exam to help you understand why bar exams are hard (even for students who did well in law school), what is involved in passing the bar exam, and what you can do to help. Significant others can either be a source of help for passing the bar or can create a risk that someone won't pass the bar. We created this handout to help you be in the former category and help the bar taker in your life avoid people in the second category.

Why bar exams are hard:
- They test some subjects students didn't learn in law school.
- They test many of the subjects students learned during law school, but unlike law school exams, bar exams test all the subjects at the same time.
- Their formats are different from law school exam formats.
- They require students to memorize thousands of pieces of information.
- They are necessary for getting a license to practice law and have a reputation for being difficult — facts that put enormous pressure on bar takers.

What's involved in passing the bar exam:
- Studying at least 600 hours.
- Attending dozens of lectures.
- Writing dozens of practice essay answers.
- Completing at least 2,000 practice multiple-choice questions.
- Memorizing thousands of pieces of information.
- Using analytical skills that are difficult to master.
- Managing time to complete all these tasks while making sure to get sufficient sleep, exercise, and nutrition.
- Managing stress so that it doesn't interfere with exam preparation or performance.

What you can do to help a bar taker pass the bar exam:
- Understand the bar review process.
- Avoid making demands on the bar taker during the preparation and exam process.
- Avoid major conflicts and confrontations with the bar taker.
- Be patient and sympathetic if the bar taker seems tense or anxious.
- Be a source of support if the bar taker needs your support.
- Help the bar taker practice recalling the law he or she needs to know by testing the bar taker's memorization.
- Run interference with people who might make demands on the bar taker's time and attention.
- Take on day-to-day tasks for the bar taker, such as doing laundry, cooking, and cleaning.

Reflection Questions

1. Why have we created a handout that you can give to the significant others in your life?

2. Who in your life would make a good point person for you? What will you ask that person to do?

3. Why are planning and communication so important in preparing your significant others for your bar exam?

PART TWO

LICENSING REQUIREMENTS, YOUR BAR EXAM, AND BAR REVIEW COURSES

CHAPTER 5

BAR EXAM COMPONENTS

Introduction

Because each state structures its own bar exam, each state's exam is unique. States usually include similar components in their bar exams, however, so that exams are more similar than different.[1] Whichever state's exam you're taking, your exam likely includes a National Conference of Bar Examiners ("NCBE") component[2] and a state-created component.

NCBE Exams

The NCBE is an entity that creates and administers national bar admission exams. Four different tests created and administered by the NCBE may be incorporated as part of a state's bar exam:

1. **The Multistate Bar Exam ("MBE").** The MBE has been adopted by almost every state as part of its bar exam.[3] The MBE is a two-hundred question, multiple-choice exam. The exam is given in two three-hour

---

1. George A. Riemer, *Bar Exam Migraine: Is a State-Based Bar Exam Obsolete?* 59 Or. St. B. Bull. 29, 29 (1999). *See also, e.g.*, Society of American Law Teachers, *Society of American Law Teachers Statement on the Bar Exam*, 52 J. Legal Educ. 446, 446 n.1 (2002) (exams similar in terms of methods of testing and subjects tested). Some states, however, are considering alternatives to a bar exam. For example, in New Hampshire a state bar committee is considering creating an alternative to the bar exam that would provide applicants the option of creating a portfolio of their work in law school to demonstrate all of the competencies that the state deems necessary to be a lawyer. Michael Hunter Schwartz Interview with Professor Sophie Sparrow, Franklin Pierce Law Center, Concord, New Hampshire (Nov. 2004).

2. The NCBE is a not-for-profit entity formed in 1931 to develop, maintain, and apply uniform standards for admission to the practice of law. NCBE, *About NCBE*, www.ncbex.org (last visited May 7, 2005). As a part of its mission, the NCBE assists bar admission entities by providing standardized exams. *Id.*

3. In 2004, the MBE was used in fifty-three jurisdictions—all states except Louisiana and Washington, plus the additional jurisdictions of the District of Columbia, Guam, Northern Mariana Islands, Palau, and the Virgin Islands. NCBE, *2004 Statistics*, The Bar Examiner 21 (May 2005), *available at* www.ncbex.org/pubs/pdf/740205_2004statistics.pdf [hereinafter *2004 Statistics*]. See the NCBE Web site for a list of jurisdictions that currently use the MBE. *Id.*

segments, with one hundred questions during each segment. Students must pace themselves through the exam at a rate of 1.8 minutes per question.

The MBE is given on the last Wednesday of every February and every July. States usually schedule the rest of their bar exams on either the Tuesday or Thursday (or both) of those same weeks so they can give the MBE as a part of their bar exams. The test includes questions from six subject areas: constitutional law, criminal law and procedure, evidence, real property, contracts (including sales), and torts.[4]

The NCBE Web site contains a thorough description of the MBE, outlines of the subject matter tested, sample questions, and publications you can order with many released test questions.[5] Because the NCBE Web site provides many sample questions that are copyrighted, visit the Web site to view the samples. Also read chapter 14, "Doing Practice Exam Questions for Your Multistate Bar Exam," and the sample MBE questions at the end of that chapter.

Note that the NCBE's purpose in providing released questions is to familiarize you with the format and nature of MBE questions. Because the NCBE's released questions sometimes (but not very frequently) address points of law that may have changed since the exams they appeared on were administered, you may come across an old answer which is no longer correct under current law.[6]

The MBE tests fundamental legal principles, usually emphasizing majority rules and exceptions to those rules.[7] Note, however, that, unlike in law school, you're not just tested on one subject at a time. Although each question only addresses a single subject, questions for each subject are randomly scrambled. So, for example, you may jump from a contracts question to a torts question to a real property question.

The MBE is a tough exam. In general, to pass your state's bar exam, you need to get 130–40 out of the 200 questions correct—that's only 65–70%![8] Because you only need to get 65–70% correct to pass the MBE exam, you may feel like you're "flunking" the exam when doing practice

---

4. For constitutional law, criminal law and procedure, evidence, and real property there are thirty-three questions per subject. For contracts (including sales) and torts there are thirty-four questions per subject. NCBE, The Multistate Bar Exam 2005 Information Booklet 11, *available at* www.ncbex.org/tests/Test%20Booklets/MBE_IB2005.pdf [hereinafter MBE Information Booklet].

5. From time to time, the NCBE releases past MBE test questions that it has retired from use. *Id.* at 1.

6. *Id.* at 46.

7. *See id.* at 2–3.

8. The NCBE computes both raw and scaled scores for each exam taker. Since raw scores are not comparable on different forms of the MBE due to differences in difficulty, scaled scores are computed using "equating," a statistical procedure that involves repeating questions from previous exams. Thus, scaled scores are comparable across administrations of the exam. *2004 Statistics, supra* note 3, at 21. For example, for the February 2004 exam, the mean raw score was a 122.89, which was scaled up to a score of 135.91. *Id.* at 22. For the July 2004 exam, the mean raw score was a 132.62, which was scaled up to 141.22. *Id.* During the past ten years, the lowest national mean scaled score was a 135.3 and the highest national mean scaled score was a 145.2. *Id.* at 23.

questions, even if you're actually doing well enough to pass.[9] This is especially so as you first start practicing MBE questions because you probably will have gaps in your knowledge of the law and it may take a while to adjust from the law school "there is no 'right' answer" view to the MBE "there is a correct answer" view.

The MBE is administered with a test booklet and a separate, computer-grid answer sheet. For each question, students are to fill in the corresponding oval space on their answer sheets with No. 2 black-lead pencils.

2. **The Multistate Professional Responsibility Exam ("MPRE").**[10] The MPRE is a fifty-question, multiple-choice exam lasting two hours and five minutes.[11] It targets ethical standards of the legal profession.[12] The MPRE has been adopted by all but three states.[13]

Each state sets its own passing score.[14] Passing scores vary from 75–85 points out of a scaled score range of 50–150 points.[15] During the 2004 administrations of the MPRE, mean scaled scores were 100.34 (March), 97.54 (August), and 99.11 (November).[16]

The test is given three times per year (March, August, and November) at times separate from states' bar exams. Most students take the MPRE during their third year of law school. Although many students choose to take the test after completing a law school ethics course, you don't need to take a law school course before taking the MPRE.[17]

The MPRE tests the law governing the conduct of lawyers, including the ABA Model Rules of Professional Conduct, the ABA Model Code of Judicial Conduct, and generally accepted principles established in leading state and federal cases.[18] The NCBE provides a subject-matter outline indicating the exam's scope of coverage.[19] A few sample questions are provided in exercise 5-1 at the end of this chapter. Sample questions and study aid order forms are also available on the NCBE Web site.[20]

---

9. For example, in February 2004 the mean raw score was 122.89 or 61% correct, and in July 2004 the mean raw score was 132.62 or 66% correct. *Id.*

10. To obtain an application and information about the administration of the MPRE, contact NCBE, MPRE Application Department, 301 ACT Drive, P.O. Box 4001, Iowa City, Iowa, 52243-4001, phone 319-341-2500, www.ncbex.org or act.org/mpre. NCBE, The Multistate Professional Responsibility Exam 2005 Information Booklet 2, *available at* www.ncbex.org/tests/Test%20Booklets/MPRE_IB2005.pdf [hereinafter MPRE Information Booklet].

11. *Id.* at 32.

12. *Id.* at 31.

13. In 2004, the MPRE was used in fifty-two jurisdictions—all states except Washington, Wisconsin, and Maryland, plus the additional jurisdictions of the District of Columbia, Guam, Northern Mariana Islands, Palau, and the Virgin Islands. *2004 Statistics, supra* note 3, at 24. See the NCBE Web site for current information about which states use the MPRE. *Id.*

14. MPRE Information Booklet, *supra* note 10, at 30.

15. *Id.* at 2, 30.

16. *2004 Statistics, supra* note 3, at 25.

17. Most bar review courses include MPRE preparation; take your bar review company's MPRE review before taking the MPRE exam.

18. MPRE Information Booklet, *supra* note 10, at 4.

19. *Id.* at 34–36.

20. NCBE, www.ncbex.org (last visited May 7, 2005).

Register for the exam six to twelve weeks before the exam is administered.[21] Before you register for the exam, though, check to make sure that you're taking it within the time window established in your state.[22]

You don't have to take the MPRE in the state where you're taking your bar exam. You may take the test at any test center in any state and have your score sent to the state where you plan to sit for the bar exam.[23] To register, read more about the exam, or obtain practice MPRE questions, see the NCBE Web site.[24]

3. **The Multistate Essay Exam ("MEE").** The MEE is a three-hour exam consisting of six essay questions.[25] Students should pace themselves through the exam at a rate of thirty minutes per essay.

The following subjects are tested on the MEE: agency, commercial paper, conflict of laws, corporations, decedents' estates, family law, federal civil procedure, future interests, limited liability companies, partnership, sales, secured transactions, and trusts.[26]

The NCBE states that the purpose of the MEE is for students to:

a. Identify legal issues raised by a factual situation;

b. Separate relevant from irrelevant information;

c. Present a reasoned analysis of the issues raised in a clear, concise, and well-organized manner;

d. Demonstrate an understanding of the law relevant to resolve the factual situation; and,

e. Demonstrate an ability to communicate effectively in writing.[27]

The MEE has been adopted by about a third of the states as part of their bar exams.[28] Students should check with their states' licensing entities to find out whether the MEE will be a part of their exams. Although the MEE is written by the NCBE, the weight accorded the MEE is determined by individual states, and the exam is graded by state examiners.[29]

---

21. *See* MPRE INFORMATION BOOKLET, *supra* note 10, at 4. You can also register for the exam late, but you'll need to pay an additional late fee. *Id.* at 6–7.

22. For example, in North Carolina students must pass the MPRE within twenty-four months before or twelve months after sitting for their bar exams. North Carolina Board of Law Examiners, *Rules, Requirements for General Applicants*, Rule .0501(6), *available at* www.ncble.org (last visited May 7, 2005).

23. MPRE INFORMATION BOOKLET, *supra* note 10, at 29–31.

24. Students can register for the MPRE online at www.ncbex.org, *MPRE Registration*, or www.act.org/mpre. *Id.*

25. NCBE, www.ncbex.org (last visited May 7, 2005).

26. NCBE, THE MULTISTATE ESSAY EXAM 2005 INFORMATION BOOKLET 1, *available at* www.ncbex.org/tests/Test%20Booklets/MEE_IB2005.pdf [hereinafter MEE INFORMATION BOOKLET].

27. *Id.* at 1–2.

28. In 2004, the MEE was used in seventeen jurisdictions (Alabama, Arkansas, District of Columbia, Guam, Hawaii, Idaho, Illinois, Kansas, Kentucky, Mississippi, Missouri, Nebraska, North Dakota, Northern Mariana Islands, South Dakota, West Virginia, and Utah). *2004 Statistics, supra* note 3, at 26. See the NCBE Web site for current information about which jurisdictions use the MEE. NCBE, www.ncbex.org (last visited May 7, 2005).

29. MEE INFORMATION BOOKLET, *supra* note 26, at 1.

The NCBE Web site contains a description of the MEE, outlines of the subject matter tested, sample questions and answers, and study aids you can order for even more sample questions and model analyses.[30]

4. **The Multistate Performance Test ("MPT").** The MPT is a performance test, requiring bar takers to perform a practical lawyering task. It has been adopted by a little more than half of the states as a part of their bar exams.[31] The NCBE provides three ninety-minute questions per exam administration.[32] States using the MPT may include one, two, or all three of the questions as part of their exams. Each state determines the weight given the MPT portion of its exam and grades the exam—there's no national grading.[33]

The MPT is like a closed office memorandum assignment. Students are given a client "File" and a "Library" with applicable law (cases, statutes, regulations, or rules) and are required to perform a specific lawyering task for a client's case.[34] The MPT doesn't test substantive knowledge; rather, the library materials provide sufficient substantive information to complete the lawyering task.[35]

Examples of tasks that students might be asked to complete include: an office memorandum, a client letter, a motion memorandum, an appellate brief, a statement of facts, a contract provision, a will, a client counseling plan, a settlement agreement, a discovery plan, a witness examination plan, or a closing argument.[36]

The NCBE states that the aim of the MPT is to test students' ability to use fundamental lawyering skills, including:

   a.   Separating relevant from irrelevant factual information;

   b.   Extracting relevant principles of law;

   c.   Resolving a client's problem by applying applicable law to relevant facts;

   d.   Identifying and resolving ethical dilemmas;

   e.   Communicating effectively in writing; and

   f.   Completing a lawyering task within time constraints.[37]

---

30. *See, e.g., id.* at 1–32.

31. In 2004, thirty-one jurisdictions used the MPT—including all states except Arizona, California, Connecticut, Florida, Kansas, Kentucky, Louisiana, Maryland, Massachusetts, Michigan, Montana, Nebraska, New Hampshire, North Carolina, Oklahoma, Pennsylvania, South Carolina, Tennessee, Virginia, Washington, Wisconsin, and Wyoming. *2004 Statistics, supra* note 3, at 27. See the NCBE Web site for current information regarding which jurisdictions use the MPT. NCBE, www.ncbex.org (last visited May 7, 2005).

32. *See* NCBE, THE MULTISTATE PERFORMANCE TEST 2005 INFORMATION BOOKLET 1, *available at* www.ncbex.org/tests/Test%20Booklets/MPT_IB2005.pdf.

33. *Id.*

34. *Id.* at 1–2.

35. *Id.* at 2.

36. *Id.*

37. *Id.*

Samples of previously administered MPT exams, including information about issues students should discuss and suggested resolutions of the issues, are on the NCBE Web site and may also be ordered from the NCBE.[38]

State-Created Exams

Almost every state's bar exam also has a state-created component. The term "state-created" means parts of a bar exam that are created by a state rather than adopted through the NCBE. State-created components use multiple-choice, essay, or performance questions (or a combination). States decide individually what subjects to test on state-created portions of their exams. Note that many questions target state laws that coincide with the majority or minority rules tested on the multistate exams.

When states design their exams, they combine both NCBE exams and state-specific portions. The resulting exam configurations are unique, but remarkably similar. Here are some examples of resulting exam formats:

1. **California:**[39]

   - Three-day exam.

   - Day one: three state-created essay questions and one state-created performance question.

   - Day two: MBE worth thirty-five percent of overall score.

   - Day three: three state-created essay questions and one state-created performance question.

   - Days one and three together are worth sixty-five percent of overall score.

2. **District of Columbia:**[40]

   - Two-day exam.

   - Day one: MPT and MEE worth fifty percent of overall score.

   - Day two: MBE worth fifty percent of overall score.

3. **New York:**[41]

   - Two-day exam.

   - Day one: MPT (ten percent), five state-created essays (forty percent), and fifty state-created multiple-choice questions (ten percent), together worth sixty percent of overall score.

   - Day two: MBE worth forty percent of overall score.

---

38. *Id.* at 15–16; *see* NCBE, www.ncbex.org (last visited May 7, 2005).

39. The State Bar of California, *Admissions*, www.calbar.ca.gov/state/calbar/calbar_generic.jsp ?cid=10115 (last visited May 7, 2005).

40. District of Columbia Courts, *Court of Appeals, Committee on Admissions*, www.dcappeals .gov/dccourts/appeals/coa (last visited May 7, 2005).

41. New York State Board of Law Examiners, *The Bar Examination* and *Admission Information*, www.nybarexam.org (last visited May 7, 2005).

4. **North Carolina:**[42]
    - Two-day exam.
    - Day one: twelve state-created essays worth sixty percent of overall score.
    - Day two: MBE worth forty percent of overall score.

Subjects Tested

Just as every state determines its own bar exam structure, each state makes an independent decision about what subjects to test on its exam. Make sure you obtain this information directly from your state's licensing office.[43] States tend to follow similar patterns, however. Frequently tested subjects include:

- Constitutional law.
- Contracts and sales.
- Criminal law and procedure.
- Evidence.
- Real property.
- Torts.
- Agency and partnership.
- Civil procedure.
- Commercial paper.
- Corporations.
- Ethics.
- Family law.
- Liens, suretyship, and mortgages.
- Remedies, including equity.
- Secured transactions.
- Tax.
- Wills and trusts.

Note that the first six subjects listed are the subjects tested on the MBE, which is a part of almost every state's bar exam. This fact means that the first six subjects are often the most important to master for bar exams (*not* that you should skip or limit your study of any of the other subjects; you should, however, make strategic studying decisions based on the likelihood of being tested on a given subject).

Finally, for any of the NCBE exams, the NCBE provides detailed subject-matter outlines that list the subjects (and topics within those subjects) that are covered on its exams.[44]

---

42. North Carolina Board of Law Examiners, www.ncble.org (last visited May 7, 2005).

43. Because state licensing entities have no obligation to provide notice of any changes to secondary sources, make sure to obtain all exam information directly from your state's office or official Web site.

44. MPRE Information Booklet, *supra* note 10, at 34–36; MEE Information Booklet, *supra* note 26, at 3–14; MBE Information Booklet, *supra* note 4, at 11–23.

Exercise 5-1: Sample MPRE Questions[*]

See the NCBE Web site, www.ncbex.org, for more sample questions.
Answers to these sample questions are provided in appendix E.

Question 1

Attorney represents Chemco, a producer of chemical products. Some of the waste products of Chemco's manufacturing are highly toxic and are likely to cause serious immediate physical harm if disposed of improperly.

Pres, president of Chemco, recently informed Attorney that a new employee mistakenly disposed of the waste products in the ground behind the company plant, an area that is part of the source of the city's water supply. Attorney advised Pres that Chemco could be liable for negligence in lawsuits brought by any persons harmed by the waste products. As a result, Attorney advised Pres to immediately report the problem to city authorities. Fearful of adverse publicity, Pres declined to do so. Attorney further advised Pres that she believed Pres's decision was immoral. Pres continued to decline to report the matter. Attorney then informed Pres that she was withdrawing from the representation and would inform the authorities herself. Immediately after withdrawing, Attorney reported Chemco's conduct to the authorities.

Is Attorney "subject to discipline"?

   A. Yes, because the information was given to Attorney in confidence and may not be revealed without the client's consent.

   B. Yes, unless Chemco's conduct was criminal.

   C. No, because Attorney reasonably believed that Chemco's disposal of the waste products was likely to cause serious physical harm.

   D. No, because Attorney reasonably believed that Pres was pursuing an imprudent course of conduct.

Question 2

Attorney Alpha represents Wife in a marriage dissolution proceeding that involves bitterly contested issues of property division and child custody. Husband is represented by Attorney Beta. After one day of trial, Husband, through Beta, made a settlement offer. Because of Husband's intense dislike for Alpha, the proposed settlement requires that Alpha agree not to represent Wife in any subsequent proceeding, brought by either party, to modify or enforce the provisions of the decree. Wife wants to accept the offer, and Alpha believes that the settlement offer made by Husband is better than any award Wife would get if the case went to judgment.

Is it "proper" for Alpha to agree that Alpha will not represent Wife in any subsequent proceeding?

   A. Yes, because the restriction on Alpha is limited to subsequent proceedings in the same matter.

---

[*] MPRE Information Booklet, *supra* note 10, at 38–39. Reprinted with permission of the NCBE. Copyright © 2005, all rights reserved.

B. Yes, if Alpha believes that it is in Wife's best interests to accept the proposed settlement.

C. No, because the proposed settlement would restrict Alpha's right to represent Wife in the future.

D. No, unless Alpha believes that Wife's interests can be adequately protected by another lawyer in the future.

Question 3

Client was an experienced oil and gas developer. Client asked Attorney for representation in a suit to establish Client's ownership of certain oil and gas royalties. Client did not have available the necessary funds to pay Attorney's reasonable hourly rate for undertaking the case. Client proposed instead to pay Attorney an amount in cash equal to twenty percent of the value of the proceeds received from the first-year royalties Client might recover as a result of the suit. Attorney accepted the proposal and took the case.

Is Attorney "subject to discipline"?

A. Yes, because the agreement gave Attorney a proprietary interest in Client's cause of action.

B. Yes, unless the fee Attorney receives does not exceed that which Attorney would have received by charging a reasonable hourly rate.

C. No, because Client rather than Attorney proposed the fee arrangement.

D. No, because Attorney may contract with Client for a reasonable contingent fee.

Reflection Questions

1. How are the formats of bar exams (combining essay, performance, and multiple-choice components) different from the formats of your law school exams? Do those differences concern you? Why?

2. How does the fact that you only need to get 65–70% of the questions correct on your MBE make you feel about your chances of passing your bar exam?

3. Why is it so crucial to understand the structure of your state's bar exam? What implications does the structure have for your study strategies?

CHAPTER 6

CAREFULLY SELECTING YOUR BAR EXAM STATE

Introduction

Many law students struggle to decide which state's bar exam to take. You're in the best position to decide this question, and we strongly encourage you to think through the issue carefully before you decide.

Before you assume that you can postpone the decision of where you want to practice law, or that taking more than one bar exam is "no big deal," think carefully through the financial and personal costs of taking a bar exam, including the costs of state licensing requirements, bar review courses, opportunity costs, use of your time, and the mental and physical sacrifices necessary to take a bar exam.

In addition to considering these costs, think through the factors that influence where you want to live and practice law, such as career opportunities, family needs, cost-of-living factors, geographic preferences, and lifestyle considerations. Finally, all other things being equal, you may want to consider bar passage rates and subjects tested on each possible state's bar exam.

The Costs of Taking a Bar Exam

Some students, particularly those who are rightfully confident they'll pass whatever bar exam they take because they're willing to do the necessary work, mistakenly assume there's no harm in choosing to take the wrong bar exam. The financial and personal costs of taking a bar exam, however, strongly weigh in favor of taking the time to pick the right state the first time.

First, consider the out-of-pocket costs of taking a bar exam. You'll need to pay your state's examiners a fee to register for and take the bar exam. Although this fee is state-specific, it often costs around $600 or more, assuming you meet the registration deadlines.[1] Most states also allow you to register late by paying an additional late fee.

Bar review costs also vary from state to state, but can easily cost $2,000 to $3,000. Even if you have recently taken a bar exam in another state, you would be wise to take a bar review course from a provider with expertise regarding your state's bar exam. Further, because most jurisdictions also require the MPRE as part of their state's bar exam, you'll likely need to pay to register and take the MPRE, too.[2]

In addition to the out-of-pocket costs to take a bar exam, also consider the opportunity costs. It's very difficult to work while studying for a bar exam; studying for a bar exam is a full-time job. Thus, you'll also lose the money you could earn by working instead of studying for and taking a bar exam.

Altogether, then, you can easily expect to spend thousands of dollars just to take a state's bar exam. Further, once you pass a bar exam, you must also pay to keep your license active. Most state bars have annual licensing fees; those fees range from approximately $200 to $500 per year. Most states also impose continuing legal education ("CLE") requirements — requiring additional expenditures to pay for CLE courses and taking time away from work to attend the courses.

Next, consider the investment of time you must make to take a state's bar exam. You'll need to spend time requesting and filling out an application. Most students spend two and one-half to three months, full-time, studying for a bar exam — and, of course, two to three days taking the exam (depending on the state).

You'll also need to spend time requesting and filling out an application for the MPRE and taking the exam. Most students spend about three to four days studying for the MPRE and a half day taking the exam.

Moreover, consider the personal costs of taking a bar exam. Few students enjoy the bar review and exam process, and many find it miserable. The experience puts stress on personal relationships; bar students tend to be grouchier, more distracted, less available, and less thoughtful than they normally would be. As a result, the selection of which bar exam to take has implications for your significant others.[3]

Consequently, if you don't need a law license to practice in a particular state, think about whether there's some other, more enjoyable and more productive way you'd like to be using your time. We've seen many students who take a bar exam just to "get it out of the way" or "prove they can do it," and then end up taking a job in another state and having to repeat the entire process. Avoid that outcome by making a thoughtful decision now.

---

1. *See, e.g.,* North Carolina Board of Law Examiners, *Rules,* www.ncble.org (last visited May 7, 2005) ($600 application fee if not already licensed in another jurisdiction; $1,200 application fee if already licensed in another jurisdiction; $250 late application fee; $400 supplemental application).

2. Check first, however, to see if a previous MPRE score can be reported to the state to eliminate the necessity of taking the MPRE again.

3. *See* chapter 4.

Some Factors to Think About in Selecting Which Bar Exam to Take

According to the National Association for Law Placement ("NALP"), success in a job search process depends on research.[4] When deciding where to work, the NALP recommends that job applicants conduct research by self-assessing their product (themselves) and their potential market (legal employers).[5]

For your self-assessment, consider your skills, temperament, preferred working style, strengths, weaknesses, values, and interests. In addition, consider the communities in which you might consider living and the organizations that do the kind of work you're interested in doing.[6] This research may require you to join a professional organization, interview practitioners in the field, investigate the job market in various locations, talk to real estate agents, and assess quality-of-life factors.[7]

We also suggest that you consider longer-term issues relating to family, personal relationships, geography, lifestyle, and living expenses. The state in which you decide to practice and take the bar is likely to be the state in which you'll spend a significant portion of the rest of your life. Consequently, while job opportunities are usually the paramount concern, other life priorities also require consideration.

In some situations, however, even if you haven't accepted a job offer and don't know where you'll practice, it might make sense to choose a state based on your best guess about where you'll end up. Because some employers won't make a job offer unless you're admitted to practice, putting off your bar exam decision could impede your job search. Other employers, however, routinely extend offers to students who haven't been admitted to a bar (contingent on passing their exams).

Although researching and evaluating all of these issues will take time, it'll be time well spent. Of course, if you're pretty sure about where you want to live and practice, and want to go ahead and get licensed, then go ahead and take that state's bar exam. If you're unsure about where you'll end up practicing, however, then research, think through your options, and take the time to make a wise decision. If you're really struggling with your decision, talk to a career counselor before deciding to invest in passing a bar exam.

---

4. NALP, www.nalp.org (last visited May 7, 2005).

5. *Id.*

6. *Id.*

7. Use a tool such as DAVID SAVAGEAU, PLACES RATED ALMANAC: SPECIAL MILLENNIUM EDITION (2000). Or, to compare quality-of-life and cost-of-living issues with respect to your choices, use one of the many Web sites that allow such comparisons such as Yahoo! Real Estate, www.realestate.yahoo.com/re/neighborhood (last visited May 7, 2005).

Exercise 6-1: Costs to Get Licensed

❏   Bar exam application fee:

❏   Bar exam application late fee (if applicable):

❏   Bar review fee:

❏   MPRE application fee:

❏   Opportunity cost: money I could be earning instead of taking time off to study:

❏   Annual license fee:

❏   Continuing education requirements and approximate cost:

❏   Total cost to get licensed: $_____.

Exercise 6-2: Career Reflection Comparison Chart

Considerations	Possible Location	Possible Location	Possible Location	Possible Location
Job opportunities in field(s) of choice:				
Job opportunities (in other field(s)):				
Preferences of significant others in your life:				
Family and friends in the area:				
Cost-of-living factors:				
Quality-of-life considerations:				
Geographic considerations:				
Additional factors (e.g., schools, health care, etc.):				
1.				
2.				
3.				
4.				

Reflection Questions

1. Do you feel ready to decide where you want to start practicing law? Why or why not? If not, what do you need to figure out to be able to make this decision?

2. To what extent has the process of deciding which bar exam to take given you insights into what you want to do as a career and how you want to live your life?

3. One theme throughout this book is taking control of your life instead of being driven by outside stimuli, such as which law firms are hiring in the city where your law school is located. Why are people who take such control over their lives generally happier? Why will taking such control over your entire bar preparation and exam process increase your likelihood of passing the bar?

CHAPTER 7

OBTAINING LICENSING
INFORMATION FOR YOUR STATE

Introduction

Passing your state's bar exam won't be all you need to do to obtain a license and practice law. Law licenses, like bar exams, are state-specific.[1] Each state sets its own licensing requirements through an entity called something like the "Board of Law Examiners" or the "State Bar Examiners." To obtain a law license, you need to comply with the licensing requirements in the state where you want to practice law.

Your State's Licensing Office

How do you locate your state's licensing office and learn your state's licensing requirements? There are several ways to find the proper office in your state. We recommend using the Web site for the National Conference of Bar Examiners ("NCBE") as a starting point.[2] The NCBE regularly updates its list of licensing entities, so it's a good

---

1. For now, that is. Many attorneys criticize the limitations imposed by state-by-state licensing given our modern economy and ways of doing business. Indeed, many attorneys agree with Anthony Davis who, serving as a panel moderator at a conference regarding multijurisdictional practice, said, "We are currently operating in a regulatory system that was created in the days when the fastest means of communication was done on the back of a horse." 73 U.S.L.W. 35, at 2559 (Mar. 22, 2005). Because of the fluid nature of modern law practice, many attorneys argue that it makes sense to provide some type of multijurisdictional licensing. In 2002, the American Bar Association ("ABA") amended its Model Rules to authorize lawyers to perform specified work outside their home states. *See id.* Since then, fifteen states have followed the ABA's lead and thirteen other states have approved multijurisdictional rules. *Id.* Thus, it appears that there will be a continuing trend toward multijurisdictional practice—and, perhaps eventually, a movement away from the state licensing process. *See also* George A. Riemer, *Bar Exam Migraine: Is a State-Based Bar Exam Obsolete?* 59 OR. ST. B. BULL. 29, 29–32 (1999) (criticizing admission rules as redundant and outdated, and advocating for easier multijurisdictional licensing given the modern economy and innumerable legal transactions that cross state lines).

2. NCBE, *Bar Admission Offices*, www.ncbex.org/offices.htm (last visited May 7, 2005).

source for current information. The American Bar Association ("ABA") Web site also maintains a contact list for state licensing entities.[3]

Once you locate the proper office in the state in which you want to take a bar exam, make sure to contact that office directly to ensure that you have current information about your state's requirements. Most state offices have Web sites on which you can find the information you need. Be sure to use an official Web site or publication for your state's exam. Other sources may not be up-to-date, and a state may change its requirements and has no obligation to provide notice to unofficial Web sites or publications.

When you contact your state's licensing office, there are several pieces of information you should obtain, including:

1. All of the state's licensing requirements (often including obtaining a law degree, submitting an application, paying a fee, taking a bar exam, taking the Multistate Professional Responsibility Exam, and passing a character/fitness-to-practice screening);

2. How to obtain an application for the bar exam, the deadline for submitting the application, and the amount of the application fee;

3. The dates and location where the bar exam will be given;

4. The format of the state's bar exam and subjects tested;

5. Whether there are any old exams or released questions and answers available to review and, if so, how to obtain them; and

6. How your exam will be scored (for example: Is there an automatic pass on a state-specific section of the exam if you obtain a certain score on your Multistate Bar Exam? Do you need to obtain a minimum score on each part of your bar exam, or does your state follow a total-points approach? Will your raw score be scaled and, if so, how?).

Character and Fitness-to-Practice Requirements

Dating back to the 1800s, bar candidates have been required to demonstrate that they have not only the legal knowledge and skills necessary to practice competently, but also the moral character necessary to be a lawyer.[4] "Such requirements have consistently withstood challenge because of their antiquity and because of the need to ensure that the bar is comprised of persons who can fulfill their duties as 'officers of the court.'"[5]

---

3. ABA, *Education Resources, Admissions to the Bar, Directory of State Bar Admission Offices,* www.abanet.org/legaled/baradmissions/barcont.html (last visited May 7, 2005).

4. Robert M. Jarvis, *An Anecdotal History of the Bar Exam,* 9 Geo. J. Legal Ethics 359, 374, 408 (1996) (citing Deborah L. Rhode, *Moral Character as a Professional Credential,* 94 Yale Law J. 491, 496–503 (1985) (providing historic overview of states' moral character requirements)).

5. *Id.* at 408 (citing *Willis v. North Carolina Bd. of Law Examiners,* 215 S.E.2d 771, 779 (N.C. 1975) ("A State can require high standards for admission to the bar, including good moral character and proficiency in the laws, so long as the qualifying standards have a rational connection with the applicant's fitness or capacity to practice law.")).

In most states, the licensing entity has the NCBE conduct a computer background check on each candidate, supplemented by references provided by bar candidates. Some states also require an interview with bar candidates.[6]

Few candidates are ever denied admission based on character; nationwide, the number of candidates rejected solely on character grounds is thought to amount to no more than two-tenths of one percent of all applicants.[7]

Even though bar examiners may inquire into candidates' character, they may not do so to exclude those whose lifestyles or values differ from their own.[8] Rather, any inquiries must be rationally related to determining whether applicants are fit to represent clients in a competent and trustworthy manner.[9]

Past substance abuse (drugs or alcohol), psychiatric counseling, having filed for bankruptcy, or criminal conduct, alone, are not usually grounds to deny applicants admission to a bar. Rather, such factors are usually reviewed in light of applicants' entire records.[10]

For example, if applicants have a past history of substance abuse, but have faced and solved their problems, that history is unlikely to prevent them from being admitted to a bar. Similarly, if applicants have recognized a need for counseling and taken appropriate action to get help, those facts are unlikely to prevent them from being admitted to a bar. In contrast, applicants who need counseling but refuse to obtain it can be denied admission if they are presently unfit to practice.[11]

Applicants cannot be denied admission simply because they avail themselves of the opportunity to start fresh by filing for bankruptcy. However, because attorneys must handle client funds responsibly, applicants may be denied admission if their records demonstrate a larger pattern of fiscal irresponsibility or that they cannot handle their personal finances.[12]

The one factor that is deadly to the fitness inquiry is dishonesty or the lack of candor.[13]

For these reasons, we have two pieces of advice about the character inquiry:

1. **Don't take it personally.** Recognize that examiners have used the character requirement for hundreds of years to uphold their responsibility to ensure that those obtaining law licenses have the moral character necessary to be lawyers; and

2. **Be honest and candid with your licensing entity.** If you have any factors in your background that you're afraid to disclose, consult with an attorney specializing in licensing issues.

---

6. *Id.*
7. *Id.* (citing RICHARD L. ABEL, AMERICAN LAWYERS 69–71 (1989)).
8. *Id.* at 408–09.
9. *Id.* at 409.
10. *Id.* at 409–12.
11. *Id.* (citing *In re Bower*, 605 N.E.2d 6, 8 (Ohio 1992)).
12. *Id.* (citing *In re Gahan*, 279 N.W.2d 826, 831 (Minn. 1979)).
13. *Id.* at 409.

Students With Disabilities

If you have any type of disability requiring an accommodation, make sure to read your examiners' procedures about obtaining accommodations and note their deadlines for doing so. Don't assume that you'll be able to obtain an accommodation, even if you were able to obtain an accommodation during law school or in other settings. The law examiners in your state may be stricter, or you might have to provide more detailed and recent documentation of your disability—which may take a significant amount of time.

Make sure to request an accommodation early—we recommend starting a year before your bar review period begins. Avoid having to spend your bar preparation time establishing either your eligibility for an accommodation or which specific accommodation you'll need. Doing so could consume valuable preparation time as well as cause you to lose your focus.

Exercise 7-1: Gathering Licensing Information

❐   State where I want to be licensed:

❐   Contact information/Web site address:

❐   Licensing requirements:

❐   Bar exam application requested.

❐   Bar exam application deadline:

❐   Bar exam application fees (regular and late):

❐   Dates and location of bar exam:

❐   Format of bar exam: day one:

❐   Format of bar exam: day two:

Exercise 7-1: (continued)

❐   Format of bar exam: day three (if applicable):

❐   Subjects tested on bar exam:

❐   Availability of old exams or released questions:

○   If available, how to obtain them:

○   Old exams obtained.

❐   How exam is scored:

Reflection Questions

1. Will your state's approach to scoring the bar exam influence how you study for the bar exam? If yes, how? If no, why not?

2. Based on what you've learned about your state's licensing requirements, what do you need to do in the next few weeks or months (aside from studying)?

3. If you've signed up for a bar review course or are planning to do so, why is it helpful to know what subjects will be tested on your state's bar exam?

CHAPTER 8

BAR REVIEW COURSES

What Are "Bar Review" Courses?

Bar review courses are classes that prepare you for a bar exam by reviewing the substantive information you're likely to be tested on as well as providing practice exam questions and exam strategies. Bar review courses are commercial products, and there are many different products on the market. Because bar exams are state-specific,[1] there are different products on the market in different states. These products vary in coverage, quality, cost, and effectiveness.

Before deciding which bar review course you should take, understand some of the differences in courses offered. Some bar review courses are comprehensive—they cover and prepare you for all components of a state's bar exam, including essay, multiple-choice, and performance questions—and some courses only cover one component of a state's bar exam. Some bar review courses cover only state-specific information for a bar exam, while others cover only multistate portions of a bar exam. What you want your bar review product (or products) to do for you—either through one product alone or several products combined—is to prepare you for your state's entire bar exam.

If you purchase a product that prepares you for your state's entire bar exam, you may or may not need to spend your money on supplemental products. We recommend being a smart consumer and considering the products available in your state, their coverage, and your level of risk for not passing your exam.[2] Make sure that you understand which products you're purchasing and make an informed decision that you need more before investing in supplemental products.[3] As an alternative, you can wait until you complete your study of the materials you've already purchased before purchasing supplemental products.

---

1. *See* chapters 5–7.
2. *See* chapter 9.
3. Also be aware that there are many free sample questions available. *See, e.g.*, National Conference of Bar Examiners, *Publications*, www.ncbex.org/pub.htm (last visited May 7, 2005).

Selecting a Bar Review Course

How do you decide which bar review course(s) to purchase? We recommend asking recently licensed attorneys in the state where you'll be taking the bar exam or administrators and faculty at your school. You can also contact employers, friends, or recent alumni. Use exercise 8-1 to collect information and decide which product is best for you.

In addition, evaluate whether a bar review's materials fit your approach to learning. Because you know what learning strategies work best for you,[4] decide which bar review's approach would work best for how you plan to study.

For example, if you memorize best by creating graphic organizers (like flowcharts or hierarchy charts), a bar review course that includes graphic organizers might seem attractive to you. You may, however, be better served by a bar review that has great outlines and no graphic organizers so that you'll have to develop graphic organizers yourself. By engaging in the act of creating graphic organizers, you'll likely memorize material more effectively.

Or, if you're a person who learns best by working in a study group, you may need to consider that fact in deciding which course to take. If your group members take different courses, a conflict in materials could be stressful. On the other hand, you may benefit by bringing information to the table from different courses and discussing the differences in your group.

Also realize that bar review courses are not operated, endorsed, or licensed by the states in which they operate. In fact, anyone can create a bar review course. Consequently, you need to do more than simply review promotional materials to make an informed decision. Take a look at the substantive law outlines and practice tests offered, ask about each course's faculty, and examine information about each course's track record. Many bar reviews sell their ability to predict which subjects will be tested on the next bar exam. Be wary of such predictions—some students fail because they over-rely on predictions and don't study every subject eligible for testing.

Once you select which bar review course to use, stick with your choice unless you discover a significant problem with your selection.[5] Inevitably, at some point during your bar study, you and your peers will talk about and compare the courses you've selected. The stress of your preparation period can easily cause these conversations to produce anxiety about your choice. Avoid these conversations like the plague; they'll inevitably waste time, interfere with your focus, and make your preparation period more stressful than necessary.

---

4. See chapter 13 for a discussion of bar review learning strategies.
5. *See* Loretta Walder, Pass This Bar: A Readiness Guide For Bar Exam Preparation 8 (1982).

Be Prepared to Work Hard

Finally, recognize the limitations of any bar review product. Bar reviews target large numbers of students (not your individual learning style) and can only lead you through the review process (they can't do your work for you). Accordingly, no matter which product(s) you choose, be prepared to do the hard work of reviewing the law, memorizing it, and doing practice questions. There are no shortcuts for the six-hundred-plus hours of work you'll need to put in to prepare for your bar exam.

Home Study Programs

Students often ask us for advice about home study programs. "Home study" programs are products sold by bar review companies for students to use to study for the bar on their own as opposed to going to a group bar review location. These products are probably just as effective as a company's other bar review products. In other words, if a bar review company has a good reputation for its group bar review courses, we'd expect its home study products to be good, too.

A more important question, however, is whether a home study program would work effectively for you. The answer depends on your own personality and learning style. Ask yourself whether you'll be able to stay motivated without the structure of a course, and whether you have a hard time studying unless someone is watching you. Some students reject home study courses because they need the structure of going to course lectures to get them up and going. Other students reject home study courses because they learn best by hearing a lecture. In contrast, for students with a high level of self-discipline who prefer to study alone and set their own schedules, home study programs could be a better choice than group bar review courses.

Exercise 8-1: Bar Review Course Comparison Chart

Characteristics	Provider	Provider	Provider	Provider
Costs:				
Multistate law, or state-specific law, or both:				
Comprehensive coverage or only one component of bar exam:				
Substantive law preparation:				
MBE preparation:				
Essay preparation:				
Performance test preparation:				
Quality of review materials:				
Fit of materials with learning strategies:				
Recommendations:				
Other reasons for selecting:				

Reflection Questions

1. What is the most important thing to you in selecting a bar review course?

2. Why are there so many bar review courses available in some states, and different products available in different states?

3. Why do you believe the bar review course you selected or plan on selecting is the best choice for you?

PART THREE

PLANNING TO PASS
YOUR BAR EXAM

CHAPTER 9

BAR EXAM STATISTICS AND INDIVIDUAL RISK FACTORS FOR NOT PASSING THE BAR

As if studying for and taking a bar exam weren't stressful enough, bar exam passage statistics are downright depressing. For example, here are a few official passage statistics:[1]

- California, 48%.
- District of Columbia, 54%.
- New York, 67%.
- North Carolina, 70%.

Having given you this information, we'll now encourage you to ignore it! Why? Because you'll either pass or you won't.[2] Further, statistics may be irrelevant as applied to you. Statistics describe past results of groups of bar takers, and can only be used to make predictions about future, similar groups of bar takers. Statistics aren't helpful for making predictions about your individual situation. Also, bar statistics usually include categories like repeaters, who generally have much lower passage rates than first-time takers.[3] Your attitude and efforts, not statistics, will determine whether you'll pass your bar exam.[4]

Further, many people who fail bar exams do so for reasons that are likely to be irrelevant to you. Common causes of bar failures include suffering a personal crisis, having to work throughout the bar review period, adopting insufficient or poor study strategies, not working hard enough, avoiding opportunities for practice and feedback, or engaging in self-defeating behavior (such as abusing alcohol or drugs or not sleeping).

---

1. Statistics are for the summer 2004 bar exams. National Conference of Bar Examiners ("NCBE"), *2004 Statistics*, The Bar Examiner 6–7 (May 2005), *available at* www.ncbex.org/pubs /pdf/740205_2004statistics.pdf [hereinafter *2004 Statistics*]. Note that the NCBE Web site contains detailed information about the most recent passage rates in all states. *See id.* at 6–16.

2. Note, however, that in some circumstances you may want to examine passage rates. For example, if you are truly undecided about whether to take one state's exam or another's, it may make sense to consider the passage rates in both states.

3. For example, some representative first-timer/repeater statistics for the July 2004 exam were as follows: California, 63%/17%; District of Columbia, 80%/45%; New York, 77%/25%; and North Carolina, 78%/32%. *2004 Statistics, supra* note 1, at 10–12.

4. *See, e.g.*, Loretta Walder, Pass This Bar: A Readiness Guide For Bar Exam Preparation 63 (1982).

The data in table 9-1 for the California, District of Columbia, New York, and North Carolina bar exams provide insight into the factors that affect a jurisdiction's overall bar passage rate.

Table 9-1: Sample Bar Passage Statistics*

Juris-diction	Overall Passage Rate	First-Time Takers, Feb.	First-Time Takers, July	Repeaters, Feb.	Repeaters, July	From ABA School	From Non-ABA School	Ten-Year Overall High/Low
CA:	44%	47%	63%	31%	17%	54%	16%	58%/44%
DC:	51%	62%	80%	47%	45%	54%	26%	59%/46%
NY:	62%	58%	77%	38%	25%	70%	N/A	67%/61%
NC:	63%	64%	78%	39%	32%	63%	N/A	79%/63%

While state bar passage rates are irrelevant to you (because they have no predictive power as to whether *you* will pass the bar), the factors that may put you at risk of not passing the bar are very important. Being aware of these factors is helpful because you can assess whether you're in a high-risk category and develop strategies to address your risks. Or, if you're not in any of the risk categories, you can feel confident that, if you do the work required, you can pass the bar.

Risk factors for not passing a bar are listed in table 9-2. Although each of the factors puts students at risk, none of them prevents students from passing. Many students have several of these risk factors yet still pass their bar exams. The factors merely reflect common characteristics of students who have failed in the past. By being aware of the risk factors and acting to minimize their effects, you can increase your likelihood of passing your bar exam.

Also note that the factors listed don't necessarily all pose the same level of risk. For example, if you've done well in law school, you probably have a low level of risk. But, if you don't always study as efficiently and effectively as you could, you may have some risk of not passing. That risk is relatively easy to remedy by following the recommendations in this text; if you do so, you should be fine.

One last point: even if you don't possess any of the listed risk factors, you should be adopting some of the suggestions in table 9-2. As you review the table, consider which suggestions really apply to all bar takers.

---

* NCBE, 2004 Statistics, The Bar Examiner 6–16 (May 2005), available at www.ncbex.org/pubs/pdf/740205_2004statistics.pdf. Unless otherwise specified, the statistics are for both the February and July 2004 bar exams.

Table 9-2: Risk Factors and Remedies

Risk Factors	Suggested Remedies
Low LSAT score, low law school GPA, or low law school class rank: If you are in the bottom twenty percent, you have this risk factor.	Carefully assess the causes of your problem and tailor your approach(es): • Analytical skills need improvement: get extra practice and consider a tutor. • Weak multiple-choice test-taking skills: get extra practice and consider a supplemental course. • Weak writing skills: write extra practice essays and consider a writing tutor. • Insufficient study: have a strict study plan, set specific study goals, and reward successes (chapters 13, 17). • Weak study skills: read chapter 13 and *Expert Learning for Law Students.***
Not taking bar-tested courses or a GPA below 2.7 (on a 4.0 scale) in bar-tested courses: Check which subjects are tested on your bar exam and review your academic history to assess this issue.	• See the list of suggestions above. • Sign up for a bar review course early and work on omitted or weaker subjects before your bar review begins.
Not taking a bar review course: Almost all students take a course.	• Take a bar review course, even if you have to borrow the money to do so.
Working (including caring for a family) during the bar review: Students who don't treat the bar review as a full-time job are at risk.	• Plan your finances to avoid having to work. • If you absolutely must work, make sure you study at least eight hours per day at times when you're mentally alert.
Nontraditional student status:*** Students who work, who are older, who have more to do (for example, parenting), and who have more real or perceived economic pressures have this risk factor.	• Get help from family and friends, or even paid help. • Develop and stick to a strict study schedule. • Use attention-focusing strategies to stay on task (chapter 13).

** MICHAEL HUNTER SCHWARTZ, EXPERT LEARNING FOR LAW STUDENTS (2005).

*** *See, e.g.,* Linda Jellum & Emmeline Paulette Reeves, *Cool Data on a Hot Issue: Empirical Evidence That a Law School Bar Support Program Enhances Bar Performance,* 5 NEV. L. J. 646, 653–55 (2005) (summarizing articles asserting that being a minority and having fewer financial resources are risk factors).

Risk Factors	Suggested Remedies
Life crises or significant changes: Significant events (such as a death in the family, getting married, moving, or ending a relationship) interfere with studying and put you at risk.	• Postpone any change you have control over until after the bar, if possible. • Seek professional help and emotional support. • Use attention-focusing strategies to keep you on task (chapter 13).
A history of poor essay or multiple-choice test skills.	• Do extra practice questions using the techniques and exercises in chapters 14 and 15.
Failure to adopt realistic and effective studying and exam-taking strategies:**** Some students do not pass the bar because they prepare poorly.	• Have a strict study plan and stick to it (chapter 17). • Use motivational and attention-focusing strategies (chapters 3, 13). • Use expert study and exam strategies (chapters 11–16, 19).
Excessive anxiety or fear of failure: Anxiety or a fear of failing may create a self-fulfilling prophecy.	• Use the techniques explained in chapter 3.

In sum, students don't just randomly fail bar exams. Rather, specific risk factors correlate with (but don't necessarily cause) failure on bar exams. Evaluate whether you possess any of these risk factors or are at risk for any other reason. Then develop a plan for dealing with your risk factor(s). If you have several risk factors, you may also want to consider getting some individual counseling or coaching before you begin and during your preparation period.

Nearly all students who study conscientiously, don't encounter a major life crisis during their preparation period, and don't have multiple risk factors, pass their bar exams.[5] You can further increase your likelihood of passing your bar exam by taking time to understand the process and formulating a winning game plan.[6]

**** The bar exam requires hundreds of hours of study—at least 600—and there's no way to avoid the necessary hard work.

5. *See, e.g.,* WALDER, *supra* note 4, at 65.

6. *See* chapter 10.

Exercise 9-1: Risk Factor Self-Assessment and Plans of Action

Bar Exam Risk Factors	Your Action Plans
❒ Low LSAT score, law school GPA, or class rank.	
❒ Not taking a bar review course.	
❒ Not taking, or earning low grades in, several subjects tested on your bar exam.	
❒ Working (including family care) during your bar exam preparation period.	
❒ Nontraditional student status.	
❒ Life crisis or significant change (either good or bad).	
❒ A history of poor essay or multiple-choice test skills.	
❒ Failure to adopt realistic and effective studying and exam-taking strategies.	
❒ Excessive fear or anxiety.	

Reflection Questions

1. How does the fact that bar takers don't just randomly fail their exams make you feel about your chances of passing the bar exam?

2. Why are bar passage statistics really irrelevant to you?

3. Which of the suggested remedies might you use even if you're not in an at-risk category?

CHAPTER 10

YOUR WINNING GAME PLAN

Introduction

You can increase your likelihood of passing your bar exam by taking the time to understand the bar review and bar exam process and by putting together a winning game plan. This approach is especially important if you have any risk factors because any risk factor can be minimized with a winning plan.

Components of Your Winning Game Plan

Your winning game plan should include the following components:

1. **A firm intent to take and pass your bar exam.** One of the frequent comments we've heard from students who don't pass their bar exams is, "But I don't know if I really want to practice law."[1] Certainly, you're not alone if you have doubts about becoming a practicing attorney, but that doubt is irrelevant to your bar exam process. Distinguish the issue of whether you want to practice law from the issue of whether you want to take and pass a bar exam. If you don't want to practice law, then you don't need a license, and you don't need to take a bar exam. You may have personal reasons, however, for wanting to become a licensed attorney (for example, a sense of closure and accomplishment or to keep your employment options flexible).

    It's perfectly fine to take a bar exam without knowing exactly how you want to proceed with your career. Just make sure to keep your career issue separate from the bar exam issue so that you don't sabotage your preparation process. The moment you decide to take a bar exam, the question of what you'll do with your license becomes (temporarily) irrelevant. For now, make sure to make a firm and final decision that, yes, you want to

---

1. *See* LORETTA WALDER, PASS THIS BAR: A READINESS GUIDE FOR BAR EXAM PREPARATION 66 (1982) ("For [students] who really don't want to be lawyers, passing looms as a threat, not an opportunity. If they pass the test, they feel that they will be doomed to a life that is not suited for them.").

take and pass the bar exam. Then, keep your focus solely on reviewing for and passing the bar exam until it's over. You'll have the rest of your life to determine what you want to do with your career.

2. **Advance planning for the bar review and bar exam process.** You'll be a step ahead if you take time to plan for your bar review and exam before you begin your review period. To plan successfully, it's necessary to understand the review and exam process—that's one of the purposes of this book. Once you understand the process, you can plan to succeed.

Your likelihood of success on the bar exam will be proportional to the degree to which you create a plan that ensures that the months during your review period are as stable and constructive as possible. For example, look at your commitments—spiritual or religious organizations, family, hobbies, or whatever else you're involved in—and ask yourself how you can limit your commitments so you'll be able to focus on studying for and taking the bar.

In addition, try to minimize nonessential life activities and any life transitions during your bar review and exam period. For example, moving or getting married during the bar review will disrupt your focus and preparation.

It's also a good idea to put off major life decisions until after you finish your bar exam. Whether you can make the best life decisions while experiencing bar review stress is questionable; making any major life decisions during this time will also distract you.

Get your significant others on board with your plans before you begin your review period. Many times, the important people in your life will assume that, after your law school graduation day, you'll *finally* have time for them. They may be upset to learn that, instead, you're entering an even more stressful, time-consuming period. Before your review period begins, help your loved ones help you by giving them a heads-up about what you expect your life to be like as well as how they can support you.[2]

Finally, as a part of your advance planning, read through the rules your state's licensing entity has promulgated that govern the bar exam. Every state has its own set of rules governing its exam, and an advance read will help you prepare as well as ensure that you don't overlook any important points during the stressful days preceding your exam.

For example, most licensing bodies will require you to bring specific items with you to your bar exam (for example, an admission document, a piece of identification, black-ink pens, and No. 2 pencils) and prohibit you from bringing other items (for example, umbrellas, backpacks, purses, and watches that make noise). Here are a few sample provisions to give you a feel for the types of rules promulgated by bar examiners for the administration of bar exams:[3]

---

2. *See* chapter 4.

3. *See, e.g.*, North Carolina Board of Law Examiners, *Exam Regulations and Code of Conduct*, www.ncble.org (last visited May 7, 2005).

- Any bar taker who engages in conduct that disrupts another bar taker or the bar exam process is subject to sanctions, including ejection from the exam site.

- Bar takers may not bring any book bags, cell phones, pagers, books, notes, written or printed material or data of any kind, or backpacks to the exam building or have any such material in their possession during the administration of the exam.

- Bar takers may not bring any type of purses, pocketbooks, or handbags to the exam site. Bar takers may bring items required for their exams (for example, photo identification, pens, and pencils) in a clear plastic bag.

- A bar taker who leaves the exam building during a session of the exam will not be permitted to re-enter during the same exam session.

- Bar takers may not gather in the restrooms or in any areas adjacent to the exam rooms while the exam is in progress.

3. **Planning for your exam logistics.** After you confirm your exam location, it's helpful to do a dry run of driving to the location and figuring out where you'll park. If you'll need to stay overnight, find a hotel and make a reservation. Depending on where your bar exam is given, accommodations may be either abundant or scarce; in either case, it's one detail that you can easily check off your list in advance so you'll be all set for exam day.

4. **A consistent investment of time.** As a lawyer, your time is money. There's a significant opportunity cost to not passing your bar exam, in addition to it being an annoyance to have to retake it. You'll likely have to pay another exam registration and bar review course fee, set aside another two to three months to study during which you won't be earning a salary, and delay starting your career and earning a salary as a lawyer. Given the hefty price you'll pay if you don't pass, it only makes sense to make a consistent investment of time to prepare for your exam.

    Studying for your bar exam should be a full-time job. Indeed, most students spend somewhere between eight to ten hours a day studying during the bar review period. See chapters 11 through 17 to get a feel for the investment of time you should make if you want to pass your bar exam. We recommend that you stay ahead of schedule so that, if a crisis arises, you'll have some cushion for taking time to deal with the situation.

5. **A financial plan.** Taking the bar exam is a financial investment. You'll be spending thousands of dollars to register for your bar exam and take your bar review course, as well as taking several months off from work to study when you could be making money instead.

    As we explained in chapter 9, students who work while they're studying for the bar exam are at risk for not passing. Thus, before you finish your last semester of law school, make sure that you have enough funds to cover your living expenses and your bar review and exam expenses so that you won't have to scramble for funds or work during the bar review process. There are loans available to students to cover bar review and exam expenses. Check with your school's financial aid or student affairs office to find out about loans that are available.[4]

6. **An academic check.** During your third year of law school, do a realistic self-assessment regarding your knowledge of the subjects tested on the bar exam. Check with the licensing entity in your state to ensure you have a current list of subjects tested.[5] Review the list, asking yourself whether there are courses you haven't taken at all or courses where your grade was in the bottom twenty percent of your class. If there are, we recommend doing remedial studying. The bar "review" is just a review; you won't have time to learn new subjects from scratch.

If you determine that remedial studying is appropriate, review our recommendations for learning the substantive law.[6] The best materials to review are bar exam outlines or black letter law commercial outlines. If you've already signed up for a bar review course, you may be able to get your outlines early. If not, ask around; you may be able to borrow someone's old bar review outlines to do your remedial studying.[7] Reviewing bar review outlines is your best bet because they target issues most frequently tested on bar exams and provide the most time-efficient way to review the material.

7. **Stress management.** Your likelihood of success on your bar exam will increase if you can be focused, mentally tough, and confident during your review and exam. This goal is a challenge because most students find the process stressful. You'll be experiencing time pressure (more to do than time to do it) and uncertainty (doubts about whether you'll pass the exam).

A key to managing stress is knowing it may be coming and planning how to deal with it. To stay as fresh, mentally tough, and as focused as possible, plan ahead for time to relax, unwind, and refresh. Think about specific activities you can engage in that'll help you stay fresh—for example, exercising, sleeping, meditating, or spending time with friends. Then, make sure to include time in your schedule for them. For example, set aside two to three hours, twice per week, to engage in one of those activities.[8]

There are many techniques you can use to deal with stress and to relax. In addition, you can reduce bar exam stress by overlearning material.[9] Finally, instead of focusing on your fear of failure, strive to imagine

---

4. Frequently used bar exam loan resources are The Access Group, www.accessgroup.org; Key Education Resources, www.key.com; Nellie Mae Loan Link, www.nelliemae.com; Sallie Mae, www.salliemae.com; and TERI Professional Education Program, www.teri.org. Denise Riebe Interview with Dean Sylvia Novinsky, Associate Dean of Student Affairs, University of North Carolina School of Law, Chapel Hill, North Carolina (Mar. 2005).

5. *See* chapter 7.

6. *See* chapter 13.

7. Make sure to use relatively recent outlines for your remedial studying. Also, even if you use borrowed outlines for your remedial studying before your bar review course begins, we strongly recommend against using old outlines as a substitute for a bar review course. Some students are tempted to save money by using old outlines and skipping a formal bar review course. Old materials may contain outdated law as well as omitting altogether law that may be tested on your exam.

8. *See* chapter 3.

9. *See* chapter 13.

yourself excelling on the bar exam. For example, imagine your answers being used as the model answers distributed by your state bar.

Exercise 10-1 will help you translate these recommendations into a set of personal plans. As you do the exercise, think through how you'll implement the suggestions in this chapter.

Exercise 10-1: Game Plan for Passing the Bar Exam

Components of a Winning Game Plan	Your Specific Plans
❐ A firm intent to take and pass the bar exam.	
❐ Development of a time management plan for the bar review and exam process (see chapter 17).	
❐ Planned consistent and substantial preparation time.	
❐ Finances arranged so there's no need to work during the preparation period.	
❐ Academic record reviewed for gaps and weaknesses, and remediation planned if necessary.	
❐ Planned stress management for both the preparation period and the bar exam.	

Reflection Questions

1. Why is planning in so many different ways a key to passing your bar exam?

2. Which of the components of your winning game plan do you think is most crucial to your success? Why?

3. Which of the components of a winning game plan discussed in this chapter are you least likely to follow? Why? What can you do to make sure you address each of the components?

PART FOUR

EXPERT STUDY STRATEGIES

Introduction

To maximize your likelihood of passing your bar exam, it's critical to think in advance about how you'll study. Before you decide how to study, make sure you understand the bar review and exam process.[1] Once you understand the overall process, review our recommendations in the following chapters and the sample study schedule in chapter 17. Then, put together your own written study plan.

We recommend that you put your study plan in writing for three reasons. First, the act of putting your study plan in writing increases your commitment to it and increases the odds that you'll stick to it. Second, vague goals (for example, "I will study eight hours a day") are not very useful. You're more likely to achieve, and feel good about achieving, narrow, specific study goals (for example, "I will test my memorization of contracts law for two hours, take a ten-minute break, write answers to two torts essay questions, break for a half-hour lunch, attend three hours of lectures on contracts law, take an hour break to exercise, and then do thirty-four MBE questions"). Third, the act of planning a schedule in writing ensures that your study goals are realistic. As one of Professor Riebe's colleagues says, "If you can't do it on paper, you can't do it."[2]

Finally, before writing your study plan, understand how your study strategies should change over time.[3] Your (written!) study plan should contain three components: (1) studying the substantive law for subjects tested on your state's bar exam;[4] (2) completing practice questions similar to those used on your state's bar exam;[5] and (3) taking time to refresh. These components are explained in more detail in the chapters that follow.

---

1. *See* chapters 1–10 and 19.

2. Denise Riebe Interview with Ruth Ann McKinney, Professor and Director, Writing and Learning Resources Center, University of North Carolina School of Law, Chapel Hill, North Carolina (Feb. 2000).

3. *See* chapter 12.

4. *See* chapter 13.

5. *See* chapters 14–16.

CHAPTER 11

THE KNOWLEDGE AND SKILLS YOU BRING TO YOUR BAR STUDY

Regardless of how well you've done in law school, you can point to a lifetime of classes, tests, quizzes, and papers on which you've performed extraordinarily well. You also performed well enough in college and on the LSAT to make it into law school, and you're about to graduate from law school. All these facts demonstrate that you possess the intellectual skills necessary to succeed on the bar exam.

You also have years of personal data regarding which approaches to learning and test-taking work best for you. If you take a moment to reflect on your past educational experiences, you probably can remember several classes in which you did well and what you did to prepare for your exams in those classes. Trust your past successes and stick to study strategies that you already know work for you.

At some point during your preparation period, family, friends, or classmates will inevitably (and probably with good intentions) give you advice about what you should do to pass the bar. Don't listen! There are many different learning styles, as well as many myths, about the bar exam; consequently, whatever you're told either may not be right for you or may be just plain wrong.

Even if there have been times in law school when you haven't performed your best, you likely have an image in your mind of what you could've done to achieve a different result. One of the best things about studying for the bar is that it's one of the few times in life when you can focus on one primary concern. Most people you know, once educated, are likely to understand and agree that preparing for the bar must be your first (and second, and third …) priority. Consequently, you'll be able to act like the model law student you either have been or would have liked to have been.

Your graduation from law school also shows that you're capable of working hard. Law school is a rigorous, demanding graduate program. You've read thousands of pages, memorized thousands of rules, and have written complex papers and exams.

Further, as a result of the work you've done in law school, you already know a lot of what you need to know for the bar exam. You know how to spot issues, state rules, apply rules to determinative facts, and analyze factual situations to predict legal conclusions.

You also know a large amount of law. Law students graduate knowing at least two-thirds of the law they need to know for the bar exam. As a result, you'll find that a large amount of the material in your bar review outlines is already familiar. While you may believe that all the law you memorized for law school exams is long gone, it's actually stored in your long-term memory. The challenge during your bar review is thus improving your ability to recall it quickly.

Finally, your success in managing the details of your life and relationships while attending law school also means that you possess the time management skills you need to succeed on a bar exam.

Because of your past academic successes, you're well situated to pass the bar if you approach it in the right way. By reading this text, using the checklists, and doing the exercises, you're on your way to succeeding with your bar exam. If, in addition, you put in the hard work required to study for the exam, using smart study techniques and adhering to your written study plan, we're confident you can pass the bar.

Excercise 11-1: Learning Self-Assessment

Think about the courses in which you've learned the most and in which you've performed the best. Think about how you studied for the exams in those courses. What study techniques worked for you? Check each of those techniques below. Use this information and what you learn in the next few chapters to help you plan how you'll study for the bar exam.

- ❏ Outlining.

- ❏ Creating gradually shrinking outlines.

- ❏ Creating graphic organizers like flowcharts or mind maps to see the relationships among concepts.

- ❏ Creating flashcards and self-testing or peer-testing your knowledge.

- ❏ Creating mnemonics.

- ❏ Discussing concepts with classmates.

- ❏ Reciting out loud what you're learning.

- ❏ Associating rules with cases you've read.

- ❏ Using color or imagery.

- ❏ Developing examples to make sure you understand concepts.

- ❏ Writing practice exam answers.

- ❏ Creating your own practice questions.

- ❏ Other techniques:

_____

_____

_____

_____

_____

_____

Reflection Questions

1. What knowledge and skills do you already have that'll be helpful to your bar study efforts?

2. Why is it important to decide for yourself what study techniques will work best for you, rather than simply doing what your friends suggest?

3. What is your image of how you would have studied in law school had you had the time, motivation, and self-discipline of an "ideal" law student? Is there anything that might keep you from being that ideal student while you study for the bar exam?

CHAPTER 12

YOUR STUDY STRATEGIES SHOULD CHANGE OVER TIME

Introduction

Before you map out your study plan, realize that your study strategies should change over time. We like to think in terms of four different preparation periods:

1. Your pre-bar review period (during your last year of law school);
2. The first forty percent of your bar review;[1]
3. The second forty percent of your bar review;[2] and
4. The final twenty percent of your bar review.[3]

The information below specifies what you should be doing during each of these preparation periods.

Your Pre-Bar Review Period

The time to plan to be successful on your bar exam is before your bar review period begins. During your pre-bar review period (your last year of law school), make sure you understand the licensing process in your state, the bar exam process, exam components, and subjects tested in your state.[4] Review chapter 2, "Action Plan Checklists," and chapter 10, "Your Winning Game Plan," for specific tasks that should be included in your pre-bar review preparation.

One crucial pre-bar review task is to remedy any risk factors you have.[5] In exercise 9-1, you identified risk factors and made plans to address those factors. Complete as many of those plans as possible before you begin your bar review.

---

1. For example, the first four weeks of a ten-week preparation period or the first three and one-quarter weeks of an eight-week preparation period.

2. For example, the second four weeks of a ten-week preparation period or the second three and one-quarter weeks of an eight-week preparation period.

3. For example, the last two weeks of a ten-week preparation period or the last week and one-half of an eight-week preparation period.

4. *See* chapters 1–7.

5. *See* chapter 9.

Exercise 9-1 directs you to list subjects tested on your bar exam that you didn't take in law school or in which you received a low grade. Your pre-review period is the time to do remedial studying to fill in those gaps. One way to do so is to get your bar review materials early and work with those materials using the study principles described in chapter 13. Old bar review outlines or black letter law commercial outlines are also good resources. If you're a person who learns best by studying with others, find a peer who needs to do remediation for the same subjects and agree upon deadlines and plans for assessing the effectiveness of each other's study efforts.

Further, take time to transition your writing style to the type appropriate for bar exam essays. Begin this process by understanding your state's essay exam; review the types of essay questions used on exams in your state and sample answers if you're in a jurisdiction where they're available. To obtain essay questions from past exams, call your licensing entity and ask whether questions are available and, if so, how to obtain them. Your law school may also have copies of past bar exams; ask your student affairs office and librarians whether your school keeps any on file that you could review. After you read a dozen questions and answers, make a list of common characteristics of the questions and passing answers. Chapter 15, "Doing Practice Exam Questions for Your Essay Exam," will provide you with more information about transitioning your writing skills.

If your state administers a performance test, the pre-bar review period is also a good time to familiarize yourself with the types of documents you'll need to create. Make sure to look at some sample questions and answers. The National Conference of Bar Examiners ("NCBE") has many samples on its Web site,[6] and your law school's library or your state bar's Web site may have past exams and answers available, too. As we recommend in chapter 16, make sure you're familiar with all of the types of documents you might be asked to create; your law school's library has practice guides with samples of the types of documents that performance questions require you to create.[7]

Finally, during the month before your bar review begins, create a written plan for success detailing how you'll prepare for your bar exam.[8]

First Forty Percent of Your Bar Review[9]

When your bar review begins, it's important to develop a routine as soon as possible. Your bar review will move quickly—for many subjects, at the pace of one law school course per day. Your routine should include reading your bar review outlines for the subjects scheduled to be covered in class, attending class, and making sure you understand and memorizing the law. Chapter 13 details best practices for these tasks. Also do at least thirty-four multiple-choice questions per day, two essays per week, and one performance question per week (if your state uses them on its exam). Chapters 14–16 describe how to practice, and learn from practicing, each of these types of questions.

---

6. NCBE, www.ncbex.org (last visited May 7, 2005).
7. For more information about preparing for performance tests, see chapter 16.
8. *See* chapter 17.
9. The first four weeks of a ten-week preparation period or the first three and one-quarter weeks of an eight-week preparation period.

Throughout your bar study, study in one- to two-hour periods of time, and make sure to take five- or ten-minute breaks every hour. Breaks allow your mind to digest what you've learned, thus making your study time more efficient and effective and saving you time in the long run.

During this phase of review, students often feel that studying for the bar isn't as hard as they had expected and, accordingly, the bar exam is passable. Make sure you also give yourself time each day (an hour or so for exercise or family time) and two longer periods of time per week to refresh (two or three hours each).

Finally, throughout your bar review period limit your intake of caffeine and alcohol, be careful taking any prescription medication (because some types of medication interfere with mental processing), and avoid illegal substances. The bar review process will push you to your mental limit and require you to be at your mental best. For this reason, avoid doing anything that might interfere with your ability to think, memorize, or analyze.

Second Forty Percent of Your Bar Review[10]

During the second forty percent of the bar review, many students start feeling overwhelmed. Keeping up with a study schedule becomes more challenging as the bar review continues to move at a pace of one semester's law school course per day. Many students struggle to keep up with their reading for class, their reviewing for reinforcement, and their practice exams. Many begin to feel like they're barely keeping their heads above water.

Instead of trying to learn everything, focus on learning what's in front of you. In other words, take it one step at a time and concentrate on completing the tasks on your study plan each day. One of the reasons we recommend that you develop and adhere to a study plan is that it helps control anxiety; you'll be more confident about your bar preparation if you have a study plan covering each aspect of your preparation.

Although it may seem counterproductive, it's also important to continue to take time to refresh during this period. You don't want to burn out before you reach the bar exam. In order to stay fresh, take (planned!) breaks—a one-hour daily break and two three-hour breaks per week—to engage in activities you enjoy, such as exercising or spending time with family.

Final Weeks of Your Bar Review[11]

Ideally, your preparation during the first eighty percent of your bar review period will enable you to efficiently review all of your bar exam subjects during the final weeks

---

10. The second four weeks of a ten-week preparation period or the second three and one-quarter weeks of an eight-week preparation period.

11. The last two weeks of a ten-week preparation period or the last week and one-half of an eight-week preparation period.

of your bar study. In addition to a review of the substantive law, do just enough practice questions to stay in the flow.

During these final weeks, take care of yourself so that you'll feel fresh for the bar exam. Continue to take at least two three-hour breaks per week to engage in activities that you enjoy. Also, start going to bed early enough to wake up at the time you'll need to wake up for the bar exam. Similarly, your studying should be done during the same hours you'll be taking the exam.

Finally, review checklists 2-5 and 2-6 to ensure that you've taken care of details for taking your exam (for example, what to take, where to go, and where to park).

Reflection Questions

1. Why should your study plan change over time?

2. Why should you do any necessary remedial studying before starting your bar review?

3. What can you do to minimize your anxiety during the second forty percent of your bar review (when most students start feeling overwhelmed)?

Chapter 13

EXPERT STUDY STRATEGIES FOR SUBSTANTIVE LAW

Introduction

Studying the substantive law tested on your state's bar exam will be the most time-consuming part of your preparation period. Specifically, we recommend devoting approximately two-thirds of your preparation time to studying the substantive law and approximately one-third of your time to doing practice questions.

Before you begin studying, make sure you have current information about what subjects your state tests on its exam. Also, take the time to understand the structure of your state's exam so that you understand whether certain subjects are more likely to be tested than others.[1] Although you shouldn't skip any subjects because they're not frequently tested, you should use frequency information to make strategic decisions about how to spend your study time. All other things being equal, you should devote greater time and effort to mastering the more frequently tested subjects and less time and effort to mastering the less frequently tested subjects. If you're taking a bar review course, study the subjects covered in an order that corresponds to your course. Also adjust your study time to allow for the fact that you'll remember and understand some subjects more readily than others.

Whatever study techniques you use, there should be four components to your study of the substantive law: (1) reading your bar review outlines; (2) attending your bar review classes; (3) making sure you understand the substantive law; and (4) memorizing the substantive law in a way that'll allow you to readily recall it during your exam. We recommend that you perform these components in the order listed. If you read your outlines before class, you're more likely to get what you need out of your bar review lectures. Because the terminology and key concepts will be familiar, it'll be easier to take good notes. You'll also already know what aspects of the law are confusing and, therefore, be ready to listen for clarification.

Your bar review preparation should be a closed-universe project; there's no need to use any materials outside of your bar review materials when studying for your

---

1. Find out the subjects tested in your state from your state's licensing entity, and ask which subjects are tested on which components. Also, look at old exams to see if there are any patterns in your state's testing practices and to find out which subjects are tested most frequently. In many states, the subjects tested on the Multistate Bar Exam are the most important to master since they are frequently tested on essay and performance exams, too.

exam.[2] Your bar review materials target the most frequently tested areas of substantive law and help you review those areas in the most time-efficient manner possible. If you can master your bar review materials, you'll be more than amply prepared. So there's no need to expand your universe of study materials any further.

The remainder of this chapter provides techniques for studying substantive law. When reading about these techniques, think of times when, in your own studying, you've used or not used them. Recall how well you learned the material. The ultimate measure of a learning technique is whether it works for you. Because you're an experienced learner with many academic successes, use what has worked for you in the past and new techniques that appeal to you.

Whatever study techniques you use, the key is making conscious, thoughtful choices about how you're going to study, constantly assessing those choices, and being willing to change if your choices aren't working. The exercises at the end of this chapter will allow you to practice using the techniques we describe below. Make sure to try any new techniques that appeal to you before you start your bar review so you can become comfortable with them.

Two Learning Models and Their Implications for Your Studying

Two learning models provide the foundation for our recommendations about studying effectively for your bar exam: (1) the information-processing model of learning; and (2) self-regulated learning. These models should inform the choices you make about where, when, how long, and how you study.

1. **The information-processing model of learning.** The information-processing model of learning,[3] depicted in diagram 13-1, suggests that human beings learn in a way that is analogous to how computers function: taking in information, processing information, and storing information in an organized fashion so that they can later retrieve it.[4] In the context of bar study, there are three important components of this process: (1) attending to information; (2) encoding information; and (3) overlearning information so that you can easily recall it.

   a. **Attending to information.** Attention plays a crucial role in whether your studying is productive or a waste of time. If you've ever read a page and then realized you don't remember a thing, or daydreamed

---

2. If you're having trouble understanding an area of law, however, make an exception to this recommendation. For such areas, consider reading a law school commercial outline or cases that deal with the subject (you can get names of cases from a professor at your law school who teaches the subject).

3. *See generally* Marcy Perkins Driscoll, Psychology Of Learning For Instruction (1994). Other works addressing cognitive learning theories include Dale H. Schunk, Learning Theories: An Educational Perspective (4th ed. 2003); Peggy A. Ertmer & Timothy J. Newby, *Behaviorism, Cognitivism, Constructivism: Comparing Critical Features from an Instructional Design Perspective*, 6(4) Performance Improvement Q. 50 (1993).

4. Michael Hunter Schwartz, Expert Learning For Law Students 21-24 (2005) [hereinafter Expert Learning].

Diagram 13-1: The Information-Processing Model of Human Learning

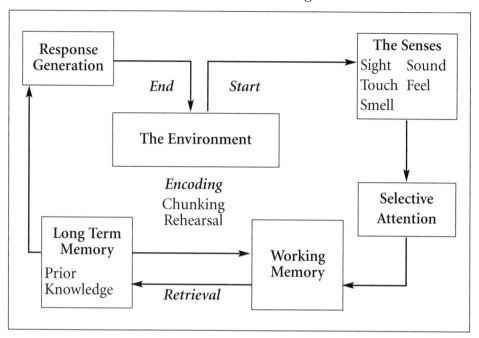

during a lecture and missed an important point, you understand that attention can determine whether you learn anything or not. Consequently, a prerequisite to successful learning is focused attention.

To ensure focused attention, there are many strategies you can use. For example, you can get plenty of rest so you're not too tired to focus; plan ten-minute study breaks every hour or so to keep your mind fresh; choose a study location that won't distract you so there's little competition for your attention; and stop every fifteen minutes during your studying to assess whether you're maintaining your focus.

b. **Encoding information.** To convert information from short-term to long-term memory, you must engage in active learning activities. Don't assume that either listening to bar review lectures or reading bar outlines, without more, will suffice. Encoding requires you to act upon material, not merely passively receive it.

You can facilitate your encoding of information in several ways. For example, just as you store information in a computer in folders, subfolders, and sub-subfolders, organize information you want to learn so that you'll have a place to store it in your brain.

You can organize materials by creating a one-page outline or graphic depiction of the material so that you have a structured map you can store in your brain. You can also organize material by identifying connections—similarities, differences, and relationships—between what you're reviewing in your bar review and what you already learned in law school.

You can also encode information through "rehearsal," which means practicing the act of remembering. In this sense, memorizing the law is like working out to build muscles; by rehearsing what you want to learn, your memory of material will be strengthened.

c.   **Overlearning information.** By overlearning, you'll know the law so well that you'll be able to recall it almost automatically, with little mental effort. For example, your knowledge of how to read is automatic. Unlike when you were a child, you no longer need to consciously think about sounding out words and piecing together sentences and paragraphs you've just read.

Similarly, if you overlearn the law, you'll be able to recall it automatically. Then, you'll spend less mental energy on recall during your bar exam and have more mental energy for analyzing and answering exam questions. Also, when you're anxious, you're devoting brain power to your anxiety; in such instances, overlearning may be necessary to recall any information at all.

2.   **Self-regulated learning.** Self-regulated learning means being aware of, taking control over, and reflecting about your own learning process. Research demonstrates that students who self-regulate their learning perform better on academic tasks, regardless of students' inherent abilities as measured by standardized tests of aptitude.[5] Self-regulated learning involves the three phases depicted in diagram 13-2: (1) planning, (2) implementation, and (3) reflection.

In the first phase, planning, you should:

- Set mastery-learning goals (for example, "By the end of the day, I'll be able to recite all the elements of all the homicide crimes,") as opposed to task completion goals (for example, "I will read pages 12–64 of my bar review criminal law outline.").

- Invoke self-efficacy (see chapter 3). For example, when you study a subject you find difficult, say to yourself, "I'm confident I'll be able to master contempt law because I mastered the rule against perpetuities, a much harder concept."

- Make careful decisions about when, how long, where, and how you'll study. Study at set, regular times (one to two hours each) with regular, short breaks (ten minutes each), and give yourself occasional rewards if you stick to your plans. Most students study best in a location that's quiet, clean, and free from distraction, and where they have easy access to help if they're struggling with material (for example, from a peer, former professor, or friend). To decide how you're going to study, consider the necessities of the task in which you're engaged, what has worked for you in the past, and

---

5. *See* Reinhard W. Lindner & Bruce Harris, *Self-Regulated Learning: Its Assessment and Instructional Implications*, 16(2) Educ. Res. Q. 29 (1992); Barry J. Zimmerman & Andrew Paulson, *Self-Monitoring During Collegiate Studying: An Invaluable Tool for Academic Self- Regulation, in* New Directions For Teaching And Learning: Understanding Self-Regulated Learning 63, at 13-14 (1995).

Diagram 13-2: Self-Regulated Bar Preparation

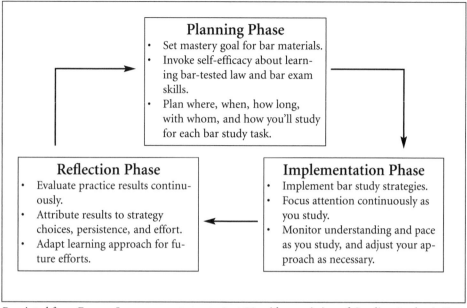

Planning Phase
- Set mastery goal for bar materials.
- Invoke self-efficacy about learning bar-tested law and bar exam skills.
- Plan where, when, how long, with whom, and how you'll study for each bar study task.

Reflection Phase
- Evaluate practice results continuously.
- Attribute results to strategy choices, persistence, and effort.
- Adapt learning approach for future efforts.

Implementation Phase
- Implement bar study strategies.
- Focus attention continuously as you study.
- Monitor understanding and pace as you study, and adjust your approach as necessary.

Reprinted from EXPERT LEARNING, *supra* note 4, at 28, with permission of Carolina Academic Press (adapted in this text to address bar study). Copyright © 2005, all rights reserved.

other information about your personality type, learning style, and preferences.[6]

In the second phase, implement the strategies you've selected. When doing so, maintain focused attention and monitor your comprehension and learning pace. For example, regularly ask yourself:

- Do I understand what I'm reading or learning?

- Am I learning as quickly and easily as I would like to be learning?

- If not, which of my strategy selections (for example, location, time, approach) is not working?

- Am I too sleepy, hungry, or frustrated to study effectively? If so, should I take a ten-minute break?

By asking yourself these and similar questions, you'll increase the likelihood that you'll learn what you need to learn in a time-efficient manner.

---

6. If you would like to learn more about your learning style, we recommend reviewing chapter 6 in EXPERT LEARNING, *supra* note 4, at 53-64. The chapter includes information about free Web site learning style assessments and about the relationship between personality type and learning law. Two good law review articles regarding law student learning styles are Vernellia R. Randall, *The Myers-Briggs Type Indicator, First-Year Law Students, and Performance*, 26 CUMBERLAND L. REV. 26 (1995), and M.H. Sam Jacobson, *A Primer on Learning Styles: Reaching Every Student*, 25 SEATTLE UNIV. L. REV. 139 (2001).

In the third phase, reflection, evaluate how well you've learned, identify any deficiencies in your studying, and plan how you'll study better. By reflecting and adapting your study approaches as you work, you'll be discarding strategies that aren't working and retaining the ones that are, resulting in better overall learning. Similarly, when doing practice tests, take the time to understand your successes and failures so you'll be able to figure out how your learning efforts went wrong. It's tempting to skip this step; but, absent reflection, you're at risk for not passing the bar because you won't know when you've gone astray. In contrast, by taking the time to reflect, you'll make your bar review as productive as possible.

Specific Bar Preparation Study Techniques

There are four study techniques that are especially important in the context of bar exam preparation: (1) reading bar review outlines productively, (2) maximizing your learning from bar review lectures, (3) making sure you've understood what you've learned, and (4) memorization. Tips for each are discussed below.

1.   **Reading bar review outlines productively.**[7] Productive reading begins with "pre-reading," creating a structure in your brain for taking in new material you're trying to learn. Pre-reading works to improve reading much like plowing a field prepares the field for planting; pre-reading readies your brain to absorb what you're going to read.

For bar outlines, pre-read by getting a feel for the big picture of the subject you're reading so that you can ascertain how concepts relate to each other. For example, criminal procedure topics relate to amendments in the Constitution and can therefore be ordered by number (for example, Fifth Amendment, Sixth Amendment) and topics within each amendment (for example, jury trial, right to counsel). Similarly, contracts law can be organized in a sort of cradle-to-grave sequence: (1) formation; (2) defenses; (3) contract interpretation; (4) third-party issues; (5) performance; (6) breach; and (7) remedies.

There are several ways to ascertain the big picture of a given subject. For example, you can read a table of contents, skim through an outline reading only headings and subheadings, or create a one-page hierarchy chart or structured outline. By doing so, you'll improve your retention and understanding because you'll have a mental structure for storing rules within subjects. You're also, in effect, creating a list of potential issue categories you can use as a tool for spotting issues on the bar exam.

Another pre-reading task you should complete is developing questions you expect to be answered by your reading. Reading research

---

7. Many of the pre-reading and reading strategies discussed in this chapter are derived from research conducted for and ideas explained in greater depth in Expert Learning, *supra* note 4, at 83-101. We also recommend an excellent text that focuses exclusively on reading strategies for law students: Ruth Ann McKinney, Reading Like A Lawyer (2005).

demonstrates that students who develop and find answers to such questions increase their reading comprehension.[8] For example, for bar review outlines, you could use pre-reading questions such as:

- I predict that the law with respect to this major concept is _____. Was I correct? Why did I (correctly, incorrectly) predict the law?

- What are the key concepts in _____ (for example, torts, civil procedure) law?

- How are _____ concept and _____ concept related?

- How are _____ concept and _____ concept similar?

- How are _____ concept and _____ concept different?

- Why is the law _____ (what's the underlying policy)?

- Do I agree with the rules in this area of law? Why or why not?

Once you have completed the pre-reading tasks, you're ready to read. There are several strategies you can use to maximize how much you understand, how quickly you read, and how effectively you maintain attention. Here are several strategies you should use:

a. **"Look back."** Use your pre-reading questions to guide your reading. As you finish reading each section of material, make sure you've answered all the questions relating to that section that you developed during your pre-reading. If you cannot find the answers, re-read the section and either get answers to your questions or determine why you cannot do so and whether you need to search elsewhere.

b. **Talk to your bar outlines.** Instead of reading passively, actively engage with your outlines.[9] For example, argue with your outline, make predictions about what's coming next, find connections between what you're reading and what you already know, restate rules in your own words, and come up with examples for each concept you read about.

c. **Take notes.** Writing as you read facilitates learning and increases the likelihood that you'll remember material. For example, for some people, the act of translating an outline to a set of flashcards causes them to remember as much as two-thirds of the material, even before they start using the cards as a self-testing tool. Alternatively, you can simply create your own condensed version of an outline. Your version should be no more than one-third the length of the outline from which you're working. Also, make sure you note any areas of the law that are confusing you so that you can ask questions about them later.

d. **Draw charts or pictures.** If you prefer to learn visually, you can convert all the rules and concepts to mind maps or hierarchy charts. A sample mind map for the elements of common law burglary is depicted in diagram 13-3. Some students who really like to be able to see the big picture at a glance create poster-sized mind maps or hierarchy

---

8. *See generally* Virginia Tech Division of Student Affairs, Cook Counseling Ctr., *SQ3R—A Reading/Study System,* www.ucc.vt.edu/stdysk/sq3r.html (last visited May 7, 2005); Arthur L. Costa & Lawrence E. Lowery, Techniques For Teaching Thinking (1989).

9. *See, e.g.,* McKinney, *supra* note 8, at 59-67.

Diagram 13-3: Mind Map of Burglary Elements and Element Definitions

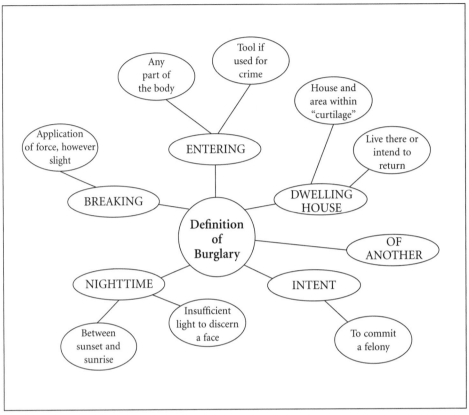

Reprinted from EXPERT LEARNING, *supra* note 4, at 152, with permission from Carolina Academic Press. Copyright © 2005, all rights reserved.

charts that depict entire subject areas; in fact, some even choose to pin their subject posters to their office or bedroom walls during the bar study process. Office supply stores sell a poster-sized version of "yellow sticky" pads, a perfect tool for this technique.

Some students go one step further and use imagery to help them understand concepts. For example, one way to understand the operation of the parol evidence rule is to draw a solid wall between a piece of evidence and a jury; the wall should appear to completely block the evidence. Then you can depict arrows going around the wall for exceptions to the rule, such as evidence of subsequent agreements, agreements for separate consideration, fraud, and mistake. Finally, you can depict arrows passing through the wall to show evidence that's subject to the rule but is nevertheless admissible under it, such as evidence of a prior term that is consistent with a partially integrated agreement.

You may enjoy and benefit from incorporating color into your studying process. For example, you could use shades of green for real property flashcards or mini-outlines because green makes you think of land, and shades of red for criminal law flashcards or mini-outlines because red makes you think of warning (and criminal law rules are warnings about how people should conduct themselves). Alternatively, you can use a variety of color within a subject area outline, such as by using green for contract law damages rules (because they deal with an award of money) and yellow for the statute of frauds (because you may consider it an old, yellowed body of law).

2. **Maximizing Your Learning From Bar Review Lectures.** To maximize your learning from bar review lectures, you must prepare before each lecture. First read your outlines using the pre-reading and reading strategies explained earlier in this chapter. Then, plan how you'll structure your notes during the bar review lecture; students who plan their notes take in more information and learn it better. Use your bar review outline to identify major concepts, subconcepts, and sub-subconcepts in a subject area and write those down with indentations to show whether a concept is a major concept, subconcept, or sub-subconcept. Leave space in between each concept for notes. Also, based on your reading, develop a list of questions for any areas in which you need clarification.

For note-taking, we recommend dividing your computer screen or note-taking pages with a vertical line one-third of the way from the left edge of the page. Use the right side of the page to take notes and the left side to write down questions, areas of confusion, exam-taking hints, and any reflections you have about what you're learning.

During lectures, regularly ask yourself whether you're paying attention. In order to stay focused, remove distractions (such as distracting people or a bad location) and actively resist fatigue, boredom, frustration, thirst, and hunger (consider bringing a snack and a bottle of water). Continue to self-monitor to make sure you understand what's being said. Take effective notes by following instructional cues (such as what is on the board or what the instructor repeats) and listen actively (for example, by trying to paraphrase rules or come up with examples for every concept you're learning). Finally, continue to refine your organization of the subject matter as you take notes.

3. **Making Sure You Understand What You've Learned.** As you read your bar outlines and attend your bar review lectures (and after you've done additional study as necessary), self-monitor your level of comprehension to move toward a mastery level of understanding for each subject you study. There are two reasons to confirm your mastery as you study. First, knowing the words of rules of law isn't enough. You're wasting your time if you memorize rules of law that you don't understand. You must also understand how to apply each rule of law to answer bar exam questions successfully. For example, it's not enough to know that a court will apply a "reasonable person" standard in torts cases. You must also understand that the reasonable person standard doesn't require people to take every precaution possible, even if an extraordinarily careful person might do so. Rather, the standard requires consideration of the particular circumstances in a given situation—for example, the cost and effort required to take action and the likelihood of harm.

The second reason to monitor your mastery is that the strategies you'll use to do so will also facilitate memorizing the material you're studying.

Five techniques that can be used to confirm your mastery are listed below. All five of these techniques can be used effectively either individually or in a study group.

a. **Paraphrasing.** Paraphrasing focuses on assessing whether you understand each rule by itself, without reference to any other rules. For each rule that you need to know, make sure that you can accurately restate the rule in your own words. The act of paraphrasing forces you to find synonyms for the words in a rule, which requires you to understand the rule well enough to be able to do so. One example should clarify this technique. Try translating the following rule into your own words before looking at the paraphrase and explanation below:

- **Rule:** An offer is the manifestation of willingness to enter into a bargain so made as to justify another person in understanding that his or her assent to that bargain is invited and will conclude it.

- **Paraphrase:** An offer is a communication of commitment.

- **Explanation of paraphrase:** This paraphrase is a good one because it captures the essence of what the rule requires, an alleged offeror must express (communicate) that, if the other party says "yes," the parties have a binding deal; the only way to do so is by expressing commitment.

To create paraphrases, it's helpful to imagine yourself as a teacher who must explain a rule to someone who knows nothing about the law. Your paraphrase should allow a novice to understand what a rule requires.

b. **Creating examples and non-examples.** Creating examples and non-examples also assesses whether you understand individual rules. Examples are short, real-world, hypothetical sets of facts that everyone would agree would satisfy a particular rule. In contrast, non-examples are sets of facts that are similar to examples, but lack one or more of the essential attributes required by a rule. For example:

- **Offer example:** "On July 2, 2006, at 2:00 p.m., I will wash and wax your car if you promise to pay me $35 next Tuesday."

- **Offer non-example:** "On July 2, 2006, at 2:00 p.m., I might wash and wax your car if you promise to pay me $35 next Tuesday."

- **Battery example:** Jane walked up to Josh and punched him in the mouth.

- **Battery non-example:** Jane walked up to Josh and tried to punch him in the mouth, but missed hitting him altogether.

If you can come up with an example and non-example of every rule, you've mastered those rules. With both this technique and paraphrasing, it's helpful to check the accuracy of your efforts. We recommend exchanging paraphrases, examples, and non-examples with someone else who is also studying for the bar exam.

Once you've mastered each rule individually, you're ready to pre-pare yourself for using the rules on the bar exam. The next three techniques listed below will help you with this task.

c. **Creating checklists of issues in each subject area that may appear on your exam.** Creating checklists of potential exam issues will assist you in spotting issues, recalling the law, and planning your essay exam answers. Consider comparing your checklists with a friend or your study group.

d. **Keeping an issues-combination log.** Your issues-combination log should include all of the various combinations of issues you encounter on practice exams. This log should identify both the general subject areas tested (for example, torts and remedies) and the specific issues within those subject areas (for example, nuisance as the specific tort and an injunction as the specific remedy) as indicated in exercise 13-5. As you get toward the end of your bar study, take a look at the log as a whole and think about the various ways you have seen issues combined. It's beneficial to do this exercise in a study group; each student is likely to have answered different questions and therefore the group's log will have more examples than any one student's log.

e. **Creating and answering your own bar exam questions.** After you've answered at least ten sample bar exam questions, try to create some of your own. To get ideas for your questions, look at your issues-combinations log. You can find ideas for your hypotheticals by looking at a newspaper, cases you've read in law school, or recently decided cases. Make sure to modify the facts to raise the issues you wish to raise. To make sure you've created good questions and answers, show them to a friend or to your study group. If you can create and answer a close imitation of a bar exam question, you've mastered the material at a very high level.

4. **Memorizing.** The final step in your efforts to master the law you need to know for your bar exam is to memorize it. Successfully taking a bar exam depends on your ability to memorize thousands of legal rules.[10] If you use the suggestions already discussed in this chapter, you should be close to the level of recall you'll need for your exam. If you've created mini-outlines, hierarchy charts, mind maps, checklists, or flashcards, then you've already established organizational structures in your mind to facilitate rapid mental access to the places in your long-term memory in which you've stored rules of law.

To cement your memorization and increase your speed and likelihood of recall, develop multiple organizational structures for each subject area you're learning. Just as having two different ways to get to work helps you get there on time if one way won't work (for example, because of a traffic

---

10. Society of American Law Teachers, *Society of American Law Teachers Statement on the Bar Exam*, 52 J. LEGAL EDUC. 446, 447 (2002); *see also* Robert M. Jarvis, *An Anecdotal History of the Bar Exam*, 9 GEO. J. LEGAL ETHICS 359, 381 (1996); Linda Jellum & Emmeline Paulette Reeves, *Cool Data on a Hot Issue: Empirical Evidence That a Law School Bar Support Program Enhances Bar Performance*, 5 NEV. L. J. 646, 652 (2005).

accident), having two paths to knowledge increases the likelihood that one of them will allow you to remember what you need to remember. Consequently, if you've created mini-outlines, then create checklists, charts, or mind maps in addition. Even if you're not a visual learner, the greater mental effort required to create charts and mind maps will help you learn material better. Similarly, even if you're not a read-write learner, the greater mental effort it takes to create an outline or checklist will supplement your charts and mind maps.

The key to using your flashcards, outlines, checklists, charts, or mind maps is to practice remembering them. Practice picturing them in your mind and then recalling and writing down the law. For example, with your flashcards, look at the name of each concept on the front of each flashcard and think about and write down the definitions that you've previously written on the back of the cards. You should practice both mentally remembering and writing down rules because on multiple-choice tests you'll need to recall rules from your short-term memory, and on essay tests you'll need to write down rules from your long-term memory. Many students find it helpful to be quizzed by a peer or even by a non-bar taker who wants to help.

Finally, you can use mnemonic techniques to help you memorize. Mnemonics are useful for bar study because they add variety to your bar study and can be fun to create. On the other hand, mnemonics are generally considered inferior memorization tools because it takes mental effort to create them and they only have meaning as a tool for memorizing. Consequently, the mental trace they leave is likely to be shorter-lived and weaker than the trace from more meaningful efforts to memorize. If you decide to use mnemonics, create them on your own. Self-created mnemonics produce a stronger mental trace than mnemonics someone else has created.

We suggest using mnemonics only to supplement study efforts rather than relying on them as exclusive bar preparation techniques. Three common mnemonic techniques that may be helpful for bar study are listed below:

a. **Single-use coding method.** Use the first letter of each word in a list of items you need to memorize to create a new word or sentence. Then memorize the new word or sentence so that you can recall it during the bar exam. For example, you can remember a checklist of contract defenses by the mnemonic sentence *DUI IS DUM*:

    Duress
    Undue influence
    Incapacity (minors, mental incapacity, intoxication)

    Illegality
    Statutes of frauds

    Deception (misrepresentation, nondisclosure, concealment)
    Unconscionability
    Mistake

b. **Familiar song.** Adapt a familiar song to address a list of items you need to remember. For example, you could use the song "Twinkle, Twinkle Little Star" to remember the requirements for adverse possession (use of land, for a specified time, in a manner that is hostile, open, notorious, and continuous, and actual and exclusive as to the whole area being claimed):[11]

Twinkle, twinkle *obvious* land use
    Why would the owner allow such *hostile* abuse?

On and on the use must *continue* to be
    And *actual, sole use* of the entire area you see

Twinkle, twinkle obvious land use
    For the statutory period without any non-use.

   c. **Place method.** Imagine a room with which you are familiar, such as the bedroom, office, or living room in your home. Scan the room in your mind and create odd associations (the odder the better) between the things in the room and a list of items you need to remember. For example, the factors considered by a court when deciding whether to grant a preliminary injunction are: (1) the likelihood of irreparable harm, (2) the balance of hardships, (3) the requesting party's likelihood of success on the merits, and (4) the general public's and third parties' interests. To remember these factors, you could create the following associations between the list of factors and your kitchen:

- For the likelihood of irreparable harm: associate the drain in the sink in your kitchen with the idea that the requesting party must be at risk of having its irreplaceable rights go down the drain;

- For the balance of hardships: associate the kitchen phone on the wall with talking with your sibling with whom you always have good arguments (balanced debates);

- For the likelihood of success: associate the stove with the fact that you're an excellent (or poor) cook by imagining how likely you would be to produce a successful meal; and

- For consideration of the general public's and third parties' interests: associate the place where you keep your newspaper with stories discussing public and personal interests.

Conclusion

The bar exam requires you to know a large quantity of information. Consequently, to be well prepared for your exam, you must maximize your use of the time you spend reading bar outlines, attending bar review lectures, checking your understanding of the law, and memorizing the law. To use your time effectively, regulate your learning by planning your study time, monitoring the effectiveness of your study time, making adjustments to your study techniques as necessary, and using study strategies (like the

---

11. Barlow Burke & Joseph A. Snoe, Property Examples And Explanations 86 (2001).

ones detailed in this chapter) that maximize your effectiveness. If you do so, you'll know the law you need to know to pass the bar.

Exercise 13-1: Using Pre-Reading and Reading Strategies to Read Bar Review Outlines Productively

This exercise offers you an opportunity to practice the recommendations for reading bar review outlines. If you're still not finished with law school and can't obtain a bar review outline, you can use a commercial outline for one of the courses in which you're currently enrolled. Choose a bar-tested subject so that you get extra bang for your effort. Respond to each of the questions below in the space provided.

Step 1: Develop an Understanding of the Big Picture of This Body of Law.

Look at the summary if your outline includes one or look at the major headings within the subject area (generally, the roman numerals, the capital letters, and the traditional numbers [1, 2, 3 ...]) and then create a one-page outline, hierarchy chart, or mind map in the space provided below.

Exercise 13-1: (continued)

Step 2: Anticipate the Questions the Outline Will Answer.

Brainstorm at least ten questions about the area of law you're learning that you expect to be answered by the outline.

1. _____

   _____

2. _____

   _____

3. _____

   _____

4. _____

   _____

5. _____

   _____

6. _____

   _____

7. _____

   _____

8. _____

   _____

9. _____

   _____

10. _____

    _____

Exercise 13-1: (continued)

Step 3: Get Answers to Your Questions as You Read the Outline.

Record your answers to your above questions in the space below.

1. _____

_____

2. _____

_____

3. _____

_____

4. _____

_____

5. _____

_____

6. _____

_____

7. _____

_____

8. _____

_____

9. _____

_____

10. _____

_____

Exercise 13-1: (continued)

Step 4: Talk to the Outline as You Read It.

In the space below, write down at least one of each of the following:

1. The points in the outline that you consider bad law:

2. Your predictions about what's coming next as you read the outline:

3. Any connections you can make between what you're reading and what you learned in your law school classes:

Exercise 13-1: (continued)

Step 5: Record Your Learning as You Read.

While you're reading, create your own interpretation by writing your own shorter version of the outline, making flashcards, creating hierarchy charts, or creating mind maps. Do this step on separate sheets of paper or index cards.

Step 6: Identify Unclear or Confusing Areas of the Law.

In the space below, write down any aspect of the law that is even slightly unclear to you.

Exercise 13-2: Checklist for Maximizing What You Learn From Bar Review Lectures[12]

Below is a checklist of activities in which you should be engaging to maximize what you learn from your bar review lectures. If you're still in law school, use this checklist to maximize what you get out of a bar-tested law school course. You may need to adapt some of the items (for example, finish reading the assigned cases and a commercial outline for the subject instead of reading the relevant bar review outline). Check each item as you complete it.

Preparation activities:

❑   Complete all reading of the relevant bar review outline.

❑   Set an explicit, mastery-learning goal regarding the subject area.

❑   Plan notes (prepare to use the one-third/two-thirds system and create a preliminary outline of the body of law into which you'll take notes).

❑   Plan attention-focusing strategies.

❑   Develop a list of questions and areas of confusion relating to the subject area.

Effective listening:

❑   Be ready mentally (remove distractions; avoid boredom, frustration, fatigue, thirst, and hunger).

❑   Self-monitor while listening to make sure you're understanding the material.

❑   Listen actively by striving to make sense of everything the instructor says.

Effective note-taking:

❑   Focus on key points and follow instructional cues.

❑   Leave lots of space for notes.

❑   Correct confusion and restate your understanding in your own words.

❑   Organize while writing.

---

12. Reprinted from EXPERT LEARNING, *supra* note 4, at 134, with permission of Carolina Academic Press (adapted to bar study principles in this text). Copyright © 2005, all rights reserved.

Exercise 13-3: Checking Your Understanding

For each rule you need to learn, provide a paraphrase and brainstorm one example and one non-example. For the first few rules, we have included a reminder of what we mean by a paraphrase, an example, and a non-example to make your efforts easier.

Rule:

Paraphrase (the rule in your own words):

Example (a short hypothetical that indisputably satisfies all requirements of the rule):

Non-example (a short hypothetical that is similar to the example, but indisputably fails to satisfy at least one requirement of the rule):

Rule:

Paraphrase (the rule in your own words):

Example (a short hypothetical that indisputably satisfies all requirements of the rule):

Non-example (a short hypothetical that is similar to the example, but indisputably fails to satisfy at least one requirement of the rule):

Exercise 13-3: (continued)

Rule:

Paraphrase (the rule in your own words):

Example (a short hypothetical that indisputably satisfies all requirements of the rule):

Non-example (a short hypothetical that is similar to the example, but indisputably fails to satisfy at least one requirement of the rule):

Rule:

Paraphrase (the rule in your own words):

Example (a short hypothetical that indisputably satisfies all requirements of the rule):

Non-example (a short hypothetical that is similar to the example, but indisputably fails to satisfy at least one requirement of the rule):

Exercise 13-3: (continued)

Rule:

Paraphrase:

Example:

Non-example :

Rule:

Paraphrase:

Example:

Non-example :

Exercise 13-3: (continued)

Rule:

Paraphrase:

Example:

Non-example:

Rule:

Paraphrase:

Example:

Non-example :

Exercise 13-3: (continued)

Rule:

Paraphrase:

Example:

Non-example :

Rule:

Paraphrase:

Example:

Non-example :

Exercise 13-4: Memorization Practice

This exercise is an opportunity to try at least two (and, if you wish, all) of the memorization strategies described in this chapter. The five memorization techniques are:

- Creating a one-page summary outline and then testing to see if you can recite and write the entire outline from memory.

- Creating flashcards and then testing to see if you can recite and write the rule statements from memory by looking at the name of each concept.

- Creating a checklist of major issues then testing to see if you can recite and write the checklist from memory.

- Creating mind maps or hierarchy charts depicting the relevant law and then testing to see if you can recreate each one from memory.

- Creating mnemonics and then testing to see if you can recite and write the rule statements from memory.

For each technique you use, complete the chart below. Although you can successfully do this exercise alone, consider working on it with a peer or in a study group.

Technique: _____

People involved:

- ❏ Self only.
- ❏ Peer.
- ❏ Study group.

Success on oral testing (select the term below that most accurately describes your level of success):

- ❏ Excellent (95%–100% correct).
- ❏ Good (85%–94% correct).
- ❏ Weak (70%–84% correct).
- ❏ Poor (less than 70% correct).

Success on written testing (select the term below that most accurately describes your level of success):

- ❏ Excellent (95%–100% correct).
- ❏ Good (85%–94% correct).
- ❏ Weak (70%–84% correct).
- ❏ Poor (less than 70% correct).

Exercise 13-4: (continued)

Technique: _____

People involved:

- ❐ Self only.
- ❐ Peer.
- ❐ Study group.

Success on oral testing (select the term below that most accurately describes your level of success):

- ❐ Excellent (95%–100% correct).
- ❐ Good (85%–94% correct).
- ❐ Weak (70%–84% correct).
- ❐ Poor (less than 70% correct).

Success on written testing (select the term below that most accurately describes your level of success):

- ❐ Excellent (95%–100% correct).
- ❐ Good (85%–94% correct).
- ❐ Weak (70%–84% correct).
- ❐ Poor (less than 70% correct).

Technique: _____

People involved:

- ❐ Self only.
- ❐ Peer.
- ❐ Study group.

Success on oral testing (select the term below that most accurately describes your level of success):

- ❐ Excellent (95%–100% correct).
- ❐ Good (85%–94% correct).
- ❐ Weak (70%–84% correct).
- ❐ Poor (less than 70% correct).

Success on written testing (select the term below that most accurately describes your level of success):

- ❐ Excellent (95%–100% correct).
- ❐ Good (85%–94% correct).
- ❐ Weak (70%–84% correct).
- ❐ Poor (less than 70% correct).

Exercise 13-4: (continued)

Technique: _____

People involved:

- ❒ Self only.
- ❒ Peer.
- ❒ Study group.

Success on oral testing (select the term below that most accurately describes your level of success):

- ❒ Excellent (95%–100% correct).
- ❒ Good (85%–94% correct).
- ❒ Weak (70%–84% correct).
- ❒ Poor (less than 70% correct).

Success on written testing (select the term below that most accurately describes your level of success):

- ❒ Excellent (95%–100% correct).
- ❒ Good (85%–94% correct).
- ❒ Weak (70%–84% correct).
- ❒ Poor (less than 70% correct).

Technique: _____

People involved:

- ❒ Self only.
- ❒ Peer.
- ❒ Study group.

Success on oral testing (select the term below that most accurately describes your level of success):

- ❒ Excellent (95%–100% correct).
- ❒ Good (85%–94% correct).
- ❒ Weak (70%–84% correct).
- ❒ Poor (less than 70% correct).

Success on written testing (select the term below that most accurately describes your level of success):

- ❒ Excellent (95%–100% correct).
- ❒ Good (85%–94% correct).
- ❒ Weak (70%–84% correct).
- ❒ Poor (less than 70% correct).

Exercise 13-5: Issue-Combination Log

This exercise will help you create a record of all the issue combinations you encounter while studying for the bar exam. Every time you look at a question or answer for an essay, complete this log.

Subject(s) at issue in the question:	Specific issues addressed:
E.g., torts, civil procedure	*E.g.,* assault, battery, motion to dismiss, venue

Reflection Questions

1. Why do self-regulated learners tend to perform better than their peers who do not use self-regulated learning techniques?

2. Which of the techniques described in this chapter have you tried before? Why did the techniques work or fail to work? Which have worked for you in the past? Which are new?

3. What will you do to make sure you've overlearned as much of the material in your bar review outlines as possible?

CHAPTER 14

DOING PRACTICE EXAM QUESTIONS FOR YOUR MULTISTATE BAR EXAM

Introduction

In addition to reviewing substantive law for your bar exam, also take time to do practice questions similar to those that will be used on your state's bar exam. The two most common types appearing on bar exams are multiple-choice and essay questions.[1] Some states also use "performance" questions that require you to perform a fundamental lawyering skill, such as writing a client letter, a memorandum, or a discovery plan.[2]

Make sure that you have current information from your state's licensing entity about the types of questions used on its exam and make sure to look at released questions as examples of what you can expect to encounter.[3] Multiple-choice, essay, and performance questions require different types of practice. Thus, in this and the following two chapters, we provide strategies tailored to each type of question.[4]

This chapter addresses multiple-choice questions in the context of the Multistate Bar Exam ("MBE") because almost all states use the MBE. Our recommendations, however, also apply to state-created multiple-choice questions, which tend to be similar to MBE questions.

Most bar review courses include in-class practice tests of some sort. Many students find in-class tests helpful, but others find them anxiety-producing. It's essential to include practice tests as part of your preparation; but, if the in-class sessions are uncomfortable, it's fine initially to do practice questions alone in a setting that works better for you. Just make sure to simulate test time allotments so you'll get a feel for how much time you can spend on each question. By one month into your bar review, start forcing yourself to take practice exams in a room with others to simulate what you'll experience during the bar exam.

---

1. For a discussion of bar exam essay testing, see chapter 15.
2. *See* chapter 16.
3. *See* chapter 7.
4. See the recommendations for multiple-choice questions in this chapter, essay questions in chapter 15, and performance questions in chapter 16.

As a general rule, the more practice MBE questions you complete the better; most bar review courses provide students with thousands of practice MBE questions for this purpose. Although this suggestion may sound obvious, we make a special note of it because the benefits of doing large numbers of practice questions are particularly significant with respect to MBE questions (and less true for essay and performance questions). While MBE questions vary, the MBE tends to test certain legal issues over and over again; thus, the more practice questions you do, the more your scores will improve.[5] This suggestion is especially important if you have a history of performing poorly on multiple-choice questions.[6] If you adhere to the suggestions in this chapter and spend time doing practice questions throughout your preparation period, you should obtain a passing score on your MBE.

The National Conference of Bar Examiners ("NCBE") discloses the subjects tested on the MBE and exactly how many questions you'll get in each subject area. The exam currently tests the following subjects:[7]

- Constitutional law: 33 questions.

- Contracts and sales: 34 questions.

- Criminal law and procedure: 33 questions.

- Evidence: 33 questions.

- Real property: 33 questions.

- Torts: 34 questions.

Typical Multiple-Choice Question Formats

Make sure to browse through sample MBE questions to familiarize yourself with typical formats for multiple-choice questions. Table 14-1 explains and illustrates the five common MBE question formats. Try answering the questions. Answers to each of these questions, with explanations, can be found in appendix D.

---

5. *See* Loretta Walder, Pass This Bar: A Readiness Guide For Bar Exam Preparation 20 (1982).

6. See chapter 9, which includes poor multiple-choice skills as a risk factor for not passing a bar exam.

7. NCBE, The Multistate Bar Exam 2005 Information Booklet 2, *available at* www.ncbex .org/tests/Test%20Booklets/MBE_IB2005.pdf [hereinafter MBE Information Booklet].

Table 14-1: The Five Common MBE Formats and Examples of Each

Formats	Examples
1. **Winner/reason questions.** These questions require students to decide which party would prevail in a lawsuit or prosecution and to choose the best explanation for that result. Thus, an answer to such a question can be incorrect because it either names the wrong prevailing party or gives the wrong reason.	1. Able and Betty entered into negotiations for a contract by which Able, an expert tour guide, would serve as Betty's tour guide for a one-week tour of New York City. Betty said, "I will pay you $1,500 to serve as my tour guide." Able replied, "Would you be willing to consider paying me $2,000?" "No," said Betty. "Then I'll take the $1,500," said Able. Two weeks later, Betty informed Able that she had hired Carl to work as her tour guide. In an action by Able against Betty for breach of contract, Able will: A. Win, because he accepted Betty's offer. B. Win, based on the doctrine of promissory estoppel. C. Lose, because he made a counter-offer and thereby terminated his power to accept Betty's offer. D. Lose, because he did not rely on the contract in any way.
2. **Result/reason questions.** These questions, which are similar to winner/reason questions, require students to predict a result on a somewhat narrower issue (for example, evidence is admissible or not admissible, the motion will succeed or not succeed, the statute is constitutional or not constitutional, the defendant will be convicted or won't be convicted) and the best explanation for that result. Thus, an answer to such a question can be incorrect because it either incorrectly predicts the result or gives the wrong reason.	2. Danielle and Paul entered into a valid and enforceable written contract for the purchase by Paul and sale by Danielle of Greenacre for $100,000. The contract was very detailed, thirty pages long, and included a merger clause. Assume the contract was made and the parties reside in a jurisdiction that has adopted Williston's approach to parol evidence rule questions. If Paul seeks to testify that, after the parties signed the agreement, Danielle promised to arrange for the hardwood floors in the house to be refinished, that evidence will be: A. Barred because the agreement is completely integrated. B. Barred, because it is inconsistent with the parties' written agreement. *(continued)*

Formats	Examples
	C. Admitted, because the parol evidence rule doesn't apply to such evidence. D. Admitted, because the agreement is not completely integrated and the writing is silent about refinishing the floors.
3. **Best argument or theory questions.** These questions, which are less common than the first two formats, end with an incomplete sentence such as "Myra's best argument for ____ is," and then the answers give alternative arguments or theories that Myra might use. Thus, an answer to such a question may be incorrect either because it's wrong or because it's not the best argument.	3. Sally, who is a manufacturer of big screen televisions, and Bob entered into a valid and enforceable written contract for the purchase by Bob from Sally of a "Sally Biggy," a seventy-five-inch big screen television set for $4,500. Sally anticipated making $1,500 in profit on the sale. Bob breached the contract, and Sally sold the Sally Biggy that Bob had agreed to purchase for $4,500. In an action seeking her lost profits, Sally's best argument would be: A. Sally is a lost-volume seller. B. Sally's lost profit is a legitimate item of consequential damages. C. Sally's lost profit compensates her for her time and money spent readvertising and reselling the television. D. Sally should be awarded the money under the doctrine of *in pari delicto*.
4. **Multiple answer questions.** This format, which is much less common than the first three formats, ends with two or three statements. The question asks the student to determine which of the two or three statements are correct, and the answers describe a variety of combinations of the statements (for example, the first and the second, the first and the third, the second and the third, or all three). Thus, an answer to this question is correct only if it describes precisely which statements are accurate.	4. Carl, who had never worked before as a grocery store clerk, and Store entered into an oral agreement whereby Carl agreed to work full-time for Store as a grocery clerk for six months, and Store agreed to pay Carl $3,000 per month. One week later, Carl announced that he refused ever to work for Store. If Store sued Carl seeking specific performance as its only remedy and the court denied Store's request, which of the following grounds would justify this result? I. The statute of frauds because the contract exceeds $5,000 and is not in writing. *(continued)*

Formats	Examples
	II. A grant of specific performance would violate the Constitution. III. Store's remedy at law is not inadequate. A. I and II only. B. I and III only. C. II and III only. D. I, II, and III.
5 and 6. Same fact pattern, multiple questions. This format is also less common than the first three formats. These questions provide a fact pattern followed by two or more questions that all rely on the same fact pattern. In many cases, the questions add facts for students to consider. The questions themselves are similar to the first three types of questions described above. Accordingly, the characteristics of correct and incorrect answers are also similar.	**Questions 5-6 are based on the following facts:** Paula, a famous painter known for her abstract painting style, entered into a valid, written contract drafted by Fred to paint a series of portraits of Fred and his family according to the following schedule: Painting of Fred: Due July 1 for $25,000. Painting of Fred's wife: Due August 1 for $25,000. Painting of Fred's house: Due September 1 for $50,000. Painting of Fred's car: Due October 1 for $20,000. The contract also included the following clause: "Fred's duty to pay Paula is expressly conditioned on Fred's satisfaction with Paula's work." At all relevant times, Fred was aware that all of Paula's past paintings were abstract. 5. Assume that Paula completed the painting of Fred on time, but Fred refused to pay for it, claiming that, while he was comfortable with abstract paintings of everyone else, he would only be satisfied with a realistic portrait of himself. In an action by Paula against Fred for breach of contract, Paula will: A. Win, because she substantially performed her promise to paint Fred's portrait. B Win, because Fred's claim of dissatisfaction lacks good faith. C. Lose, because Paula did not substantially perform her promise. *(continued)*

Formats	Examples
	D. Lose, because Fred's duty to pay was expressly conditioned on his satisfaction with the painting, and Fred was not satisfied.
	6. Assume all of the facts stated in Question 1. Also assume, *for the purposes of this question only*, that Fred's refusal to pay Paula was justified and therefore that Fred did not have to pay Paula for her portrait of Fred. If Fred thereafter repudiates the entire contract, Paula's best argument for enforcing the contract would be:
	A. She painted Fred's portrait in good faith.
	B. Fred is estopped from repudiating the contract because he acknowledged that abstract paintings of everyone else would be satisfactory to him.
	C. Contra proferentem.
	D. The contract is divisible.

Recommendations for Scoring Well on Your MBE

We have developed a set of ten recommendations for scoring well on the MBE portion of your bar exam:

1. **Do practice MBE questions religiously.** Practicing MBE questions is an effective way to increase your MBE scores. Accordingly, we recommend that you practice MBE questions six days a week during your entire bar review period.

2. **Do thirty-four questions per practice session.** Thirty-four questions translates into the number of questions you should complete in one hour during the bar exam. Accordingly, by consistently practicing thirty-four questions a day, you'll be able to track how you're doing timewise on your MBE questions. This is important information to have so you'll know whether you need to pick up your pace or whether you have enough extra time to slow down. There tends to be an inverse relationship between speed and accuracy. So, if you're finishing your practice questions with a lot of time left over, slow down and aim for a higher level of accuracy.

3. **Develop endurance and a rhythm.** You'll likely find that practicing MBE questions gets boring rather quickly! Doing thirty-four questions per day is a good way to "train"—build your endurance for sitting through 200 questions in one day—and provides enough questions to develop a rhythm.

4. **Narrow the answer to two possibilities and take your best guess.** When you answer MBE questions, try to narrow your answer to two possibilities. Then, make your answer selection and stick with it! Don't go back and change an answer unless you're certain your first choice was wrong; your first selection will usually be a better bet.

5. **Track your practice MBE percentages.** When you practice MBEs, keep a log of the percentage you're getting right (use exercise 14-2 at the end of this chapter). If you're getting above 50% right when you begin your preparation, you're doing well. And, if you can get up to 65–70% correct by the time you sit for the bar exam, you'll be doing well and be in the passing zone.[8] But be forewarned: you won't feel like you're doing well at all! During your entire academic career, 65% would be the equivalent of a "D." Most students feel terrible when taking the MBE because they feel they're getting too many answers wrong. They're likely getting a lot wrong, but they're probably also getting enough correct to pass the bar. Tracking your scores will likely build your confidence level as you compile objective evidence that you're approaching the 65–70% mark.

6. **Practice one subject at a time to review and reinforce the substantive law.** For a significant portion of your bar review preparation period, practice multiple-choice questions one subject at a time. Because your goal during most of your review period is to review and reinforce the substantive law,

---

8. *See* Richard Cabrera, *Working to Improve: A Plan of Action for Improving the Bar Exam Pass Rate*, 27 Wm. Mitchell L. Rev. 1169, 1184 (2000) (asserting that a MBE scaled score over 140 is high enough to ensure passing the bar).

you'll be most effective practicing one subject at a time. Also, because you want to be reviewing and reinforcing the legal principles tested on your bar exam, make sure to review all your answers—not just the questions you get wrong. Identify why each correct answer is correct and why each wrong answer is wrong. An answer can be wrong for one of four reasons, because it:

- Relies on the wrong issue or element;

- Reflects a reading-comprehension error;

- Misstates the law; or

- Misapplies the law.

Make sure to ascertain which error explains why you get questions wrong so that you can identify patterns in your errors and alter your approach to reading questions or studying accordingly. Exercises 14-3 and 14-4 at the end of this chapter will help you identify patterns and plan how to avoid such errors in the future.

7. **Do mixed-subject MBE sets during the last part of your bar preparation period.** During the last part of your preparation period, your reason for doing practice MBEs should shift from reviewing and reinforcing legal principles to simulating test conditions. Accordingly, use mixed-subject sets of practice MBEs during the last part of your preparation period.

8. **Aim for *at least* 2,000 total practice MBE questions.**[9] If you take the time to do the math, you'll discover that, at thirty-four questions per day, you should do *at least* 2,000 MBE questions during your bar review period! Thus, cumulatively, just thirty-four questions a day should result in a passing MBE score.[10]

9. **Answer every question as you take the MBE.** When you take the MBE, you are given computer-graded sheets with ovals to fill in for your answers. Because your score will be based on the number of questions you answer correctly, you should answer every question on the exam—including those you don't know and those you don't get to (by filling in ovals for any unanswered questions during the final moments of your exam).

One of the saddest bar exam stories we've heard was about a student who finished question number one hundred, just to realize that her answer was written in the row for question number ninety-nine. She had skipped a question, and marked her answers for almost the entire exam in the wrong rows!

A good way to avoid this problem is to force yourself to select an answer for every question, even if you have doubts. Place a question mark in your exam booklet next to questions you're not sure of, so that if you have extra time, you can go back to those questions. This approach has two advantages. First, it helps you avoid spending too much time on a few hard questions and getting off pace. Second, by marking an answer for every

---

9. Note that this is a *minimum* recommended number of MBE practice questions. Indeed, many experts recommend doing significantly more practice MBE questions. *See, e.g., id.* at 1180 n.71 (recommending a minimum of 3,500 practice MBE questions).

10. Thirty-four questions per day, six days a week, for ten weeks equals 2,040 practice questions.

question, you'll ensure that you have answered every one and that you'll never face question one hundred when you're at answer space ninety-nine.

Although the NCBE states that no credit will be given for anything written in your exam booklet,[11] we recommend circling your answers in your test booklet. In the event there is any problem with your computer grid sheet, or you discover you got off track in filling in the correct ovals, you'll be able to redo your answers relatively quickly by looking in your test booklet.

10. **Read the instructions for the MBE well in advance of the exam.** Make sure to read the directions for the MBE exam in advance.[12] That way, you'll only need to take time to skim the instructions during your actual exam to ensure there aren't any changes. Specifically, note the following directions:[13]

- Choose the best of the possible answers.

- Answer all questions according to the generally accepted view unless noted otherwise.

- Assume that UCC Articles 1, 2, and 9 (fixtures) have been adopted.

- Assume the Federal Rules of Evidence control.

- The terms "constitutional" and "unconstitutional" refer to the federal constitution.

- Assume there are no applicable statutes unless stated otherwise.

- Assume joint and several liability.

---

11. MBE Information Booklet, *supra* note 7, at 44.
12. *Id.* at 24.
13. *Id.*

*Exercise 14-1: Sample MBE Questions**

Below are three sample MBE questions to give you a sense of their length, style, and format. Try answering them; the answers are in appendix D at the end of this book. More samples are available on the NCBE Web site, www.ncbex.org.

Question 1

Neighbor, who lived next door to Homeowner, went into Homeowner's garage without permission and borrowed Homeowner's chain saw. Neighbor used the saw to clear broken branches from the trees on Neighbor's property. After he had finished, Neighbor noticed several broken branches on Homeowner's trees that were in danger of falling on Homeowner's roof. While Neighbor was cutting Homeowner's branches, the saw broke.

In a suit for conversion by Homeowner against Neighbor, will Homeowner recover?

A. Yes, for the actual damage to the saw.

B. Yes, for the value of the saw before Neighbor borrowed it.

C. No, because when the saw broke Neighbor was using it to benefit Homeowner.

D. No, because Neighbor did not intend to keep the saw.

Question 2

Defendant is on trial for nighttime breaking and entering of a warehouse. The warehouse owner had set up a camera to take infrared pictures of any intruders. After an expert establishes the reliability of infrared photography, the prosecutor offers the authenticated infrared picture of the intruder to show the similarities to Defendant.

The photograph is:

A. Admissible, provided an expert witness points out to the jury the similarities between the person in the photograph and Defendant.

B. Admissible, allowing the jury to compare the person in the photograph and Defendant.

C. Inadmissible, because there was no eyewitness to the scene available to authenticate the photograph.

D. Inadmissible, because infrared photography deprives a defendant of the right to confront witnesses.

Question 3

Water District is an independent municipal water-supply district incorporated under the applicable laws of the state of Green. The district was created solely to supply water to an entirely new community in a recently developed area of Green. That new community is racially, ethnically, and socioeconomically diverse, and the community has never engaged in any discrimination against members of minority groups.

The five-member, elected governing board of the newly created Water District contains two persons who are members of racial minority groups. At its first meeting, the governing board of Water District adopted a rule unqualifiedly setting aside twenty-five percent of all positions on the staff of the District and twenty-five percent of all contracts to be awarded by the District to members of racial minority groups. The purpose of the rule was "to help redress the historical discrimination against these groups in this country and to help them achieve economic parity with other groups in our society." Assume that no federal statute applies.

A suit by appropriate parties challenges the constitutionality of these set-asides. In this suit, the most appropriate ruling on the basis of applicable United States Supreme Court precedent would be that the set-asides are:

A. Unconstitutional, because they would deny other potential employees or potential contractors the equal protection of the laws.

B. Unconstitutional, because they would impermissibly impair the right to contract of other potential employees or potential contractors.

C. Constitutional, because they would assure members of racial minority groups the equal protection of the laws.

D. Constitutional, because the function and activities of Water District are of a proprietary nature rather than a governmental nature and, therefore, are not subject to the usual requirements of the Fourteenth Amendment.

Exercise 14-2: MBE Practice Question Statistics

Date	Subject	Number Correct/34	Percent Correct	Time
		/34		
		/34		
		/34		
		/34		
		/34		
		/34		
		/34		
		/34		
		/34		
		/34		
		/34		
		/34		
		/34		
		/34		
		/34		
		/34		
		/34		
		/34		
		/34		
		/34		
		/34		
		/34		
		/34		
		/34		
		/34		
		/34		
		/34		
		/34		
		/34		
		/34		
		/34		
		/34		
		/34		
		/34		
		/34		
		/34		

Exercise 14-2: MBE Practice Question Statistics

Date	Subject	Number Correct/34	Percent Correct	Time
		/34		
		/34		
		/34		
		/34		
		/34		
		/34		
		/34		
		/34		
		/34		
		/34		
		/34		
		/34		
		/34		
		/34		
		/34		
		/34		
		/34		
		/34		
		/34		
		/34		
		/34		
		/34		
		/34		
		/34		
		/34		
		/34		
		/34		
		/34		
		/34		
		/34		
		/34		
		/34		
		/34		
		/34		
		/34		
		/34		
		/34		

Exercise 14-3: Incorrect MBE Answer Assessment Form

Use this form to help you analyze your errors on MBE practice questions and to plan how to improve your MBE scores. Make multiple copies of this form so you can use it throughout your bar study period.

Q#	Subject Area	Why the Correct Answer Was Correct	Why My Answer Was Wrong	Type of Error(s) (check all that apply) RC: Reading comprehension I: Missed issue L: Error of law A: Applied law incorrectly
				❑ RC ❑ I ❑ L ❑ A
				❑ RC ❑ I ❑ L ❑ A
				❑ RC ❑ I ❑ L ❑ A
				❑ RC ❑ I ❑ L ❑ A
				❑ RC ❑ I ❑ L ❑ A
				❑ RC ❑ I ❑ L ❑ A

Exercise 14-4: Plan of Action for Improving My MBE Scores

After you have taken several sets of thirty-four multiple-choice questions, assess how you can improve. Review your answers in exercise 14-3 and identify your most common errors. List all errors that are a significant concern to you and your plan for avoiding those errors on the bar below.

My Most Common Error(s)	My Plan for Addressing Those Errors

Reflection Questions

1. In which of the subject areas tested on the MBE are you strongest? Weakest?

2. Why is it important to assess why you missed MBE questions?

3. How do you feel about a test on which 65–70% correct is passing? Why shouldn't such a low required passing score influence how you study for the MBE?

CHAPTER 15

DOING PRACTICE EXAM QUESTIONS FOR YOUR ESSAY EXAM

Introduction

Because all states use essay questions on their bar exams, you'll need to include practice essay questions in your study plan. Some states use the National Conference of Bar Examiners ("NCBE") essay exam—the Multistate Essay Exam or "MEE"—some use state-created essays, and some use both.

If your state uses the MEE, review the information in chapter 5 about the format of the exam and subjects tested. Make sure to visit the NCBE Web site where both exam information and sample questions are provided.[1] The NCBE Web site has additional sample questions available for purchase.[2] Remember, even if your state incorporates the MEE, it's still graded by examiners in your state—there's no national grading.[3]

If your state uses its own state-created essay questions, find out from your state's licensing entity what subjects are tested on the essay portion of its exam and the format, length, number of questions, and time allotted for the essay portion.

If you've made it into and graduated from law school, odds are you're already a "good" writer. Regardless, to do well on bar exam essays, it's necessary to understand the types of questions asked as well as how to adapt your writing style to write the type of essay answers expected by law examiners. For most students, adapting takes a little thought and tweaking, but has a big payoff with your bar exam essay graders.

---

1. NCBE, *Multistate Tests*, www.ncbex.org/tests.htm (last visited May 7, 2005).
2. *Id.*
3. NCBE, The Multistate Essay Exam 2005 Information Booklet 1, *available at* www.ncbex .org/tests/Test%20Booklets/MEE_IB2005.pdf.

Transitioning Your Writing Style
to Produce Effective Bar Exam Essays

Below are the steps you should be taking to transition your writing to the style expected on bar exam essays. We also recommend that you use exercise 15-1, an essay checklist, to guide your transition.

1. **Understand the types of essay questions used on your state's bar exam.**
    Most states release sample essay questions and model answers or examples of passing answers. Questions and answers may be available on the Web site of your licensing entity,[4] directly from your licensing entity upon request, through your bar review company, or from your law school (for example, many schools have sample questions on reserve in their libraries). If your state uses the MEE, you can view sample questions on the NCBE Web site; additional questions are available for purchase from the NCBE.[5]

    Although essay questions vary from state to state, they tend to be fairly similar. In general, they're more specific, concrete, and concise than the long hypothetical questions traditionally used on law school essay exams. They don't ask students to analyze broad questions of public policy or theorize; rather, they tend to require students to identify issues, apply rules to facts, and predict outcomes. Sometimes, but not frequently, they ask students to apply and distinguish major cases.

    Just as exam questions are concise, your answers should also be concise. But "concise" is a relative term. Don't make the mistake of being too concise—writing so little that you don't get full credit on your essay answers. You only get credit for what appears on your paper. Thus, aim to spot all the issues, spend the largest amount of time on the most significant issues, and spend the least amount of time on the least significant issues. Each essay will require you to exercise judgment regarding which issues to discuss and in what depth.

    What else can you do to achieve the correct level of conciseness? First, be aware that law-trained readers expect a certain structure—it's how we communicate in the profession. To meet the expectations of your examiners, law-trained readers, structure your essays according to the CRAC template we describe below.

    Second, make sure to use the full time you allot to each essay. For example, if you need to pace yourself at a rate of thirty minutes per essay to finish your exam, use thirty minutes—no more and not much less—to answer each question.

    Third, some examiners provide you a certain amount of space in which to write your essay answers; if so, make sure to use the allotted space. In short, by forcing yourself to structure your essays to meet the ex-

---

4. *See, e.g.,* State Bar of California, *California Bar Examination, Examination Statistics, Selected Answers, Study Aids,* www.calbar.ca.gov/state/calbar/calbar_generic.jsp?cid=10397&id=1010 (last visited July 8, 2005).

5. NCBE, *Multistate Tests, supra* note 1.

pectations of your law-trained readers and by adhering to the time and space allotments for each essay question, you'll likely achieve the correct level of conciseness.

2.   **Be prepared for bar exam questions that weave multiple law school subjects together in a single essay question.** Another distinction in the types of questions asked on bar exam essays is that, unlike law school questions, which come with subject labels ("contracts," "criminal procedure") and focus only on a single law school course, bar exam essay questions often combine multiple law school subjects in a single essay question. By creating your own issues-combination log as suggested in chapter 13, you'll get a feel for some of the many possible combinations, such as:

- Issues of substantive law (for example, breach of contract) combined with issues of remedial law (for example, specific performance or damages);

- Issues of substantive law (for example, criminal law) combined with issues of constitutional law (for example, criminal procedure);

- Issues of substantive law (for example, family law) combined with issues of professional responsibility;

- Issues of substantive law (for example, tort law) combined with issues of evidence law; and

- Issues of substantive law (for example, tort law) combined with procedural rules or appellate standards of review.

Examiners frequently use the last combination (substantive law combined with a procedural rule or appellate standard of review), and that one seems to be the trickiest for students to address. Here are some types of "calls" (questions) you might see that weave substance and procedure together:

- Did the trial court err in granting the motion to dismiss on the contract claim?

- Should the trial court grant Defendant's motion for summary judgment on the tort claim?

- Did the trial court err in denying Defendant's motion for judgment of acquittal?

As long as you know the applicable standards, it's a relatively quick task to weave them into your essay answers. It often works well to simply state the applicable standards at the beginning of your answers and then to proceed with the substantive issues. Here are a few examples of how to state a standard at the beginning of essay answers:

- **Example 1: Motion to dismiss a criminal charge in a larceny case:**[6]

---

6. Reprinted with permission from Ruth Ann McKinney with Kenneth S. Broun and Richard Rosen, Guide to North Carolina Standards for Consideration of Trial Court Motions (Feb. 2000) (unpublished handout available from the Writing and Learning Resources Center at the University of North Carolina School of Law, Chapel Hill, North Carolina). Copyright © 2000, all rights reserved.

In ruling on a motion to dismiss a criminal charge, a judge must consider the evidence in the light most favorable to the state, with all inferences going to the state. The question is whether the evidence considered in this light is sufficient to allow a reasonable fact finder to reach a guilty verdict.

Accordingly, a judge must address whether there is sufficient evidence to support a charge for larceny. To convict a defendant of larceny, the state must provide sufficient evidence of [continue on, stating the elements of a larceny offense, and then addressing the elements of the offense one at a time].

- **Example 2: Summary judgment:**

Summary judgment is appropriate when there is no genuine issue of material fact and the moving party is entitled to judgment as a matter of law. The motion is decided based on the record before a court, including pleadings, discovery, and affidavits. The moving party has the burden of establishing summary judgment is appropriate, and all facts are construed in the light most favorable to the non-moving party.

Here, [continue with essay, discussing the relevant issues presented by the question. Make sure to address both prongs of summary judgment: whether there are any material issues of fact in dispute, and whether a party is entitled to judgment as a matter of law (in other words, analyze the relevant substantive law)].

- **Example 3: Standard of review for appeals of questions of law:**

On appeal, questions of law are reviewed under the *de novo* standard of review. In other words, an appellate court uses "fresh eyes," granting no deference to a lower court's determination. An appellate court reviews questions of law using its own judgment and determines whether there was any legal error. [Continue the essay, addressing whether there is any legal error].

3. **Understand the purpose, tone, and audience of bar exam essays.** Thinking through purpose, tone, and audience factors will also help you target essay answers appropriately. In particular, think about how the purpose, tone, and audience factors for bar exam essay questions differ from the type of writing you've done during your law school career.

   The purpose of bar exam essays—to show your bar examiners that you're competent to practice law—is different from the purpose of your law school exam essays—to show your professors that you've mastered the body of substantive law they've covered over the course of a semester.

   The tone of bar exam essay answers—specifically, the extent to which your writing is objective (like an office memo) or persuasive (like a motion memo or appellate brief)—may be similar to or different from the tone you've used in your law school essay exams, depending on your professors' preferences. Aim for the tone you would use in a motion memo or appellate brief—formal, assertive, logical, and confident.

   The audience for your bar exam essays depends on who will be grading your essays, which is a question to ask your state's licensing entity. Generally, bar exam graders are fairly similar. Graders are often practicing attorneys, who grade hundreds of essays rapidly. If you have relatively con-cise and specific questions graded by practicing attorneys who are trying to determine whether you are competent to practice law, it follows that your answers need to be direct, concise, easy-to-read, and responsive to the questions asked. Again, thinking in terms of a motion memo or appel-late brief addressing a specific point about a specific client's situation is often a good point of reference.

In addition to considering your readers' perspectives, avoid thinking in terms of "right" or "wrong" answers. Instead, focus on writing solid essay answers. Needless to say, if you produce the "right" answer, that out-come would be ideal. But, just as in many law school exams, you can do well on the essay portion of bar exams by writing strong essays regardless of whether your answers are "right" or "wrong."

An analogy to motion memoranda and appellate briefs is helpful. In the "real" world, there are attorneys arguing both sides of a motion or ap-peal. Both attorneys may write strong memos or briefs, identifying the issue in dispute and couching their arguments about what the law is or how it applies within the correct legal framework, but only one side will prevail. Similarly, you can write a strong bar exam answer even if your conclusion turns out to be "wrong."[7]

4. **Develop your own "template" for writing bar exam essays.** After you've taken the time to understand the types of essay questions asked on your state's bar exam and have thought through the purpose, tone, and audi-ence factors, begin developing a "template" that you can use when answer-ing any essay question.

Here's what we mean by a "template": If we asked you to visualize an office memo or appellate brief, you could probably immediately visualize them. You have mental templates for these types of legal documents, which makes it easier to write them: you don't need to spend time imagin-ing what one might look like. Accordingly, we recommend that you de-velop a template to use as a basic structure for answering bar essay ques-tions.

By developing a template, you should have an easier time structuring and writing your essays. If you've integrated a template into your thinking, your essays should flow smoothly. You should almost be able to be on "au-topilot" when structuring and writing your answers. More importantly, on exam day you should be able to focus most of your effort on the substance of your essays, rather than on the writing process.

When developing your essay answer template and practicing essay exam answers, focus on the *process* of writing as much as on the substance of your answers. What you shouldn't be doing while practicing essays is spending a lot of time trying to recall the law if you don't yet know it. We're aware of some students who answer as many as six essay questions

---

7. This point assumes that you're correctly identifying the legal issues and legal framework and are making logical arguments within that framework about what rules should apply, or how they should apply to a specific factual situation. In contrast, if your answer is totally off base (missing the issue, misunderstanding the law), it'll be hard to save your essay with good writing skills.

per week because they're trying to use practice essay questions as a tool for learning the substantive law. This approach is inefficient (because it's such a slow way to go about learning the substantive law) and ineffective (because it's impossible to find and write answers to essays addressing even half of the rules you need to know). To learn the substantive law, use one of the many more effective and efficient methods detailed in chapter 13.

We encourage you to create your own essay answer template because you need to tailor your template to the types of questions asked on your state's essay exam. In addition, you'll need to adapt a template to your personal writing style, and you'll be much more likely to remember your template if you have created it on your own. Here are our general suggestions, however, for your essay answer template:

- **Overall conclusion:** State your overall conclusion at the beginning of each essay answer.

- **Introductory paragraph:** Use an introductory paragraph after the initial conclusion to address a procedural standard, appellate standard of review, or to set out overarching rules (for example, elements of an offense) that will be discussed in the body of your answer.

- **CRAC:** Address each individual issue using the CRAC paradigm (Conclusion, Rule, Application, Conclusion) or a similar paradigm (for example, IRAC—Issue, Rule, Application, Conclusion). Make sure to use transitional phrases to lead your examiners through your CRAC analysis, for example:

  ○ C: Yes, Myra will be able to recover …

  ○ R: As a general rule, …

  ○ A: Here, …

  ○ C: Thus, …

- **Overall conclusion:** End your essay by repeating your overall conclusion.

As you work on developing your template, also experiment with varying your template to adapt to the different types of essay questions you may face. For example, for a question with multiple, narrow calls (questions at the end of a fact pattern), use several short CRACs. In contrast, for a question with one broad call, use one longer CRAC.[8] Notice how the use of a paradigm like CRAC will help ensure that you touch all the bases of a solid legal analysis (identifying the legal issue, stating applicable rules, applying the rules to the key facts in a question, and reaching a conclusion) and ensure that your essays have a logical, easy-to-follow flow.

5. **Follow the same process for every essay answer you write.** By following the same process for every essay answer you write, you can minimize your focus on the writing process and maximize your focus on the substance of your answers. Thus, you should be developing and following the same process for each essay answer you write. We recommend the following process:

---

8. The sample essay questions in exercise 15-5 and the sample answers in appendix F provide good examples of adapting a template to different types of essay questions.

a. **Allot time for each essay.** Before you begin each essay question, make sure to jot down your starting time and the time you should finish so that you can keep yourself on track to finish all of your essay questions. You'll likely be under some time pressure, and examiners don't often start exams exactly on the hour, half-hour, or other easily tracked time increments. In addition, while focusing on the substance of your essay answers, it's easy to forget when you started and when you need to stop.

b. **Follow the order of the questions.** On your essay exam, you'll likely be given several questions to answer during a block of time. In what order should you tackle the questions? There are two schools of thought on this point. The first is to look for an "easy" question to answer first so that you'll gain confidence that'll carry over to more difficult questions. The second school of thought advocates going in order, so you avoid spending precious exam minutes flipping through the exam questions. While the first approach may be tempting, we strongly recommend the second approach. Students who flip through questions risk wasting time, losing their focus, and becoming overwhelmed. This choice violates two important principles that you should follow during both your preparation period and on the exam itself: use your time efficiently and stay focused. Looking for an "easy" question is a fear-based reaction to the bar exam. To head off fear, invoke your self-efficacy, manage your fear, and trust the preparation you've done and the excellent skills you bring to your exam.

c. **Start and end with the call of the question.** A "call" is the specific question (or questions) posed at the end of a hypothetical scenario. A true but seemingly apocryphal story illustrates the importance of the call. Professor Schwartz once attended a calibration meeting of graders of a state bar exam.[9] The graders were discussing a one-hour essay question that had four specific calls relating to criminal law and procedure. The hypothetical, however, arguably also raised a professional responsibility issue that several bar takers chose to answer. Sadly, because none of the calls of the question directed bar takers to address the professional responsibility issue, the examinees who did so, even those who wrote beautiful analyses, at best wasted their time and, at worst, failed that question.[10] In short, your task on bar exam essay questions is to answer the call.

Consequently, we recommend that you start and finish your essay-writing process by reading the call of each question. Starting by reading the call will help you focus your attention on the relevant facts

---

9. Bar exam graders often meet during the early portion of the grading process to ensure that they're grading answers in the same way and by the same standards.

10. Note that in several states you may get credit, not lose it, by adding relevant points that examiners did not anticipate when they drafted a question. However, make sure to use your time answering the specific calls of the questions first, before adding in any extra points that you think are relevant. Do not, however, add in irrelevant points in the hope of obtaining more points.

in the exam hypothetical. Most states' bar exams test over twenty subjects, and often a call will tip you off as to the subject of a certain question. For example, if you get a call such as "Can Bert recover from Beatrice for his broken leg?" you should automatically think "torts."[11] Thus, you can read the entire question more quickly and with the correct focus—looking for torts issues.

This approach makes even more sense when you consider a possible error that might occur if you hadn't read the call of the question first. Imagine reading a long hypothetical in which parties have a fight and one ends up with a broken leg. A student who didn't read the call first might address criminal law issues, assessing whether the elements of criminal assault and battery are present.[12]

Although the call of a question won't always provide sufficient information for you to target the right subject area, many times it will. This immediate focus on the call of the question will also ensure that you adopt the one essential principle in organizing bar exam essays: organize your answer according to the call of the question. If there are four calls for a question, your essay should have four headings that label four distinct discussions.

Finish your essay-writing process by rereading the call. This gives you a last opportunity to check your work and make sure that you've completed your assigned task: to answer the call.

d. **Outline your essay answer.** We don't recommend spending a lot of time outlining because you only get credit for what you actually write as part of your answer. If you quickly jot down key words about relevant issues, rules, and key facts, however, and take a few minutes to think about a logical order in which to address them, you'll be less likely to omit key points and your essay will read more fluidly.

e. **Make your essay look professional.** In some states, you'll handwrite your answers, while in others, you may have the option of using a laptop to type your answers.[13] Regardless of whether you write or type, produce answers that look professional. What makes an essay answer look professional? Professional-looking essays are neat and organized, include sufficient white space between paragraphs, use margins, have paragraphs with half-inch indentations, and use headings to lead your examiners through your answers. Transitions between sentences are also important for reader-friendly writing. See table 15-1 for a list of transitional phrases.

---

11. Anytime a question asks about the rights of a private party against another private party, you should immediately think of civil causes of action.

12. This would be incorrect because you should only discuss criminal causes of action if the examiners ask about what actions the government (a state or the United States) could pursue.

13. Make sure to check with your licensing entity if you want to use a laptop. You may have to apply by a certain deadline to do so, and you may need to pay an additional fee.

Table 15-1: Transitions*

Sequence: • First • Second • Next • Finally **Addition:** • Also • And • Furthermore • In addition • In fact • Moreover • Then **Comparison:** • Both • Likewise • In comparison **Contrast:** • Instead • In contrast • Despite • However	**Concession:** • Although • Though **Illustration:** • For example • For instance • Specifically **Result:** • Accordingly • Therefore • Because • Consequently • Since **Summary:** • Accordingly • In sum • Therefore **Emphasis:** • More important • Above all

Although a neat, professional look and clear transitions do not ensure that you'll succeed on your bar exam, they can help. A professional-looking, easy-to-read answer creates an impression of credibility and helps an examiner reach the conclusion that, yes, you're competent to practice law. In addition, because examiners typically must read many answers rapidly, the easier you make it for them to find your smart insights, the more likely they will, in fact, find them!

f. **Use the same type of legal reasoning you used in law school.** The backbone of legal analysis is deductive (or syllogistic) reasoning. This is the same type of reasoning you've used in your law school writing courses and your law school essay exams (better known as "CRAC" or "IRAC"). Just as these rubrics kept you on track in your legal reasoning in law school, they'll ensure you touch the bases you need to cover to get points on your essay exam. Make sure to use transitional phrases to lead your reader through each CRAC. Also, if you are dealing with a multiple-element or multiple-factor rule, make sure you do a CRAC for each element or factor and that you also take the time to

---

* *E.g.*, Linda H. Edwards, Legal Writing: Process, Analysis, And Organization 96–97 (3d ed. 2002).

weigh factors against each other and reach an overall conclusion. Table 15-2 details the CRAC paradigm and table 15-3 provides a sample demonstrating how to use a template and the CRAC paradigm in an answer.

Table 15-2: CRAC Paradigm

Paradigm Components	What to Include	Sample Transitional Phrases to Use
C: Conclusion	State an explicit conclusion.	Yes, … No, …
R: Rules	State the applicable rules.	As a general rule, … Under [your state's] law, …
A: Application	Apply the rules to the relevant facts.	Here, … In this case, …
C: Conclusion	Repeat your explicit conclusion.	In sum, … Therefore, … Thus, …

g. **Be precise and concise.** It's worth repeating that most examiners have a "real-world" perspective and are interested in relatively concise and specific answers that demonstrate your competence to analyze specific clients' cases. Thus, aim for precise, concise essays. Be aware, though, that you can't get credit for what you don't say. So, make sure to write solid answers that cover the issues raised by your questions.

h. **If you have time, proofread your essays.** If you have time to proofread your essay answers, do so. If you reread your answers, make sure to make any edits as neatly as possible. If you don't have time to proof your essays, however, don't let it distress you; many students who pass their bar exams don't have time to go back and proofread their answers.

i. **After answering each question, take a deep breath, clear your head, and move on.** There are likely to be some answers you'll feel relatively good about, and others you'll find more difficult or feel that you didn't address adequately. Regardless, when you're done with an answer, take a moment to take a deep breath and clear your head before beginning another question. Most importantly, don't let uncertainty about an answer you've already finished detract from your focus as you move to subsequent questions. Instead, calculate and write down the time at which you need to finish your next answer and move on. Think of every exam question as a new opportunity to shine. Professional athletes and musicians know they cannot allow themselves to think about their performances in a previous game, inning, half, or concert. As a professional student, you, too, know that it's a waste of time and a needless distraction to ponder past performances, even on immediately preceding questions.

Table 15-3: Sample Essay Answer Demonstrating Template and CRAC Paradigm

Below is a sample essay answer demonstrating how you can use the recommended template and CRAC paradigm to structure your essay answers. We have labeled and shaded the parts of the CRAC paradigm to help you understand our use of the paradigm.

This answer is based on a hypothetical situation involving Marci and her friend, Barb, at a local bar. Dave, who had been in the bar for quite awhile and had had many drinks, pulled an unloaded gun from his pocket and threatened to shoot Marci. Marci knew that Dave had carried an unloaded gun on previous occasions. Bruce walked in on the scene, picked up a cue stick, and told Dave to drop his gun. When Dave refused, Bruce hit Dave, who fell to the floor. Marci fainted, fell to the floor, and broke her arm. The questions presented are: (1) whether Marci can recover from Dave, and (2) whether Dave can recover from Bruce.**

---

1. Marci v. Dave

[Overall conclusion***] Yes, Marci may recover from Dave since she has a cause of action against Dave for assault. [Umbrella rule****] Assault is a tort arising from an intentional act that places another in reasonable apprehension of an imminent harmful or offensive contact. To recover for assault, there must be intent, a reasonable apprehension of imminent harm, causation, and damages.+

[Conclusion, beginning with transition] In this case, there was a reasonable apprehension of imminent harm when Dave pointed a gun at Marci and threat-

---

** This essay hypothetical is adapted from a question asked on a North Carolina bar exam essay question. The answer was written by Denise Riebe and edited by Professor Ruth Ann McKinney, University of North Carolina School of Law, Chapel Hill, North Carolina. Special thanks to Professor Charles Daye, UNC, for providing legal principles to integrate in the answer and for reviewing the answer for accuracy. As you read through the sample answer, notice that the tone is confident and assertive (not hesitant and uncertain) and the writing style is clear and concise (not rambling and difficult to follow). Note that headings are used that match the calls of the question, and notice how they provide a reader easy access to the macro-organization of the answer.

*** Begin and end each section of your essay answers with an explicit, overall conclusion.

**** For this question, there is an "umbrella" rule—an overarching rule (assault and its elements) that provides a structure for the analysis. If there's an umbrella rule that applies to an essay question, state it explicitly, immediately after your overall conclusion, and use it to organize your analysis.

+ Notice how providing the applicable umbrella rule—assault and its elements—provides a reader a roadmap for the analysis to come. After your umbrella paragraph is complete, proceed with the body of your essay, CRACing each element. For this question, each CRAC is rather short and tight. Note that in another question, in a different context, your CRAC may be much longer—maybe several paragraphs, maybe several pages. Some elements might require long CRACs, whereas others will be short and straightforward. As you read the body of this essay, also notice how transitional phrases are used to lead a reader through the essay answer.

ened to shoot her. [Rule, beginning with transition] As a general rule, an objective standard is used to determine whether there is reasonable apprehension. [Application, beginning with transition] Accordingly, the fact that Marci was aware that Dave carried an unloaded gun on previous occasions does not diminish the character of Dave's conduct. A gun may create harmful contact. [Conclusion, beginning with transition] Thus, a reasonable person would be afraid of imminent contact from a gun, as Marci was here.

[Conclusion, beginning with transition] Next, Dave's conduct was intentional. [Rule] Intent is another element required for an assault cause of action. Intent requires that a defendant act with the purpose of causing a harmful result or substantial certainty that a harmful result will result from the defendant's purposeful actions. [Combined application and conclusion] Although Dave was drinking, he could anticipate that his choice to aim a gun at Marci would cause her to fear he would shoot her. Thus, he did not appear to be so drunk that he lost his capacity to form the requisite intent for assault.

[Conclusion, beginning with transition] Further, there is causation. [Rule] For intentional torts, a defendant is responsible for the full scope of damages caused, not just those that are strictly foreseeable. [Application, beginning with transition] Here, but for the series of events that Dave's behavior set in motion, Marci would not have fallen off her chair. Marci broke her arm when she fainted and fell. [Conclusion, beginning with transition] Thus, damages would be established.

[Overall conclusion++] Therefore, Marci has a cause of action for assault and may recover from Dave.

---

2. Dave v. Bruce+++

[Overall conclusion, beginning with an explicit answer] No, Dave may not recover from Bruce for Dave's bodily injury.

[Conclusion, beginning with transition] First, Bruce had a privilege to defend Marci. [Rule, beginning with transition] As a general rule, one may defend another by going to the other's aid. When doing so, a defender steps into the shoes of the person being attacked and may only defend to the extent that the person being attacked could rely on self-defense as a privilege. The standard is that of an objectively reasonable person; that is, a person may only defend against what a reasonable person would think was a legitimate threat.

[Application, beginning with transition] In this case, Marci was the target of an unprovoked attack and self-defense would be permitted. [Conclusion, beginning with transition] Accordingly, Bruce had a privilege to defend Marci and could defend to the extent that Marci could have defended herself.

[Conclusion, beginning with transition] Second, Bruce used reasonable force in defending Marci. [Rule, beginning with transition] As a general rule, the amount of force that may be used for self-defense is only so much as is reasonably necessary to eliminate the threat. In general, force may only be used after an attacker has been asked to cease and the attacker refuses.

++ Note that the subsection ends with an explicit overall conclusion.
+++ Again, note that the subheading matches the call of the question.

[Application, beginning with transition] Here, Bruce demanded that Dave lower his gun. Dave ignored him and continued to point the gun at Marci. Thus, a demand and refusal to stop the attack occurred. Only then did Bruce hit Dave over the head. The hit over the head would likely be considered a reasonable amount of force, especially when weighed against the danger presented by a gun. [Conclusion, beginning with transition] Thus, Bruce used reasonable force in defending Marci.

[Overall conclusion] Therefore, Dave may not recover from Bruce for his bodily injuries. ++++

Essay Answer Self-Evaluation or Peer Evaluation

When you write practice essay answers, take advantage of *every* opportunity to get feedback—from your bar review provider, study group members, or classmates. If the feedback is critical, it doesn't mean you won't pass the bar. Rather, by getting feedback you'll increase your chances of passing because critical feedback is a prerequisite to improvement.

Although some students have a hard time being critical of their own work because they feel attached to it, others are too hard on themselves. Force yourself to be objective and clinical. Ideally, you should team up with a friend or study group and engage in peer reviews of practice essays. Both receiving and giving feedback will help you prepare for the bar exam; in fact, if you learn to accurately and constructively assess another person's work, you'll increase the likelihood you'll be able to produce a good essay yourself.

When choosing peers for this purpose, select people you're comfortable with and who are likely to give you honest feedback. Tell them you're looking for critical feedback. Exercise 15-3 provides a checklist for evaluating bar essays; use it to ensure that you and your peers are accurately assessing your work. Then, use exercise 15-4 to maximize what you learn from the feedback you receive.

++++ When you finish your essay answers, remember to proofread your essays with any remaining time, then take a deep breath to clear your mind.

Exercise 15-1: Checklist for Writing Effective Bar Exam Essays

Notes / To Do

❏ I understand the types of essay questions used on my state's bar exam.

❏ I'm familiar with samples of how bar exam essays often weave together topics from multiple courses.

❏ I understand the purpose, tone, and audience factors for bar exam essays.

❏ I've developed my own "template" and process for answering bar exam essay questions.

❏ I understand that I should follow the same process for every essay answer I write. Specifically, I will:

○ Allot time and mark the time on my scrap paper.

○ Answer the questions in the order asked.

○ Start and end with a conclusion responding to the call of the question.

○ Take time to briefly outline the issues, rules, and key facts.

○ Make my essay look professional (*e.g.*, white space, margins, neat, transitions).

○ Use the legal reasoning techniques I used in law school (CRAC).

○ Be concise and precise.

○ Proofread my answers if time permits.

○ Take a deep breath and clear my head before moving on to each new question.

Exercise 15-2: Commonly Tested Motion Standards and Appellate Standards of Review and Their Rules

The left column of this chart details the motions and appellate standards of review frequently tested on bar exams. In the right column, fill in the appropriate standards. After you've completed this chart, we encourage you to create flashcards so that you can periodically test your knowledge of this important information.

Motion/Appeal	Rules
Rule 12(b)(6) motion to dismiss.	
Rule 56 summary judgment motion.	
Rule 41 motion to dismiss.	
Rule 50 motion for a directed verdict.	
Rule 50 motion for a JNOV.	
Motion to compel discovery.	

Exercise 15-2: (continued)

Motion/Appeal	Rules
Evidentiary rulings (*e.g.*, admitting or excluding evidence).	
Criminal motion to dismiss.	
Criminal defendant's request for jury instructions on a defense.	
Criminal request for instructions regarding lesser included offenses.	
De novo standard of review.	
Any competent evidence standard of review.	
Abuse of discretion standard of review.	
Substantial evidence standard of review.	

Exercise 15-3: Self-Evaluation or Peer-Evaluation Checklist+++++

1. Before reading an essay answer, assess whether the appearance is professional. Specifically:

    ❐ Is the essay neat and legible with no scribbles?

    ❐ Is sufficient white space provided for margins and between paragraphs?

    ❐ Are paragraphs clearly indented (at least one-half inch)?

    ❐ Has the writer used headings well to lead a reader through the answer?

2. Read through the answer, getting a feel for the tone and writing style.

    ❐ Is the tone confident and assertive (not hesitant and uncertain)?

    ❐ Is the writing style clear and concise (not rambling and difficult to follow)?

3. Read through the answer again, focusing on the organization and content.

    ❐ Has the writer answered all calls of the question?

    ❐ Does the macro-organization (overall structure) make sense?

    ❐ Does the micro-organization (paragraphing, sentence links) make sense?

    ❐ Does the essay (and do any subparts of the essay) begin with an explicit conclusion answering the question posed?

    ❐ Does the essay correctly identify the issues raised?

    ❐ Is there an explicit and accurate explanation of the applicable law?

    ❐ Does the author use the CRAC format?

    ❐ Is the law properly applied to the specific factual scenario in the question asked, dealing specifically with determinative facts in the question?

    ❐ Does the essay (and do any subparts of the essay) end with an express conclusion?

    ❐ Are headings and appropriate transitional phrases used to guide a reader through the answer?

4. Finally, take a moment to list one or two things for the writer to focus on improving as well as one or two things done well in the answer. Be sure to also write constructive, detailed comments on the paper itself; your comments should suggest specific improvements.

+++++ This checklist is adapted from an unpublished handout created by Professor Riebe and Professor Bobbi Jo Boyd, University of North Carolina School of Law, Chapel Hill, North Carolina, for UNC's bar preparation workshops.

Exercise 15-4: Reflection Exercise: Analyzing Peer or Bar Review-Provider Feedback◊

This exercise will assist you in maximizing what you learn from the bar review or peer feedback you receive. Answer each of the questions below each time you get feedback on a practice essay.

How well did you think you had learned the material before you took the practice essay? Check the item that best describes your perception of the degree to which you thought you had learned the material:

- ❐   Excellence◊◊
- ❐   Mastery◊◊◊
- ❐   Competence◊◊◊◊
- ❐   Approaching competence◊◊◊◊◊
- ❐   Poor◊◊◊◊◊◊

How well did you do on the practice essay? Check the description that best describes your outcome, how well you actually performed on the essay:

- ❐   Excellence
- ❐   Mastery
- ❐   Competence
- ❐   Approaching competence
- ❐   Poor

Given your results on the practice essay, how accurately did you assess your learning? Check the description that best describes the accuracy of your assessment:

- ❐   Very accurately
- ❐   Okay
- ❐   Poorly

◊ Reprinted from Michael Hunter Schwartz, Expert Learning For Law Students Workbook 143–45 (with modifications for bar study in this text), with permission from Carolina Academic Press. Copyright © 2005, all rights reserved.

◊◊ "Excellence" refers to a performance that is almost flawless and reflects having produced an answer that is at least 90% correct or which would receive an "A" grade.

◊◊◊ "Mastery" refers to producing a very good answer—one that is better than the minimum necessary to pass (more than 70% correct), but is not close to flawless. The answer should have no significant flaws, and few minor flaws.

◊◊◊◊ "Competence" refers to a performance that is passing, but just the minimum necessary to pass (70% correct).

◊◊◊◊◊ "Approaching competence" refers to an answer that is not passing (less than 70%). It contains more than one major flaw and several minor flaws.

◊◊◊◊◊◊ "Poor" refers to an answer that is not even close to passing. It has a significant number of major flaws.

Exercise 15-4: (continued)

If you did not check "very accurately," or if you "very accurately" predicted a poor outcome, discuss why your assessment was inaccurate or why you predicted a poor outcome:

Given your results, discuss how efficient and effective your learning strategies were:

If you did not perform as well as you would've liked to have performed, or if you believe that your learning process, although effective, was inefficient, identify the cause of your performance issue. Below is a checklist of possible causes; check all that apply:

❐ Failure to set mastery-learning goals.

❐ Failure to invoke self-efficacy.

❐ Poor motivational-strategy choices (you couldn't stay motivated).

❐ Poor environmental choices (you made bad location, timing, rest, or sequence choices).

❐ Poor cognitive-strategy choices (the strategy choices proved unsuited to the task or you should've used additional strategies).

❐ Incorrect implementation of strategy choices (you incorrectly used the strategies).

❐ Failure to maintain focused attention (you were unable to focus while studying).

❐ Failure to self-monitor (you failed to recognize a breakdown in the studying process while it was ongoing).

❐ Insufficient persistence (you needed to work harder).

❐ Failure to pursue opportunities for self-assessment (you did not take advantage of or create opportunities for practice and feedback).

Exercise 15-4: (continued)

How did you do on this practice essay in comparison to how you did on your law school exams? Why did you do better or worse on this practice essay?

What is the most common feedback you received from your peer or bar review evaluator? What did your peer or bar review evaluator mean by this comment?

List all of the errors that you made in your answer based on the checklist in exercise 15-3:

Based on your outcome and your response to the above questions, how will you change your approach to studying and writing essay answers?

Exercise 15-5: Sample State-Created and MEE Essay Questions

Set aside thirty uninterrupted minutes to answer each of the following essay questions. *You will only understand the essay-writing process and "own" the information explained in the answers if you take the time to work through the questions and write your own answers first.* After you write your own answers, see the sample answers for these questions in appendix F at the end of this book. Use exercise 15-3 to analyze the effectiveness of your essays or a peer's essays and exercise 15-4 to analyze what you can learn from essay feedback.

Note that the practice essays used in this chapter come from three different sources. Questions 1–7 are simulated state-created questions that are representative of the types of questions used on bar exams. Questions 8–12 are released state-created questions that appeared on the July 2004 Maryland bar exam.[14] Questions 13–15 are released MEE questions.[15]

For more practice essay questions, see appendix H which lists other essays available from various Web sites and MEE essays available on the NCBE Web site.

---

14. Reprinted with permission of the Maryland State Bar. Copyright © 2004, all rights reserved.
15. Reprinted with permission of the NCBE. Copyright © 1998, all rights reserved.

Exercise 15-5: (continued)

Question 1[16]

[Authors' note: Before you begin this question, refer back to the recommended process for answering essay questions in chapter 15. Then, try to use the recommended process to approach and answer this question on your own before looking at the answer in the appendix. Be thoughtful about the process you utilize. The time you spend doing this will be well spent; once you master a process for answering essay questions, you'll be able to answer questions more efficiently and your answers will flow smoothly.]

Ralph Client recently had an epileptic seizure in the lobby of First National Bank. Afterward, the Bank manager approached Client and, using a raised voice, told him the Bank was closing his account. Client said he felt dazed as the manager gave him a check for the balance of his account and escorted him out to the parking lot. He remembers the manager saying, "The Bank does not need your business."

Client is a male in his fifties who lives a fairly limited life consisting mostly of working at a donut shop and banking at the Bank. Client was a Bank client for twenty years and had his entire life savings on deposit at the Bank.

Before the most recent seizure, Client had three previous seizures at the Bank. After the first two, Client cried for help, remained standing, and a few minutes later walked up to a teller and made transactions. The third seizure was more severe: Client collapsed and the Bank manager called 911. The emergency team escorted Client to the hospital for further testing.

The Bank manager claims he has no medical training, did not know Client had epilepsy, and had never seen any other person have a seizure. The manager said he closed Client's account because he disturbed Bank personnel and customers.

Client says he was embarrassed and humiliated at the time of the incident. Since then, he has felt angry and "down." He says he replays the incident over and over, and it prevents him from falling asleep. When he does sleep, he frequently has nightmares about the incident. He has seen a counselor twice, but does not think he ever was diagnosed with any emotional disorder. He also says he took several days off work and left work early several times because he was feeling down.

Can Client recover for the intentional infliction of emotional distress against the Bank based on the Bank manager's conduct?

---

16. This essay is based on Nebraska law.

Exercise 15-5: (continued)

Question 2[17]

Law student Larry was home for spring break visiting his sweetheart, Sophie. Sophie had turned sixteen several months earlier and had obtained a driver's license. She was dying to buy herself a new car. While Larry was home, she asked Larry to take her to see a car she had eyed at a used-car dealership in the town next to the one where they lived.

The car Sophie had eyed was a used Honda Civic for sale for $4,000. Sophie had been saving her babysitting money for years and, along with a generous gift of cash from her grandmother at Christmas, had just enough money to pay for the car. She planned on having Larry help her test-drive and purchase the car.

Sophie and Larry went to the used-car dealership on a Saturday afternoon. Larry, in his law school sweatshirt, asked the salesman if they could test-drive the car. Larry gave the salesman his license, which showed he was twenty-one, and Larry and Sophie went for a spin.

When they returned, Larry said they wanted to purchase the car. After a low-ball offer and some haggling, they agreed on a $4,000 purchase price. Larry and Sophie went into the salesman's office to complete the paperwork for the purchase. While doing so, Larry instructed the salesman to put the contract in Sophie's name. Sophie signed the contract after a quick skim. The contract contained a clause stating, "Buyer represents that he or she is of the age of majority."

Larry and Sophie decided to "celebrate" the new purchase by driving around for hours. Just as they were headed back to Sophie's house, with Sophie driving, Sophie ran a red light, crashed into another car, and totaled her new Civic.

As you can imagine, Sophie's parents are furious—especially about the car dealership's sale of the car to their minor daughter. Do Sophie's parents have any basis for recourse against the dealership?

---

17. This essay is based on multistate contracts rules.

Exercise 15-5: (continued)

Question 3[18]

Lou Lawyer was recently terminated from his position as an associate with a law firm. He had worked for the firm for three years, mostly under the supervision of Patty Partner. Partner gave him top employment evaluations and said on many occasions that Lawyer's working style was a great fit with the firm.

After Lawyer had been with the firm two years, Amanda Associate joined the firm as a new associate. Lawyer and Associate clashed from day one. Lawyer reported several "run ins" with Associate. Lawyer also believes Associate tried to undermine him and make him look bad in several ways. For example, Lawyer says that Associate falsely told partners at the firm that Lawyer made inappropriate remarks about clients' attire, mannerisms, and legal affairs.

Lawyer also believes Associate discussed her desire to have Lawyer terminated with partners in the firm. When Lawyer confronted Associate, Associate admitted her dislike for him and her desire for him to leave the firm. Soon thereafter, the firm terminated Lawyer's employment stating that his skills and experience did not fit with the firm's long-range plans.

Lawyer believes that Associate's actions caused his termination. Will he be able to prevail with a tortious interference claim against Associate?

---

18. This essay is based on North Carolina law.

Exercise 15-5: (continued)

Question 4[19]

On the evening of March 12, Dave, a twenty-three-year-old male with two prior criminal convictions, broke into the apartment of his former girlfriend, Vicki. Vicki, nineteen, was asleep at the time. Dave held a knife to her throat and said, "Come with me and be quiet if you don't want to be hurt."

Vicki cooperated with Dave; she went outside and got in Dave's car. Dave began driving without saying a word. Vicki lived in Greenville, South Carolina, and Dave drove from her home toward Myrtle Beach, South Carolina. After a half hour of driving, Vicki spoke up and said, "Please take me home." Dave said, "Don't talk," and continued driving.

About a half hour later they stopped for gas. While Dave was filling the tank, Vicki went into the gas station and used the restroom. Then Dave came in, paid for the gas, and bought them both a drink. The two then returned to the car and Dave continued driving toward Myrtle Beach. As Dave drove, Vicki said, "Please take me back home." Dave ignored her.

When the two arrived in Myrtle Beach, Dave said he wanted to take a walk on the beach. Dave held Vicki's hand while they walked on the beach. Many other people were also out walking on the beach. After walking awhile, they stopped and played in the waves coming up on the sand. Then, they started walking back in the direction of the car. Halfway back, Dave gave Vicki a piggyback ride.

When they got back to the car, Dave said he wanted to drive up to Sunset Beach, North Carolina. He started driving, and Vicki was silent. After awhile, she fell asleep and didn't wake up until Dave stopped in Sunset Beach. They stayed at a hotel in Sunset Beach for two nights, and then Dave took Vicki back home to Greenville.

After Vicki returned home, she called the police and told them what had happened. Dave was subsequently charged with kidnapping. Dave's attorney has filed a motion for judgment of acquittal in the case. Should the motion be granted?

---

19. This essay is based on the federal kidnapping statute and cases construing the statute's requirements.

Exercise 15-5: (continued)

Question 5[20]

Hank and Wilma met about fourteen years ago when both were in their twenties. At the time, Hank was a bouncer at a night club and Wilma worked in the Human Resources department of a Fortune 500 corporation.

After thirteen years of marriage, Wilma said she was no longer happy and wanted a divorce. Wilma then moved out of the marital home. At the time, Hank was earning $29,000 as a security guard, and Wilma was earning $106,000.

At several points after the separation, Wilma called Hank to see if they could meet to divide up their property. Each time she called, Hank started crying and saying he wasn't up to it. Hank started seeing a psychiatrist and taking an antidepressant.

After being separated a year, Wilma retained an attorney to file a petition for dissolution of the marriage. At the same time, Wilma called Hank and told him to think about hiring an attorney, too. Hank complained that attorneys were too expensive, and asked Wilma if her attorney could represent them both. Wilma said she didn't think that was a good idea, and mailed Hank an appearance and consent form along with a note. The note said that Hank should sign the form indicating he was proceeding *pro se* if he wasn't going to get an attorney. Hank signed the form and mailed it back to Wilma, and Wilma filed it at the court.

Shortly thereafter, Wilma called Hank again and said they really needed to meet about dividing their marital property. Although Hank was reluctant, they agreed to meet at a park near their homes on Saturday afternoon, May 23. When they met, Wilma made a list of the property they discussed dividing. They agreed that Hank would keep the marital home (valued at $265,000 less a $115,000 outstanding mortgage) and that Wilma would keep her retirement account ($75,000) and the couple's vacation cabin (valued at $115,000 with no mortgage). Hank was visibly upset during the meeting; he started crying and finally said he had to leave and couldn't discuss the matter further.

Wilma called Hank again the next day, Sunday, and said they needed to finish dividing their property before the upcoming marital dissolution hearing scheduled for Tuesday, May 26, at 2:00 p.m. They agreed to meet at a diner next to the courthouse at 11:00 a.m. on Tuesday, before the dissolution hearing. Wilma told Hank her attorney would be with her, and that Hank was welcome to bring an attorney, too.

Hank and Wilma met as planned, along with Wilma's attorney. Hank said he was anxious and upset during the meeting, and felt pressured to reach an agreement regarding their property division before their hearing. They decided Hank would keep the following property: Honda, $16,000; Hank's retirement account, $25,000; Hank's checking account, $3,200; and the marital household furnishings, $20,000. They decided Wilma would keep the following property: Camry, $15,000; mutual fund account, $10,000; privately owned company stock, $25,000; and her checking account, $2,600. Wilma's attorney took some notes, but nothing else was put in writing.

At the hearing, the court granted the dissolution of marriage and Wilma's attorney presented the settlement agreement orally. Both Wilma and Hank stated on the record that Wilma's attorney accurately stated their agreement. The court concluded the hearing by asking Wilma's attorney to prepare a written order to be entered by the court.

---

20. This essay is based on Illinois law.

Exercise 15-5: Question 5 (continued)

Subsequently, a judgment for dissolution of marriage incorporating the agreement as presented in court was entered.

The month after the hearing, Hank found out that Wilma had a new boyfriend. He also read in the paper that the company in which Wilma owned private stock had been purchased by a public corporation and that the value of her stock had doubled. Hank started questioning whether their property agreement was really fair—after all, he could never bridge the earning gap between them, and Wilma was the one who "drove the wagon" during the property negotiations. Hank does not think that Wilma failed to disclose or misrepresented any information, but he doesn't think he got a very good deal and wants to get out of the property agreement.

Will Hank prevail with a motion to vacate the judgment incorporating the marital settlement?

Exercise 15-5: (continued)

Question 6[21]

Wendy recently separated from her husband, Harry. The two had met in college and married in their early twenties. Their first year of marriage was "ideal," but, during their second year of marriage, they had almost constant conflict. They decided to try a separation. After two months, they decided to return to the marriage.

For the next year, their marriage was relatively peaceful, but the year after they again experienced a lot of conflict. Harry started working long hours and avoided spending time at home. Wendy then discovered Harry was having an affair. They again separated for some "cooling off" time, and they went to counseling.

Harry and Wendy eventually reconciled, and Wendy forgave Harry. At the same time, Harry was offered a job out of town, so the couple moved. The move felt like a "fresh start" to both of them, and they became closer than they had been for years.

A year later they had a son, Sam. They were joyous initially, but then struggled to adapt to their new family status.

When Sam started school, Wendy took a part-time job as an assistant at her church. At that time, Harry noticed a change in Wendy: she acted "cool" and started wearing makeup and fashionable clothing. Harry believes that at that point Wendy became involved with Don, the chair of the church's Building Committee.

Wendy started spending less time at home, lied about her whereabouts on several occasions, and spoke on the phone with lots of giggling and whispers. Harry found a card on Wendy's desk that said, "Just because...." Inside the card, in handwriting, was written: "I wish I could put on paper the satisfaction it gives me to work with you. Thank you for your assistance and kindness. Fondly, Don." The couple separated again the next month.

Harry is very distraught. He acknowledged that his marriage was not as happy as some, but felt that he and Wendy shared a genuine love. He said that both relatives and neighbors would attest to the fact that they seemed like a happy couple. Also, videos from the previous Christmas show the couple happy together.

Harry blames Don for the breakup of the marriage and wants to know if there is any legal action he can pursue against Don for alienating his wife's affections.

Wendy claims the marriage had been going downhill ever since Sam was born. She said she was the one that initiated contact with Don while married, and that after the separation they started dating. When Harry asked Wendy if she still loved him, Wendy responded, "I love both you and Don, just in different ways. I'll always love you as the father of my son."

If Harry pursues legal action against Don, will he prevail?

---

21. This essay is based on the majority and minority rules for alienation of affection claims; the analysis based on the minority view is based on North Carolina law.

Exercise 15-5: (continued)

Question 7[22]

Lou is a law student at Penn State. For spring break, he and a few of his pals were planning on going to Daytona Beach. Unfortunately, just a few days before spring break, their plans fell through when they discovered they wouldn't be able to use a friend's timeshare as planned.

Bummed at the prospect of a boring break, Lou called his older brother, Bob, who lives in Chicago, whom he hadn't seen in almost a year. Lou asked whether he could visit and crash with Bob for the week. Bob said Lou was definitely welcome; Bob noted, though, that he would be leaving town midweek for a trip himself.

When Lou arrived in Chicago, he and Bob had a couple of great days together. They hung out at the lakefront and some local bars and ate meals together at Bob's place. Before Bob left for his trip, he asked Lou to water the plants and bring in the mail, but asked Lou not to accept any deliveries for him. He invited Lou to "have at it," "not worry about a thing," and enjoy his stay.

The day after Bob left, Lou answered the door at Bob's place. There was a sheriff with an envelope for Bob. The sheriff asked Lou if he lived there, and Lou said, "It's my brother's place." The sheriff said, "Good, then you can just give this to him."

Lou placed the envelope on the kitchen counter along with Bob's other mail before he left town to return to school. Lou didn't see Bob again before he left. And, though he meant to call and thank Bob and tell him about the sheriff, he completely forgot about it once classes started.

In the meantime, Bob returned from his trip. Unbeknownst to him, a few weeks later a default judgment was entered against him. The envelope that was delivered to Lou was a summons and complaint. Although Lou had left it on Bob's cupboard, the envelope had fallen behind the cupboard and Bob never saw it. Bob didn't receive any other information to inform him about the summons and complaint.

The state where Bob lives has a statute that provides that a complaint and summons may be served on an individual personally or "by leaving a copy at Defendant's usual place of abode with some person of the family."

Bob has come in for a consultation regarding what to do about the default judgment. Are there any grounds for Bob to obtain relief?

---

22. This essay is based on Illinois' substitute service statute and Illinois cases construing the service statute.

Exercise 15-5: (continued)

Question 8[23]

On December 29, Seller entered into a written contract with Buyer for the sale and purchase of Seller's house at 803 Westgate Lane in Howard County for the sum of $175,000.

The pertinent provisions of the contract provided for a down payment of $5,000, which Buyer paid upon execution of the contract, with the balance to be paid in cash "at time of settlement, which shall take place on February 27, at which time, and upon payment as herein provided, possession of the premises shall be given, and a deed containing a covenant of special warranty shall be executed and delivered to Buyer."

The contract included a clause that stated "time is of the essence" and further provided: "This Contract contains the final and entire agreement between the parties, and neither shall be bound by any terms, conditions, or representations not contained herein."

During negotiations between the parties prior to signing the contract, Seller told Buyer that he was not certain when a new house he had under construction in Ocean City, Maryland, would be finished and ready for his occupancy, but that his best estimate was two months.

On February 27, neither Seller nor Buyer had taken any steps toward settlement. However, on March 1, the settlement date was extended to March 11 by mutual agreement.

Buyer did not tender payment or notify Seller that he was ready for settlement on March 11; nor did Seller notify Buyer of his readiness to settle on that date. In fact, Buyer's attorney had not completed the title examination, and Seller's house was not ready for occupancy.

On March 19, Seller's attorney notified Buyer by letter that, inasmuch as the property settlement had not taken place within the time stipulated in the contract as extended, and because time was "of the essence," Seller considered the contract void and of no further effect. On March 28, Seller contracted to sell the property to a third party.

Can Buyer obtain specific performance?

---

23. Reprinted with permission of the Maryland State Bar. Copyright © 2004, all rights reserved. This essay is based on Maryland law.

Exercise 15-5: (continued)

Question 9[24]

Molly Miser, a meter maid employed by the Town of Beverly, dreams of becoming a police officer for the Town. One day, while in uniform and on duty checking for expired meters in a residential neighborhood, she noticed two young men, Wally and Eddie, engaged in what appeared to be a scuffle in the front yard of a residence. Sensing an opportunity for a true law enforcement experience, Molly charged across the street to investigate.

At that moment, Wally's mom, June, looked out of the window and saw a stranger running toward her minor son and his friend. Fearing for their safety, she opened her front door and let the family pit bull "Vichuss" out without its muzzle, as required by the Town's animal-control ordinance. Shocked by the sight of Vichuss, Eddie darted to the edge of the property to escape the dog. Molly, running from the other direction, whipped out her personal 22-caliber pistol and fired off a warning shot to scare Vichuss. However, the bullet struck Eddie in his left thigh.

As Eddie lay incapacitated in the street, Vichuss pounced on him and bit him in the thigh. Startled by the sequence of events, Molly stood frozen in the street and was hit by Ward who came careening around the corner in an SUV. Because he was changing his compact disc at the time, he did not see Molly in the street until too late to avoid an accident.

Eddie was treated at the local hospital for Vichuss' bite and the bullet wound in his thigh. After his release, Eddie experienced insomnia, headaches, and nightmares. Molly suffered two broken legs and three broken ribs and was placed in traction for a full month. Fearing that she will never become the police officer of her dreams, she also suffers from recurring anxiety.

1. Can Eddie bring any causes of action?

2. Can Molly bring any causes of action?

---

24. Reprinted with permission of the Maryland State Bar. Copyright © 2004, all rights reserved. This essay is based on Maryland law.

Exercise 15-5: (continued)

Question 10[25]

Max and Morley are identical twin brothers who inherited, in equal shares, all of the member interests of Doughnut Heaven, LLC ("Heaven"), a successful Maryland limited liability company.

Max and Morley were unable to agree on significant management decisions. Among other things, a dispute arose over the repayment of money loaned by Max to Heaven that was used by Morley for both business and personal purposes.

Max decided that he can no longer work with Morley and consulted with Heaven's lawyer, Amanda Attorney, to find out how he could personally remove Morley from the business. Amanda is a recent law graduate who practices law in Lewes, Delaware. She is not a member of the Maryland Bar. Amanda advised Max that, to assist him, she expected to receive an interest in the business as part of her fee.

During one of Heaven's business meetings at its headquarters in Easton, Maryland, Max, without Morley's knowledge, instructed Amanda immediately to (1) create Doughnut Universe, LLC ("Universe"), a Maryland limited liability company, (2) issue the member interests 90% to Max and 10% to Amanda, and (3) prepare any documents to transfer all of Heaven's assets to Universe. Amanda agreed to do so. Max and Amanda agreed that, in addition to an ownership interest, Amanda would receive from Max her hourly rate of $350 for preparing the necessary documents.

Max and Amanda refused to answer Morley's telephone calls regarding Heaven. Consequently, Morley filed a complaint with the Attorney Grievance Commission of Maryland. Max and Amanda failed to respond to the Commission's several requests for information.

You are the assistant bar counsel assigned to investigate Morley's complaint, and you have confirmed the above facts. Is there any basis for disciplinary action against Amanda?

---

25. Reprinted with permission of the Maryland State Bar. Copyright © 2004, all rights reserved. This essay is based on Maryland law.

Exercise 15-5: (continued)

Question 11[26]

Al and Brenda began living together in Brenda's apartment in Pittsburgh, Pennsylvania, in 1998. In 1999, Brenda gave birth to the couple's only child, Sally. Because of complications arising out of Sally's birth, Brenda became disabled and began receiving $1,200 per month in Social Security disability payments. At the same time, Sally began receiving Social Security dependency benefits of $400 per month.

In 2000, Al purchased, in his own name, a townhouse rental property in Cumberland, Maryland, for $100,000. He put $50,000 down from his savings and secured a first mortgage for $50,000. The rent received from the townhouse each month was sufficient to satisfy the monthly mortgage payments in their entirety.

In 2003, Al and Brenda were married in Pennsylvania. As a wedding present, Al's father gave him 1,000 shares in Turk, Inc. In December 2003, Al used his employment bonus to purchase a $12,000 interest in a mutual fund in his own name.

In December 2004, Al and Brenda moved to Maryland and set up residence in Al's Cumberland townhouse. Al paid his monthly mortgage payments from his earnings. Al also received an additional 500 shares of Turk, Inc., based on a stock split in December 2004.

In June 2005, Al learned that Brenda was having an affair when he caught Brenda in bed with his next-door neighbor.

Al contacted Charles, an attorney who regularly handles domestic relations matters, concerning his domestic situation.

1. Can Al file for an absolute divorce in Maryland at this time?

2. Is he entitled to any of Brenda's Social Security disability benefits?

3. Does Brenda have any entitlement to Al's previously acquired assets?

4. Do Sally's Social Security dependency payments have any impact on child support that might be payable by Al or Brenda?

---

26. Reprinted with permission of the Maryland State Bar. Copyright © 2004, all rights reserved. This essay is based on Maryland law.

Exercise 15-5: (continued)

Question 12[27]

Pete owns Pete's Pizza Planet, an unincorporated business consisting of six highly successful pizza delivery shops in Maryland. On June 1, 2002, Pete entered into a written four-year contract with Cheeze, Inc., whereby Cheeze agreed to become Pete's "exclusive supplier of Grade A pizza cheese." This cheese is readily available on the market and its specific ingredients are widely known in the food business. Pete purchases approximately $1,000,000 worth of products from Cheeze each year.

Pete was very happy with his agreement with Cheeze and the superior customer service it provided. In fact, he was so happy that on June 1, 2003, Pete entered into a second written contract with Cheeze for the next three years to serve as his advertising agency to design, produce, and coordinate Pizza Planet's marketing campaign. Pete agreed to spend, through Cheeze, $250,000 per year in advertising because he liked Cheeze's creativity and proven success in conducting advertising campaigns for pizza businesses.

On April 30, 2005, Mega-Mini, Inc., purchased all of Cheeze, Inc.'s assets. The sale included an assignment of Cheeze's ongoing supply and advertising contracts with Pete.

Although Mega-Mini assumed the contracts and continued to supply products and services as required, Pete did not like the new sales and advertising personnel he was now forced to work with at Mega-Mini. Therefore, on June 1, 2005, with one year still remaining on each contract, Pete notified Mega-Mini that he refused to accept an assignment of the contracts and was terminating both contracts.

Mega-Mini consults you, its newly hired in-house counsel and a recently admitted Maryland attorney. Can Mega-Mini enforce the supply and advertising contracts, and can Mega-Mini recover any damages?

---

27. Reprinted with permission of the Maryland State Bar. Copyright © 2004, all rights reserved. This essay is based on Maryland law.

Exercise 15-5: (continued)

Question 13[28]

Husband's valid will provides:

I, Husband, leave my entire estate to Wife, or, if she predeceases me, I leave my entire estate in equal shares to my son, Son, and my daughter, Daughter.

Wife's valid will bequeaths her entire estate to Husband. It does not provide for an alternate gift if Husband predeceases her.

Husband and Wife recently died in a fire in their home. The fire was set by Son in his second-floor bedroom at 2:00 a.m. Wife's body was found in her nightclothes in the second-floor bedroom she shared with Husband. Husband's body was found in his nightclothes at the base of the stairs on the first floor of their home with his head facing the front door, his feet toward the upstairs landing, and red marks on his stomach indicating that he had been crawling down the stairs when he had been overcome by smoke.

Husband and Wife were survived by Son and Daughter and by Son's daughter, Granddaughter.

Son claims the fire was set inadvertently when a cigarette he was smoking in bed dropped to the mattress, causing it to ignite. The fire marshal has found traces of a combustible substance on the premises, suggesting the possibility that the fire may have been set intentionally. The local prosecutors, however, have declined to seek an indictment because although the available evidence indicates that it is more likely than not that Son intentionally set the fire, the evidence is insufficient to support a criminal conviction.

The intestate succession statute of this jurisdiction provides that a decedent's surviving spouse is his or her sole heir. If there is no surviving spouse, the decedent's issue take the estate per stirpes. This jurisdiction also has enacted the Uniform Simultaneous Death Act.

1. To whom should Husband's estate be distributed? Explain.

2. To whom should Wife's estate be distributed? Explain.

---

28. Reprinted with permission of the NCBE. Copyright © 1998, all rights reserved. This is a released MEE question.

Exercise 15-5: (continued)

Question 14[29]

Wareco is a corporation that operates a small commercial storage warehouse. Pres is the president of Wareco and Sec is the secretary of Wareco. Both Pres and Sec regularly attend board meetings, although neither of them is a director or shareholder of Wareco. At a January 1 board meeting, the Wareco board of directors passed a resolution stating that the president of the corporation may not enter into any contract for over $1,000,000 without the express prior approval of the board.

On February 1, Pres signed a contract as president of Wareco providing that Wareco would purchase a fleet of fifty trucks from Able, Wareco's usual supplier of trucks. The purchase price specified in the contract was $20,000,000. Able was unaware that the board of directors of Wareco had never approved this transaction, but he did know that Wareco had never owned more than five trucks at any one time. On February 2, the board learned of the contract with Able and immediately repudiated it.

On March 1, Pres proposed to the board of directors of Wareco that the corporation purchase a forklift from Beta. Forklifts are essential to Wareco's business and it owns several of them. Because the board did not believe Wareco needed an additional forklift, it passed a resolution disapproving the proposed purchase. Nevertheless, without the board's knowledge, on March 5, Pres signed a contract as president of Wareco to purchase a forklift from Beta for $2,000. Beta had no knowledge of the board's disapproval. On March 6, the board learned of the contract with Beta and immediately repudiated it.

On April 1, Pres signed a contract as president of Wareco providing that Wareco would purchase a herd of cattle from Rancher for $2,000,000. Sec, as secretary of Wareco, signed and delivered a document certifying to Rancher that the Wareco board of directors had earlier approved the execution of this contract by Pres in a resolution validly passed at a duly called meeting of the board. Sec attached a copy of the text of the resolution to the certificate. Sec frequently signed such certificates as part of Sec's duties as secretary. In fact, the execution of this contract had not been approved at a board meeting, but instead was previously approved without a meeting by a consent resolution signed by four of the five members of the Wareco board of directors. Rancher was unaware that Sec's certificate was incorrect. On April 2, the board learned of the contract with Rancher and immediately repudiated it.

1. Can Able recover damages from Wareco? From Pres? Explain.

2. Can Beta recover damages from Wareco, and, if so, does Wareco have a cause of action against Pres? Explain.

3. Can Rancher recover damages from Wareco?

---

29. Reprinted with permission of the NCBE. Copyright © 1998, all rights reserved. This is a released MEE question.

Exercise 15-5: (continued)

Question 15[30]

Software, Inc., applied to Bank for a $250,000 loan to finance an expansion of its business. Bank was unwilling to make the loan unless Investor, an independently wealthy businessman with a substantial stock interest in Software, agreed to co-sign the loan. Despite the fact that he held stock in Software, Investor played no role in managing the company and did not serve on its board of directors.

Software's chief executive officer ("CEO") asked Investor to co-sign the loan. After studying Software's expansion plans, Investor urged CEO to seek a $500,000 loan, arguing that $250,000 was not enough to finance fully the proposed expansion. CEO, however, was adamantly opposed to incurring any debt beyond $250,000 and refused to consider seeking a larger loan. Nonetheless, Investor agreed to talk further with Bank about co-signing the loan.

In separate negotiations with Bank, to which neither CEO nor Software was a party, Investor explained his belief that a $500,000 loan was necessary to finance the proposed expansion and indicated his unwillingness to co-sign a loan for $250,000, which he felt would prove inadequate. Investor agreed to co-sign the $250,000 loan on the condition that Bank agree to lend Software an additional $250,000 within six months, if necessary to complete the project. Bank agreed and wrote a letter to Investor to that effect. This agreement and letter were not disclosed to Software or CEO.

On January 15, Bank made Software a $250,000 loan with a due date of November 1. A negotiable promissory note was signed both by CEO on behalf of Software and by Investor personally. Software and Investor were designated co-makers on the note.

Within three months, Software had spent the full $250,000 and had still not completed the expansion project. Software approached Bank about a second loan for $250,000. Bank, fearful that Software was in a shaky financial situation, refused the second loan. As a result, Software was unable to complete the expansion project.

When the $250,000 loan came due on November 1, Investor told Software of the secret agreement between Investor and Bank. Both Software and Investor refused to pay Bank. After several requests for payment, Bank sold the overdue note to Collection Agency for $150,000. Bank endorsed the note and transferred it to Collection Agency on December 15.

Collection Agency has now sued both Software and Investor seeking payment of the note. State law permits the introduction of evidence of contemporaneous or previous agreements in suits for breach of contract. What are the rights and liabilities of Investor, Software, and Collection Agency on the note? Explain.

---

30. Reprinted with permission of the NCBE. Copyright © 1998, all rights reserved. This is a released MEE question.

Reflection Questions

1. How are bar exam essay questions similar to the essay questions you've answered in law school? How are they different? Do the differences make the bar exam questions seem easier or harder?

2. Why is practicing and getting feedback important to your success on bar essay questions?

3. Why does this text place so much emphasis on reflecting on your practice tests? What do we hope you'll learn from doing so?

CHAPTER 16

DOING PRACTICE EXAM QUESTIONS FOR YOUR PERFORMANCE EXAM

Introduction

Some bar exams include a performance component to test students' abilities to use fundamental lawyering skills to complete tasks that newly licensed lawyers should be able to complete.[1] States including a performance component on their exams either use state-created questions or the National Conference of Bar Examiners ("NCBE") Multistate Performance Test ("MPT").[2] This chapter primarily addresses performance exams in the context of the MPT; the general principles we explain, however, apply to all types of performance exams.

Performance exams are like closed office memo assignments. For example, for the MPT, students are given a client "File" and a "Library" with applicable law (including cases, statutes, regulations, and rules) and are required to perform a specific lawyering task for a client's case.[3] Performance tests don't test knowledge of substantive law; rather, library materials are included which provide sufficient substantive information to complete an assigned lawyering task.[4]

Examples of tasks that students might be asked to complete include an office memorandum, a client letter, a motion memorandum, an appellate brief, a statement of facts, a contract provision, a will, a client counseling plan, a settlement agreement, a discovery plan, a witness examination plan, and a closing argument.[5] Table 16-1 provides additional information about the types of tasks assigned and the frequency with which the MPT has asked students to perform them.

---

1. NCBE, The Multistate Performance Test 2005 Information Booklet 1, *available at* www .ncbex.org/tests/Test%20Booklets/MPT_IB2005.pdf [hereinafter MPT Information Booklet].

2. Make sure to look at sample MPTs on the NCBE Web site, www.ncbex.org, so that you understand what a client "File" and "Library" are. Even if the MPT is used, grading is done by the state administering the exam (there's no national grading). *Id.*

3. *Id.*

4. *Id.* at 2.

5. *Id.*

Table 16-1: Frequency of MPT Tasks Tested*

Most Frequent:
- Memorandum.
- Persuasive brief.

Least Frequent:
- Client letter.
- Letter to opposing counsel.
- Interrogatories.
- Mediation statement.
- Will.
- Opinion letter.

The NCBE states that the aim of the MPT is to test students' ability to use fundamental lawyering skills, including:

1. Separating relevant from irrelevant factual information;
2. Extracting relevant principles of law;
3. Resolving a client's problem by applying applicable law to relevant facts;
4. Identifying and resolving ethical dilemmas;
5. Communicating effectively in writing; and
6. Completing a lawyering task within time constraints.[6]

Samples of previously administered MPT exams, including information about issues students should discuss and suggested resolutions of the problems, are on the NCBE Web site and may also be ordered from the NCBE.[7] In states using state-created performance exams, students should ask their licensing entities whether any sample questions are available. Table 16-2 provides examples of past MPT task assignments.

---

* *E.g.*, Suzanne Darrow-Kleinhaus, 37 Gonzaga L. Rev. 17, 28 (2001–02).

6. MPT Information Booklet, *supra* note 1, at 2.

7. NCBE, *NCBE Free Publications*, www.ncbex.org/pub.htm (last visited May 7, 2005).

Table 16-2: Sample MPT Tasks**

Every MPT question includes a "File" and "Library" that provide sufficient substantive information to complete an assigned task.*** Below are examples of tasks assessed on previous exams. See the NCBE Web site for more samples of MPT questions.****

- Write a brief supporting a motion for summary judgment in a negligence action based on assumption of the risk. The file contains a memo on brief writing, a medical summary, and deposition excerpts. The library consists of case law.

- Write an office memorandum regarding ethical issues involved in representing a client. The file contains client interview notes. The library contains case law and excerpts from the jurisdiction's rules of professional conduct.

- Write a client opinion letter advising the client about potential liability. The file contains guidelines for preparing opinion letters and copies of contracts between the parties. The library consists of case law and excerpts from the state's commercial code.

- Write a persuasive trial brief arguing for the admission of testimony regarding prior criminal conduct in a criminal case. The file contains a memo regarding how to write trial briefs, a trial transcript, and an arrest report. The library contains applicable criminal statutes, rules of evidence, and case law.

- Write a persuasive brief in support of a motion to compel the production of documents. The file contains a memo regarding how to write trial briefs and deposition excerpts. The library contains relevant rules of civil procedure and case law.

- Write a memorandum assessing the constitutionality of a code proposed to a board of education. The file includes a copy of the proposed code. The library contains relevant constitutional provisions, statutes, and case law.

- Draft introductory and dispositive clauses of a will, giving reasons why the provisions are drafted the way they are. The file contains excerpts from a client interview, a copy of the client's previous will, and a memo describing the firm's format for wills. The library contains case law and an excerpt from a treatise on wills.

- Draft six interrogatories designed to elicit specified information in a lawsuit, following each interrogatory with an explanation of how it will serve its intended purpose. The file contains interview notes and three interrogatories drafted by a supervising attorney. The library includes excerpts from a treatise on discovery, case law, and applicable statutory provisions.

- Write a persuasive mediation statement to use in a mandatory mediation. The file includes an interview, mediation procedures, a complaint, and correspondence relating to the case. The library includes case law.

** *See* NCBE, *Publications, Study Aids*, www.ncbex.org/pub.htm (last visited May 7, 2005).
*** MPT Information Booklet, *supra* note 1, at 1–2.
**** *See* NCBE, *NCBE Free Publications*, www.ncbex.org/pub.htm (last visited May 7, 2005).

Performance Exam Instructions

Take the time to read the performance exam instructions carefully during your preparation period. Then, you'll only need to spend time skimming the instructions during your exam to ensure no provisions have changed. For the MPT, instructions are available on the NCBE Web site.[8] Note the following points included in the MPT instructions:

1. **Jurisdiction and court structure.** Jurisdiction and court structure information allow you to determine which state's law applies and the weight you should accord authority (based on the hierarchy of the courts).[9]

2. **Test materials.** Students are given both a "File" containing client information and a "Library" containing legal authorities to be used in completing the assigned task.[10] A few points about the file and library materials are important to note:

   • In the file, there will be a memo telling you what task you are to complete.[11]

   • The file may include some factual information that is irrelevant.[12]

   • Likewise, the library may contain some legal information that is irrelevant.[13]

   • The authorities in the library may be real, modified, or written solely for the exam. Thus, even if legal authorities look familiar to students, students should read them thoroughly, as if they were new.[14]

   • Citations should be provided for legal authorities and facts in the documents students are asked to write. Citations don't have to be in *Bluebook* format. For cases, students may use abbreviations for case names and omit page references (for example, Reliable Ins. Co.).[15] For facts, students may just cite to the record page (for example, R. 4.).

   • Students should only use the client file and library in completing assigned tasks. Performance exams do not test knowledge of law as much as the ability to extract legal principles and facts relevant to a specific case. Thus, although students' legal educations and experiences provide general background information, students should complete assigned tasks based on the specific materials provided.[16]

---

8. MPT Information Booklet, *supra* note 1, at 4–5.
9. *Id.*
10. *Id.*
11. *Id.*
12. *Id.*
13. *Id.*
14. *Id.*
15. *Id.*
16. *Id.*

Keys to Doing Well on Performance Exams

There are four keys that are particularly important to doing well on performance exams:

1. **Manage time effectively.** Just like other types of bar exam questions, performance exams present a time challenge.[17] You must use your time efficiently. The most common problem students have on performance tests is not finishing them. The MPT is designed to be completed in ninety minutes.[18] The NCBE advises you to use half of that time reading and digesting the file and library materials and organizing an answer.[19] The other half of your time should be used writing.[20] To learn to manage time efficiently on performance exams, do practice questions. After working through several samples, time will be easier to manage.

2. **Practice and get feedback.** There are many released exams available on the NCBE Web site. Do a couple of exams to get a feel for them and to work out a system for approaching MPTs during your pre-bar review period. Then, do at least one practice MPT question a week during your entire bar review period.

   As with essay exams, it's important not only to take practice performance exams, but also to get feedback on your practice efforts. It may be helpful to write your first one or two practice tests with your bar study group. One effective technique for doing so is called "think-pair-share." Using this technique, each member reads a performance exam packet and develops his or her own outline of an answer. Next, members pair off and negotiate a consensus for an improved version of their outlines. Finally, the entire group reconvenes and negotiates a consensus as to an ideal outline.

   Some bar reviews will allow you to submit practice performance tests for feedback. In addition, we strongly recommend that you pair up with a classmate or work with a study group to get feedback on practice tests. In either case, we encourage you to reflect on the feedback you receive using the exercises at the end of this chapter so you can improve your exam performance.

3. **Isolate the overarching rule.** To do well on performance exams, you should focus on isolating the overarching, applicable rule.[21] The applicable rule may be provided by a rule, statute, or cases. It may be clear-cut and

---

17. *E.g.*, Suzanne Darrow-Kleinhaus, 37 GONZAGA L. REV. 17, 26 (2001–02).

18. MPT INFORMATION BOOKLET, *supra* note 1, at 1. State-created performance exams are usually similar, but with some slight variations. For example, students who take the California bar exam must answer two performance questions during three hours. State Bar of California, *General Bar Examination vs. Attorneys' Examination*, www.calbar.xap.com/Applications/CalBar/California_Bar_Exam/default.asp (last visited June 7, 2005).

19. MPT INFORMATION BOOKLET, *supra* note 1, at 4.

20. *Id.*

21. *E.g.*, Darrow-Kleinhaus, *supra* note 17, at 31–32.

readily identifiable, or you may need to synthesize the applicable rule from several authorities.

As many legal writing texts advocate, once you have isolated the applicable rule, you can use it to organize whatever document you'll be writing.[22] For example, for a federal kidnapping offense, the overarching, applicable rule establishes three requirements of an offense: (1) seizure; (2) holding; and (3) interstate transportation.[23] Once the overarching rule is broken down into these components, the components can serve as the organizational structure for a written document. For example, if you are asked to write a trial brief for a defendant in a federal kidnapping case, the argument section of the brief could be organized as shown in table 16-3.

Table 16-3: Using a Rule's Structure to Organize

Argument

THE STATE CANNOT PROVE A FEDERAL KIDNAPPING OFFENSE BECAUSE THERE WAS NO SEIZURE, HOLDING, OR INTERSTATE TRANSPORTATION.

I.   There was no illegal seizure because [add key facts].

II.   There was no illegal holding because [add key facts].

III.   There was no interstate transportation because [add key facts].

---

4. **Become familiar with the types of performance tasks assigned on exams.** Familiarize yourself with the various types of documents you may be asked to create. Tables 16-1 and 16-2 list the types of documents historically tested on the MPT. If your state uses state-created performance tests, contact your state bar to determine whether it publishes a list of tasks tested on its exam and, if so, get the list. If not, obtain past state questions and go through each one to determine what task each test asks students to complete. Once you know the range of possibilities, make sure you've created such a document in the past, or find a few examples in practice guides in your law library.[24]

Although it's possible that the NCBE or your state bar will come up with a new task you've never seen before, becoming familiar with past tasks assigned is worth your time. Just as having a template will help you focus on the analytical issues in essays, having a template for each type of document you may be asked to create will free up mental energy for doing the analytical and writing tasks you're asked to complete. Even if a ques-

---

22. *See, e.g.,* Linda H. Edwards, Legal Writing: Process, Analysis, And Organization 29–38 (3d ed. 2002).

23. Federal Kidnapping Act, 18 U.S.C. § 1201 (2000).

24. This task should be finished before you start your bar review course. *See* chapter 2.

tion asks you to create a document you've never seen before, the fact that you've seen many different types of legal documents will assist you in producing an effective product because you'll have seen analogous documents.

Recommended Approach to Performance Exams

Just as with writing bar exam essays, developing a system for answering performance exam questions will allow you to use your time efficiently and focus on the substance of the assigned task. Below is the system we recommend for answering performance exams:

1. **Allot time.** The MPT's performance questions are allotted ninety minutes. Allot half of your time to reading the question materials and organizing an answer, and half of your time to writing your answer. Make sure to write down the halfway time and finish time on a scrap piece of paper before you begin.

2. **Skim the general instructions.** You should've read the MPT instructions or your state's performance exam instructions during your preparation period. Assuming you've done so, you'll only need to skim through the instructions during your exam to make sure nothing has changed.[25]

3. **Read the memo in the file providing instructions for the performance question.** Before reading anything else, make sure to understand the specific lawyering task you're being asked to accomplish. Because the MPT is task specific, it's critical that you understand the exact task you're being asked to accomplish.[26] Write the assigned task at the top of a piece of scrap paper to make sure you keep your focus.[27] Also, note any concessions made and positions taken, and the tone you're to use in your assignment. For example, if you're asked to write a memo exploring the pros and cons of a position, you should use an objective tone. If you're asked to write a trial brief advocating a position for a client, you should use a persuasive tone. A few other distinctions should also influence your tone and writing: Is the document you're being asked to draft informal or formal? Will it be read by a public audience (for example, a court) or a private audience (for example, a client or supervisor)?[28]

4. **Skim over the items provided in the file and library.** By getting a quick feel for what is included in your file and library, you'll be able to tell which areas of law are involved and whether you're dealing with a statutory or common-law problem. Then, you can read the library more thoroughly knowing which rules might be most relevant.

---

25. *See* Darrow-Kleinhaus, *supra* note 17, at 27.
26. *See, e.g., id.* at 29.
27. *Id.*
28. *See, e.g.,* Steven D. Jamar, Director, Howard University School of Law, Legal Reasoning, Research, and Writing Program, *Prof. Jamar's MPT Exam Tips,* www.academic.udayton.edu/legaled/barpass/Performance/mpt05.htm (last visited May 7, 2005).

5. **Read the library.** Read the library next, even before you read the file. This approach is similar to reading the call of a question before reading a hypothetical. You won't know which facts are relevant until you understand the applicable law. In other words, the library will inform your subsequent reading of the file.

   As you read through the library, organize relevant law and discard irrelevant law. Use an authorities chart to organize your authority. Table 16-4 provides a sample chart that you could use, or develop your own summary system. Whichever tool you use, make notes about the authorities you have in the order of their authoritative value. For cases, provide key facts, holdings, and reasoning. Using an organizational tool will make it much easier to see the big picture and organize your document, and you'll be better able to write your document without having to go back and weed through the library over and over. In other words, a little extra work up front will save you time.

   Although you may not use every piece of information in the library (because part of your challenge is to identify what's relevant and irrelevant), it's unlikely that the bar examiners have included multiple authorities that are totally inapplicable. As you read through the library, ask yourself, "Why is this case in my library?" and "How do I use this case?"[29] For example, consider whether an authority provides a rule, an exception to a rule, or is distinguishable from a rule.

6. **Read the file.** As you read the file, your challenge will be to organize relevant facts and discard irrelevant ones. Again, use an authorities chart like the one provided in table 16-4, and write any key facts from the file next to the rules to which the facts correspond. In other words, you're slotting the evidence that is relevant to each of the requirements imposed by the rule(s). Remember, you should provide record cites for your facts. Accordingly, it's helpful to put a page number next to your facts as you organize them.

7. **Outline your document.** No matter what type of legal document you're asked to write, your central task will always be the same: to organize your answer based on the legal rules and to apply the rules to your client's facts.[30] This task is therefore really the same thing you've done over and over again on your law school exams and in any memos or briefs you've written. The context may change, but the skills and approach are almost always the same.

   Accordingly, when outlining your document, outline both the law and its application. Remember, the easiest way to organize is to use a rule's structure. Break down the elements or requirements of the overarching rule, and then address each part one at a time. If you've used an authorities chart like table 16-4, you can save time by numbering the parts in the order you want to address them instead of writing a separate outline.

---

29. Darrow-Kleinhaus, *supra* note 17, at 30.
30. *E.g., id.* at 27.

8. **Write your document.** If you've done a good job organizing, writing your document should be relatively easy. A few points are worth noting:

- Target the tone appropriately by taking a moment to check on whether you are writing an objective or persuasive document and whether your audience is private or public.

- The CRAC rubric will keep you on track: Start with your overall position, state the applicable rules, apply the rules, and end with your overall position.

- Effective writing is clear, concise, and precise. Say what you have to say, and then stop.

- Remember to cite to the record for facts and legal authorities for points of law. Record facts can be cited with a "R. 4." Legal authorities can be cited by names or abbreviations; no page numbers are necessary.

- Even if you handwrite your exam, try to make it look as professional as possible. Use headings, include white space in between paragraphs and to create margins, and add closing or signature lines.

Table 16-4: Performance Exam Organizational Chart

Legal Sources (Rules, Statutes, Cases)	Rules	Key Facts in Source Cases	Analogous or Counter-Analogous Client Facts

Exercise 16-1: Sample MPT Question

Below is a released MPT question. Answer it using the exam approach described in this chapter and the organizational chart, table 16-4. If this is the first performance test you've ever tried to complete, give yourself two hours instead of the hour and a half actually allotted. After you've completed your answer, exchange it with a peer's and compare your answers to the model in appendix G. Use exercises 16-2 and 16-3 to ascertain what you've learned.

In re Steven Wallace[31]

File

Memorandum from Eva Morales.

Notes of meeting with Steven Wallace.

Inventory Receipt.

Appraisal of Artwork.

Letter from Martin R. Feldner.

Library

Walker on Bankruptcy.

Franklin Commercial Code.

Franklin Civil Code.

First National Bank v. Marigold Farms, Inc. (1997).

In re Levy (1993).

---

31. Reprinted from NCBE, *Publications*, www.ncbex.org/pub.htm (last visited May 7, 2005), with permission from the NCBE. Copyright © 2000, all rights reserved.

Piper, Morales & Singh
Attorneys at Law
One Dalton Place
West Keystone, Franklin 33322

MEMORANDUM

To: Applicant

From: Eva Morales

Date: July 27, 1999

Subject: Steven Wallace: Painting Titled "Hare Castle"

Steven Wallace, a long-time friend of mine, recently retired as chair of the English Department at the University of Franklin to pursue full time what has until now been his avocation as an artist. He came in yesterday to get my advice and brought the documents I've included in the file. On reviewing the file, I can see that there are other facts we need in order to advise him properly.

About a year ago, Steven left one of his paintings, a canvas he had titled "Hare Castle," with Lottie Zelinka, an art dealer friend of his, with the understanding that she would try to sell it for him. Ms. Zelinka is the owner of Artists' Exchange, an art gallery here in West Keystone. Ten days or so ago, Ms. Zelinka returned the painting to Steven. A few days ago, he received a letter from Martin Feldner, a bankruptcy practitioner here in town. Mr. Feldner represents Charles Sims, the court-appointed trustee in bankruptcy. The letter advises Steven that Ms. Zelinka has filed for bankruptcy and demands that Steven turn "Hare Castle" over to the trustee in bankruptcy. Naturally, Steven is upset by this turn of events and wants to know how to respond.

Please draft for me a two-part memorandum:

First, analyze the legal and factual bases of the trustee's claim that the painting is an asset of the bankruptcy estate under the Bankruptcy Act and the Franklin Commercial Code (FCC).

Second, for each of the four defenses under FCC section 2-326(3), discuss how the facts we already know support the defense, identify additional facts that might be helpful to us, state why they would be helpful, and indicate from what sources we might be able to obtain them.

Notes of July 26, 1999, Meeting with Steven Wallace

Steven can't believe this letter he got (copy attached) two days ago. A bankruptcy attorney is demanding that Steven turn over one of his best paintings ("Hare Castle") to a trustee.

A friend of his, Lottie Zelinka, has an art gallery in West Keystone. The gallery is called Artists' Exchange. She operates it as a sole proprietorship.

Lottie has a sizeable inventory of paintings and sculptures. Steven thinks (but isn't sure) that most of the art in the gallery is on consignment from artists and that Lottie doesn't really own it. That's how Steven and every other artist he knows deal with the galleries in town—i.e., by consignment. He's pretty sure that's how galleries work everywhere. Maybe Lottie owns some of the art, but, mainly, she shows the art, sells it for the artists, and makes her money on the sales commissions.

Steven thinks (but is not sure) Lottie had placed a sign in the window at the front of the gallery that said something like, "All offers will be considered and forwarded to the artists."

About a year ago, Lottie was at Steven's house for dinner with Steven and Ella, his wife. Lottie saw "Hare Castle" (oil on canvas, about 2 x 3 feet) hanging on the dining room wall. She admired it and said she thought she could sell it for "a lot of money," maybe as much as $25,000. (Some of Steven's recent paintings have been fetching pretty good prices, but he'd never thought about trying to sell "Hare Castle." It was one of his favorite paintings and had been hanging in his dining room since he finished it a couple of years ago.) Lottie told Steven, if he was interested, he should bring it to her gallery, and she'd put it up for sale.

Steven and Ella talked it over and, although they had recently purchased a new rug for their dining room that coordinated with the colors in the painting, $25,000 sounded like a lot of money. So, they decided to see if Lottie was right. Steven took "Hare Castle" to Lottie's gallery, they did some paperwork (copies attached), and Steven left the painting with Lottie. He had put a label (about 2 x 3 inches) on the back of the painting that said: "Hare Castle C Property of Steven Wallace (plus his address and phone number)."

From time to time, Lottie called Steven to tell him about offers for the canvas (three offers all told, the highest one for $6,000). Steven rejected them; not enough money.

Maybe ten days ago, Lottie called Steven at about 10:00 p.m., told him she was going to come right over and leave "Hare Castle" at his house. She didn't think she could sell it and she needed the space in the gallery. He thought it was strange, but he didn't ask any questions, and Lottie didn't let on that anything was unusual. Now he realizes she tried to do him a favor by returning the painting. Apparently, she filed for bankruptcy.

Steven is now painting full time, because he retired from the University of Franklin at the end of the last school year. His paintings seem to have caught on, and he's been selling more and more of them (in fact, he has offered to buy back for $750 paintings he originally sold for $500 because he says he can probably sell them now for $2,500).

He now has a studio in a loft on Parker Street. Up until now, he's been working out of a spare room at home.

Steven can't believe he jeopardizes his paintings every time he puts them up for sale in a gallery!

ARTISTS' EXCHANGE
West Keystone's Premier Gallery
9 Wharf Alley
West Keystone, Franklin 33322
(555) 942-5060

Inventory Receipt

Date: August 15, 1998

Artist: Steven Wallace

Agent: None

Address: 749 Galewood Circle
            West Keystone, Franklin 33322

Phone: (555) 942-3342

Medium	Inventory Number	Size	Title	Artist's Net
Oil/Canvas	C 6076	2' x 3'	Hare Castle	Sale price minus 40% commission to Gallery

General Conditions:

The item(s) of artwork listed above is (are) being placed by the Artist or his/her agent, as consignor, on consignment with Artists' Exchange (Gallery), as consignee, to be sold by Gallery for the account of Artist. Artist retains title to the artwork until sold by Gallery. Gallery makes no representations regarding its ability to sell any or all of said artwork or the sales price thereof. Gallery may return artwork to Artist at any time if not sold. All offers shall be communicated to Artist by Gallery, and Artist shall have the right to accept or reject any offers. Artist shall have the right to determine price of sale, except that if an offer exceeds the appraised value of the artwork plus the amount of Gallery's commission, Artist shall be required to accept the offer. Risk of loss over and above amount of Gallery's liability and hazard insurance shall be borne by Artist. Artist's net shall be paid to Artist upon payment in full of sale price by buyer.

Artists' Exchange   **Artist or Agent**
By: Lottie Zelinka   By: Steven Wallace

APPRAISAL OF ARTWORK

Date: August 15, 1998

Title: "Hare Castle"

Artist: Steven Wallace

Medium: Original Oil on Canvas

Value: $25,000.00

Owner: Steven Wallace

THE ABOVE INFORMATION IS TRUE AND CORRECT
TO THE BEST OF OUR KNOWLEDGE.

Signed: Lottie Zelinka

Title: Owner, Artists' Exchange

Martin R. Feldner
Attorney at Law
2298 West Arden Boulevard
West Keystone, Franklin 33322
(555) 942-4324

July 23, 1999

Mr. Steven Wallace
749 Galewood Circle
West Keystone, Franklin 33322

Re: In the Matter of Lottie Zelinka dba
Artists' Exchange
<u>Bkpcy No. 980-7 (99)</u>

Dear Mr. Wallace:

I represent Charles A. Sims, trustee in bankruptcy in the Chapter 7 bankruptcy case of Lottie Zelinka dba Artists' Exchange ("Debtor"). The Debtor filed a petition for bankruptcy under Chapter 11 of the Bankruptcy Act on May 25, 1999. She converted the case to a liquidation under Chapter 7 on July 19, 1999, on which date Mr. Sims was appointed trustee.

The Debtor has recently provided us with an accounting and business records detailing certain actions taken by her after the filing of the petition. According to Ms. Zelinka, she transferred a piece of artwork titled "Hare Castle" to you on July 20, 1999. The transfer was improper under Franklin Commercial Code section 2-326 and section 544 of the Bankruptcy Act.

The trustee has elected to exercise his power under section 549 of the Bankruptcy Act to avoid improper transfers made during the pendency of a bankruptcy case. Accordingly, demand is hereby made that you forthwith return to the trustee the artwork titled "Hare Castle" or all proceeds from the sale thereof. If you fail to do so within fifteen days of the date of this letter, the trustee will commence legal action to recover the artwork or the proceeds.

Very truly yours,

Martin R. Feldner

Walker on Bankruptcy (3d ed. 1995)
A Short Course for the Non-Bankruptcy Lawyer

Section 4 - Definitions:

* * *

Section 4.07 - Chapter 11: A petition for a Chapter 11 "reorganization" commences a proceeding in which the insolvent debtor continues to operate as an ongoing business with certain restrictions. The business operates by the direction of the Bankruptcy Court under the management either of a court-appointed trustee or the debtor (debtor-in-possession). The Bankruptcy Act provides for an automatic stay of legal and self-help proceedings against the debtor pending the preparation and execution of a "plan of arrangement" pursuant to which the debtor "works out" its obligations to its creditors over an extended period of time.

Section 4.08 - Chapter 7: Often, Chapter 11 proceedings that fail are converted to Chapter 7 cases. A petition for bankruptcy under Chapter 7 commences a proceeding for liquidation of the debtor's assets for the benefit of its creditors. A court-appointed trustee takes possession of the business, including all items in inventory, which thereafter come under the exclusive control of the trustee. The trustee is vested with all the rights possessed by the creditors of the bankrupt debtor prior to the filing of the petition. The trustee's principal function is to marshal and, subject to the rights of secured creditors, sell the assets and distribute the proceeds proportionately to the creditors in accordance with their interests. Under section 549 of the Bankruptcy Act, "The trustee may avoid a transfer of property of the estate ... that occurs after commencement of the case...."

* * *

Section 4.27 - Schedules of Assets, Debts, and Creditors: It is incumbent on the debtor in any bankruptcy proceeding to file with the court schedules of its assets, debts, and creditors. All property, including goods delivered on consignment and accounts receivable, in which the debtor has any interest must be described and its location shown on the schedule of assets. Likewise, the amount of each debt and the name and address of the creditor to whom each debt is owed are required to be listed on the schedules of debts and creditors, with designations in each case as to whether the particular creditor is secured or unsecured. The schedules of secured creditors must describe with particularity the property of the debtor in which the creditor has a security interest.

Franklin Commercial Code

* * *

Section 2-326. Sale on Approval and Sale or Return;
  Consignment Sales and Rights of Creditors.

(1) Unless otherwise agreed, if delivered goods may be returned by the buyer even though they conform to the contract, the transaction is:

   (a) a "sale on approval" if the goods are delivered primarily for use; and

   (b) a "sale or return" if the goods are delivered primarily for resale.

(2) Except as provided in subsection (3), goods held on approval are not subject to claims of the buyer's creditors until acceptance; goods held on sale or return are subject to such claims while in the buyer's possession.

(3) Where goods are delivered to a person for sale and such person maintains a place of business at which he deals in goods of the kind involved, under a name other than the name of the person making the delivery, then, with respect to claims of creditors of the person conducting the business, the goods are deemed to be on sale or return. The provisions of this subsection are applicable even though an agreement purports to reserve title to the person making delivery until payment or resale or uses such words as "on consignment" or "on memorandum." However, this subsection is not applicable if the person making the delivery:

   (a) complies with an applicable law providing for a consignor's interest or the like to be evidenced by a sign; or

   (b) establishes that the person conducting the business is generally known by his creditors to be substantially engaged in selling goods of others; or

   (c) complies with the filing of provisions of the Article on Secured Transactions (Article 9); or

   (d) delivers goods which the person making delivery used or bought for personal, family, or household purposes.

* * *

Franklin Civil Code

Section 3533 - Sign Law.

If a person transacts business and identifies his place of business by a sign and fails by another sign or signs in letters easy to read and posted conspicuously in his place of business to state that he is dealing in property in which others have an interest and identifying such property, then all the property, stock of goods, money, and choses in action used or acquired in such business shall, as to the creditors of such person, be liable for his debts and be in all respects treated in favor of his creditors as his property unless the provisions of Franklin Commercial Code section 2-326(3)(b) through (d) are applicable.

First National Bank v. Marigold Farms, Inc.

Franklin Court of Appeal (1997)

In this case, we determine the priority of the claims of First National Bank (the Bank) and Marigold Farms, Inc. (Marigold) to $139,000 in a bank account (the Fund) of Pacific Wholesalers (Pacific). The trial court held that the Bank was entitled to the Fund. Marigold appeals.

The Bank had loaned $600,000 to Pacific, and Pacific, in turn, had executed a security agreement granting the Bank a security interest in certain assets of Pacific. The Bank had perfected its security interest by filing a financing statement with the Secretary of State. Pacific defaulted on the loan and the Bank sued. Pacific and the Bank negotiated a settlement pursuant to which cash received by Pacific in the conduct of its business would be delivered to the Bank and applied to the balance of the loan. Marigold asserted claims to the same cash and also asserted that its claims had priority over any claim of the Bank. The court approved the settlement subject to resolution of the competing claims of Marigold and the Bank and ordered $139,000 of Pacific's cash receipts held in a "blocked" account (that is, the Fund).

The facts of the relationship between Marigold and Pacific are undisputed. Marigold was a grower of flowers. Pacific was a flower wholesaler. They had a long-standing relationship under which Marigold would deliver flowers to Pacific and obtain a delivery receipt. Pacific would mark the flowers with Marigold's name, package them, and attempt to sell them to retail florists at prices determined by Pacific. If the flowers were sold and Pacific received payment, Pacific would remit to Marigold 75% of the sales price, retaining 25% as its commission. If the flowers were not sold, Pacific would, with Marigold's approval, discard them, and Marigold would receive nothing for those flowers. It is also undisputed that the Bank had no actual knowledge of the nature of the commercial arrangement between Marigold and Pacific.

The Bank's financing statement and the security agreement between Pacific and the Bank describe the collateral as "all inventory used in Pacific's business now owned or hereafter acquired; and all accounts and rights to payment of every kind now or hereafter arising in favor of Pacific out of Pacific's business, including all proceeds from the sale of inventory."

Under the Franklin Commercial Code ("FCC"), it is clear that, upon delivery of Marigold's flowers to Pacific, the flowers became part of Pacific's "inventory" because they were held by Pacific for sale. The Fund consists of "proceeds" of this inventory.

Marigold contends that its sale of flowers to Pacific was a "consignment sale," that Pacific never had title to the flowers and that, therefore, Pacific never owned the collateral (inventory) to which the Bank's security interest could attach. Marigold also asserts that FCC section 2-326(3) is inapplicable in this case.

A consignment sale is one in which the merchant takes possession of goods and holds them for sale with the obligation to pay the owner of the goods from the proceeds of the sale. If the merchant does not sell the goods, the merchant may return them to the owner (or, as in this case of perishable flowers, discard them) without obligation. In a consignment sale transaction, title to the goods generally remains with the original owner. The arrangement between Marigold and Pacific was a consignment sale arrangement; Marigold was the consignor and Pacific was the consignee. Under FCC section 2-

326(3), which clearly governs this transaction, the retention of title by Marigold is irrelevant to the ability of the Bank to obtain a security interest in the collateral.

Marigold does not contend that it complied with the filing requirement under the secured transactions division of the FCC as provided for in section 2-326(3)(c). Nor does Marigold claim that it complied with an applicable "sign law" under section 2-326(3)(a) or that it had delivered goods it had "used or bought for personal, family, or household purposes" as provided for in section 2-326(3)(d).[1] Rather, Marigold claims that, as provided for in section 2-326(3)(b), Pacific was generally known by its creditors "to be substantially engaged in selling goods of others."

At the evidentiary hearing, Bank officials testified unequivocally that the Bank was unaware that Pacific was selling the goods of others. Three flower growers who also consigned flowers to Pacific testified that Pacific was "well-known as a commission selling agent" and that other flower growers knew it as well. Although it is true that consignors, all of whom are necessarily also creditors, might know that Pacific deals in the goods of others, such knowledge cannot be extrapolated into a fact "generally known by its creditors." The purpose of section 2-326(3) is to protect general creditors of the consignee from claims of consignors who have undisclosed arrangements with the consignee. To impute as a matter of law the self-interested knowledge of the consignors/creditors to the general creditors does not give general creditors the opportunity to protect themselves from the undisclosed interests of the consignors.[2]

A consignor asserting that the consignee is "generally known by his creditors to be substantially engaged in selling the goods of others" must establish such general knowledge by proof other than that a few other consignors know that fact. He must establish that non-consignor creditors possess the requisite knowledge. Marigold failed to meet that burden of proof.

Accordingly, we affirm.

---

1. The obvious reason for the exception for goods "used or bought for personal, family, or household purposes" is to avoid the situation in which one who is not a merchant, and who should not therefore be deemed to know of the intricacies by which merchants protect their interests under the commercial code, unwittingly loses his right to property. If a householder occasionally delivers an item of property to a dealer to see if the dealer can sell it for him, the FCC protects that item from claims of the dealer's creditors. On the other hand, if the deliverer is one who deals in goods of the kind sold by the person to whom he delivers the goods, he should be held to the rules in the FCC that bind merchants. There are hybrid situations such as, for example, when one collects gemstones for his personal use and enjoyment but also regularly places the gems on consignment with jewelers to test the market and sells if the price is right. At some point, the casual collector crosses over the line from being the householder, whom the personal goods exception is designed to protect, to being a merchant or dealer, who is bound by the filing or other protective provisions of section 2-326. In this case, Marigold is clearly at the extreme end of the merchant spectrum.

2. The result might be different if all or most of Pacific's creditors were flower consignors, but that fact does not appear from the evidence in this case. If all or most of the creditors *were* consignors, then one might be able to conclude that the creditors did have such "general knowledge."

In re Levy

Bankruptcy No. 29054
United States District Court, E. D. Pa. (1993)

In December 1992, Bernard Levy, owner of a retail shoe store in Reading, Pennsylvania, filed a voluntary petition in bankruptcy. One of his suppliers, Acme Shoe Co. (Acme), had delivered a stock of shoes to Levy for resale in his store under the terms of a written agreement in which Levy, the bankrupt, acknowledged that the shoes were "on consignment" and could be returned to the consignor at any time.

Acme has filed a reclamation petition to recover the shoes it delivered to the bankrupt. The trustee resists the petition on the ground that the transaction was one of "sale or return," and, since there had been no compliance with section 2-326(3) of the Pennsylvania Uniform Commercial Code ("UCC"), the stock of shoes while in Levy's possession was subject to the claims of Levy's creditors.

Acme concedes that it had not filed any financing statements in the public records office. Acme did, however, produce evidence that small cards had been placed upon certain sections of shelving in Levy's store where Acme's shoes were stored and displayed, identifying the shoes placed on those sections of the shelving as shoes manufactured by Acme.

Under section 2-326 of the UCC, if goods are delivered to a consignor primarily for resale with the understanding that they may be returned by the consignor, the transaction is one of "sale or return" and such goods are subject to the claims of the buyer's creditors while in the buyer's possession even though the consignee has retained title. The consignee may avoid the consequences of having the goods subjected to the claims of the consignor's creditors by doing one or more of three things: (a) complying with "an applicable law" evidencing a consignor's interest or the like by a sign to that effect; or (b) establishing that the consignor is generally known by his creditors to be substantially engaged in selling the goods of others; or (c) complying with the provisions for filing financing statements and other notice documents under UCC Article 9 having to do with secured transactions.

There was no filing under Article 9. There was an effort by Acme to protect its goods by posting signs on the sections of shelving where its shoes were kept, but Acme has failed to show that there is in Pennsylvania "an applicable [sign] law" as that term is used in section 2-326(3)(a). The phrase "an applicable law" means a statute, and there is no such statute in Pennsylvania. Absent such a statute or an Article 9 filing, Acme is left with the burden of proving that Levy was generally known by his creditors to be substantially engaged in selling the goods of others.

Acme argues that, although the absence of a sign law might mean that the cards Acme caused to be placed on the shelves did not invoke the "sign law" subsection of section 2-326, the cards nonetheless served to impart knowledge that Levy was selling the goods of others. That argument might have had some merit if Acme could have shown that the cards did in fact impart such knowledge to Levy's creditors to such an extent that it was "generally known" by the creditors, and if the cards also suggested that Levy was "substantially engaged" in selling goods not owned by him. On the record before the court, however, the most that can be said is that the cards were designed to impart to Levy's *customers*, not his creditors, the knowledge that the shoes were Acme's. Thus, Acme's proof fell short.

Under section 544 of the Bankruptcy Act, the trustee is vested with the rights that the creditors had prior to the filing of the petition in bankruptcy. Section 2-326(2) of the UCC expressly makes goods held on sale or return subject to the claims of the debtor's creditors. That is the situation in this case.

Acme's petition for reclamation is denied.

Exercise 16-2: Self-Evaluation or Peer-Evaluation Checklist

1. Before reading an answer, assess whether the appearance is professional. Specifically:

    ❏   Is the document neat and legible with no scribbles?
    ❏   Is sufficient white space provided for margins and in between paragraphs?
    ❏   Are paragraphs clearly indented (at least half an inch)?
    ❏   Has the writer used headings to lead a reader through the answer?

2. Read through the answer, getting a feel for the tone and writing style.

    ❏   Is the tone confident and assertive (not hesitant and uncertain)?
    ❏   Is the writing style clear and concise (not rambling and difficult to follow)?

3. Read through the answer again, focusing on the organization and content.

    ❏   Has the writer answered all calls of the question?
    ❏   Has the writer produced a document that comports with the requirements of the assignment and looks like what it's supposed to look like (for example, if it's supposed to be a motion, does it look like a motion; if it's a set of interrogatories, does it look like a set of interrogatories)?
    ❏   Does the macro-organization (overall structure) make sense and work well?
    ❏   Does the micro-organization (paragraphing, sentence links) make sense and work well?
    ❏   If appropriate, does the document (and do any subparts) begin with an explicit conclusion answering the question posed?
    ❏   Does the document correctly identify the issues raised?
    ❏   Is there an explicit and accurate explanation of the applicable law?
    ❏   Is the law properly applied to the specific factual scenario, dealing with determinative facts in the question?
    ❏   Does the answer (and do subanswers) end with an express conclusion?
    ❏   Are headings and appropriate transitional phrases used to guide a reader through the answer?

4. Finally, in the space provided, take a moment to list one or two things for the writer to focus on improving as well as one or two things done well in the answer. Also provide constructive comments on the paper itself that suggest specific improvements.

Exercise 16-3: Reflection Exercise Analyzing Peer or Bar Review-Provider Feedback[+]

This exercise will assist you in maximizing what you learn from the bar review and peer feedback you receive. Answer each of the questions below each time you get feedback on a practice performance test.

How ready did you feel for the performance test before you took it? Check the item that best describes your perception of the degree to which you felt prepared:

- ❑   Excellence[++]
- ❑   Mastery[+++]
- ❑   Competence[++++]
- ❑   Approaching competence[+++++]
- ❑   Poor[++++++]

How well did you do on the practice performance test? Check the description that best describes your outcome:

- ❑   Excellence
- ❑   Mastery
- ❑   Competence
- ❑   Approaching competence
- ❑   Poor

Given your results on the test, how accurately did you assess your learning? Check the description that best describes your outcome:

- ❑   Very accurately
- ❑   Okay
- ❑   Poorly

+ Reprinted from Michael Hunter Schwartz, Expert Learning For Law Students Workbook 143–45, with permission from Carolina Academic Press (with modifications for bar study in this text). Copyright © 2005, all rights reserved.

++ "Excellence" refers to a performance that is almost flawless and reflects having produced an answer that is at least 90% correct or which would receive an "A" grade.

+++ "Mastery" refers to producing a very good answer—one that is better than the minimum necessary to pass (more than 70% correct), but is not close to flawless. The answer should have no significant flaws, and few minor flaws.

++++ "Competence" refers to a performance that is passing, but just the minimum necessary to pass (70% correct).

+++++ "Approaching competence" refers to an answer that is not passing (less than 70%). It contains more than one major flaw and several minor flaws.

++++++ "Poor" refers to an answer that is not even close to passing. It has a significant number of major flaws.

Exercise 16-3: (continued)

If you did not check "very accurately," or if you "very accurately" predicted a poor outcome, discuss why your assessment was inaccurate or why you predicted a poor outcome:

Given your results, discuss how efficient and effective your test-taking strategies were:

If you didn't perform as well as you would've liked to have performed, identify why you didn't perform well. Below is a checklist of possible causes; check all that apply:

❐   Failure to set mastery-learning goal.

❐   Failure to invoke self-efficacy.

❐   Poor motivational strategy choices (you couldn't stay motivated).

❐   Poor environmental choices (you made bad location, timing, rest, or sequence choices).

❐   Failure to maintain focused attention (you were unable to focus while taking the test).

❐   Failure to self-monitor.

❐   Insufficient persistence (you needed to take more practice performance tests).

❐   Failure to adequately investigate the range of documents you might be asked to create.

Exercise 16-3: (continued)

How did you do on this practice performance test in comparison to your law school exams? Why did you do better or worse on this practice test?

What is the most common feedback you received from your peer or bar review evaluator? What did your peer or bar review evaluator mean by this comment?

List all of the possible errors detailed in exercise 16-2 that you made in your practice answer:

Based on your outcome and your response to the above questions, how will you change your approach to performance tests?

Reflection Questions

1. Many students have told us that their performance exam was their favorite part of the bar exam. Why do you think that so many students like this part of the bar exam?

2. Why is practicing and getting feedback important to your success on bar exam performance questions?

3. Have you previously drafted all of the types of documents that you might be asked to draft on the bar exam? If not, what is your plan for familiarizing yourself with the drafting of such documents?

CHAPTER 17

PUTTING IT ALL TOGETHER: YOUR INDIVIDUALIZED STUDY PLAN

Now that you understand the components you need to include in a successful study plan, take the time to map out your own plan in writing. Before you do, it'll help to look at the sample study plan in table 17-1. Plot out your individualized plan as follows:

The Big Picture

Start with a blank calendar. Mark all the weeks from the start to the end of your bar preparation period. Block out any days that you won't be available for bar preparation—for example, for attending a wedding, a family member's birthday celebration, or similar event you don't want to miss. You shouldn't take more than one day a week off; so, count any time you'll be unavailable as part of that one day per week. You should have six days per week, eight to ten hours per day, available for studying (forty-eight to sixty hours per week).

Day-by-Day Calendar

Having developed a sense of the big picture, you're ready to develop a day-by-day calendar. On your calendar, mark:

1. **Your bar review.** Blocks of time when you'll be in your bar review course and the subjects covered during each day of your course.

2. **Time to refresh.** Blocks of time you want to take off to refresh (include one one-hour break per day and at least two three-hour breaks per week).

3. **Study time.** Blocks of time you'll have available for studying (structure your study time in two-, three-, or four-hour blocks with ten-minute breaks every hour or so).

Study Time

Next, fill in your study time as follows:

1. **Multistate Bar Exam ("MBE") questions** . Block out two hours every day to do thirty-four practice MBE questions (one hour to do the questions and one hour to review your answers and complete exercise 14-3, the MBE self-assessment form).

2. **Practice essays.** Block out two to five hours per week to do and review two practice essay questions (depending on whether your state has half-hour, one-hour, or two-hour essay questions). Review your essays on your own or with a peer using the essay evaluation checklists in exercises 15-1 and 15-3. Analyze any peer or bar review feedback that you receive using exercise 15-4.

3. **Practice performance tests.** If your state includes a performance test, block out enough time to take one test per week plus an additional hour to review your work product on your own or with peers using exercise 16-2. Review any peer or bar review feedback using exercise 16-3. (Note that you should've already taken time during your pre-bar review preparation to familiarize yourself with performance test instructions and the types of documents you may be asked to create).

4. **Substantive law.** All the remaining time blocks should be devoted to studying and reinforcing the substantive law. Of course, the subjects you'll include will depend on the specific subjects tested on your state's bar exam. Start with a list of all the subjects tested. If you're taking a bar review course, your study schedule should correspond to your review course's subject area coverage so that you read each course outline before the corresponding bar review lecture. (You should've already taken time during your pre-bar review preparation to remediate your understanding of subject areas you didn't study in law school or in which you didn't do well.)

   If you don't have a review course schedule to follow, you'll need to develop a schedule on your own. Make sure you include a significant amount of time to study every subject, allocating more time to subjects most frequently tested on your bar exam and the subjects with which you have the greatest difficulty.

5. **Last two weeks.** Most bar review schedules leave the last two weeks open for students to study on their own. This time frame should be devoted to self-testing to make sure your recall of the law is as automatic as possible. Also, do a few practice tests just to stay in the flow.

Sample Schedule

Table 17-1 provides one week of a sample schedule that adopts these principles. We recommend that you create a schedule for your entire bar review period. Tailor a schedule to your specific needs considering the structure of your state's bar exam and your bar review. Research demonstrates that students who plan their study time are more successful than students who don't.[1] Thus, by making a specific plan and adhering to it, you'll increase your likelihood of passing your bar exam.

Table 17-1: Sample Day-by-Day Study Schedule

Below is a sample schedule for one week. This schedule is offered solely for illustrative purposes. Make sure to create your own schedule for your entire bar review period individualized to meet your needs. The schedule assumes the student is in a state that has adopted the MBE, MEE, and MPT for its bar exam. Also note that you should integrate breaks as necessary to stay fresh throughout your study time; we recommend a five- to ten-minute break every hour.

Day	Subjects to Study	Schedule of Activities	Time to Refresh
Day 1	Constitutional law	**8:00–9:00:** Answer thirty-four MBEs **9:15–10:15:** Evaluate MBEs **10:30–12:30:** Study law* **12:30–1:30:** Lunch **1:30–2:30:** Study law **2:30–3:00:** Answer one essay question **3:00–4:00:** Study law **4:00–4:30:** Travel to bar review **4:30–end:** Attend bar review lecture **Dinner** **After dinner:** Time to refresh/exercise	
Day 2	Constitutional law	**8:00–9:00:** Answer thirty-four MBEs **9:15–10:15:** Evaluate MBEs **10:30–12:30:** Study law** **12:30–1:30:** Lunch **1:30–2:30:** Study law **2:30–3:00:** Evaluate answer to essay (on own, with peer, or in group) **3:00–4:00:** Study law **4:00–4:30:** Travel to bar review **4:30–end:** Attend bar review lecture **Dinner** **After dinner:** Time to refresh/exercise *(continued)*	Movie

1. Peggy A. Ertmer & Timothy J. Newby, *The Expert Learner: Strategic, Self-Regulated, and Reflective*, 24 INSTRUCTIONAL SCIENCE 1 (1996).

* The sample schedule assumes that the first day for each subject is focused on reading your bar review outline and preparing for that day's bar review lecture. During each study period, take a five- to ten-minute break at least once every two hours to stretch and walk around. Short breaks refresh you, thereby making your studying more productive.

** The sample schedule assumes that the second day of study of each subject is focused on assessing mastery by creating paraphrases, examples, and non-examples. *See* chapter 13.

Day	Subjects to Study	Schedule of Activities	Time to Refresh
Day 3	Criminal law and criminal procedure	**8:00–9:00:** Answer thirty-four MBEs **9:15–10:15:** Evaluate MBEs **10:30–12:30:** Study law **12:30–1:30:** Lunch **1:30–2:30:** Study law **2:30–4:00:** Answer one performance question **4:00–4:30:** Travel to bar review **4:30–end:** Attend bar review lecture **Dinner** **After dinner:** Time to refresh/friends	
Day 4	Criminal law and criminal procedure	**8:00–9:00:** Answer thirty-four MBEs **9:15–10:15:** Evaluate MBEs **10:30–12:30:** Study law **12:30–1:30:** Lunch **1:30–2:30:** Study law **2:30–3:00:** Evaluate answer to performance test (on own, with peer, or in group) **3:00–4:00:** Study law **4:00–4:30:** Travel to bar review **4:30–end:** Attend bar review lecture **Dinner** **After dinner:** Time to refresh/exercise	
Day 5	Criminal law and criminal procedure	**8:00–9:00:** Answer thirty-four MBEs **9:15–10:15:** Evaluate MBEs **10:30–12:30:** Study law **12:30–1:30:** Lunch **1:30–2:30:** Study law **2:30–3:00:** Answer one essay question **3:00–4:00:** Study law **4:00–4:30:** Travel to bar review **4:30–end:** Attend bar review lecture **Dinner** **After dinner:** Time to refresh/friends *(continued)*	Dinner out with significant other

Day	Subjects to Study	Schedule of Activities	Time to Refresh
Day 6***	Contracts/sales	**8:00–9:00:** Answer thirty-four MBEs **9:15–10:15:** Evaluate MBEs **10:30–12:30:** Study law **12:30–1:30:** Lunch **1:30–2:30:** Study law **2:30–3:00:** Evaluate answer to essay (on own, with peer, or in group) **3:00–6:00:** Study law **Dinner** **After dinner:** Time to refresh/exercise	
Day 7	Day off	Day off (Note, however, that if you've taken extra time off during the week or fallen behind your study schedule, you may use your day off to get back on track so you'll be able to start the next week caught up with your schedule. If you do this, fit in at least one two- to three- hour break at some point during the day to refresh.)	

*** The sample schedule assumes that the bar review course doesn't have lectures on Saturdays and Sundays.

Exercise 17-1: Your Individualized Study Schedule

Create your own, individualized study schedule according to the principles discussed in this chapter. You *don't* need to adopt the format below; it is offered solely as an example. *Do* be specific about times, activities, and subjects, and tailor your schedule to your specific bar exam. After you've finished, exchange your schedule with a peer and evaluate each other's schedules according to the following criteria:

❏ Does it include thirty-four multiple-choice questions per day and time to evaluate them?

❏ Does it include two essay questions per week and time to evaluate them?

❏ Does it include one performance test per week and time to evaluate it?

❏ Does it include time for bar review lectures?

❏ Does it include time for studying the substantive law several hours per day?

❏ Does it include time to refresh for two to three hours, twice per week?

❏ Does it plan activities on an hour-by-hour basis?

❏ Does it include sufficient time to study all the subjects tested on the bar?

❏ Does it leave the last two weeks for focusing on memorization?

Day	Subjects to Study	Schedule of Activities	Time to Refresh
Day 1			
Day 2			
Day 3			
Day 4			
Day 5			
Day 6			
Day 7			

Reflection Questions

1. Why is creating a detailed, individualized schedule so critical to passing the bar?

2. (Answer this question after completing your schedule.) What will be your greatest difficulty in sticking to your schedule? What can you do about it?

3. (Answer this question after completing your schedule.) Now that you've had time to look over your schedule, do you think a written schedule, adapted to your law school studies, would've improved your law school time management? Why or why not?

CHAPTER 18

"WHAT-IFS": DEALING WITH AN UNEXPECTED CRISIS DURING YOUR PREPARATION PERIOD

Unfortunately, some students experience a life crisis during the bar exam preparation period—a sick parent, a death in the family, a break up with a significant other, and similar situations. These crises may be either positive (a wedding) or negative (a funeral). Whatever the context, they interfere with bar preparation, consuming time needed to prepare and causing stress, anxiety, and unstable emotions.

So, what should you do if you experience some type of crisis during your preparation period? Should you postpone your bar exam? To answer these questions, ask yourself:

- "Will I still be able to focus on my studying?"
- "Will I still have enough time to study?"
- "Will my emotional state undermine my preparation efforts?"
- "How much time have I lost already?"

After assessing your situation, you'll need to make a "go" or "no go" decision. This is often a difficult decision to make; thus, use exercise 18-1 to help assess your situation. It may also be helpful to talk through your options with a friend, trusted professor, or professional counselor. If you think you can still do it, then go ahead. After all, you don't want to lose all the time and effort you've already spent preparing for your exam.

On the other hand, if you have serious doubts about your ability to stay focused and about whether you'll have enough time to prepare adequately, think seriously about deferring the bar exam. Often students in this situation will say something to this effect: "Well, I'll just wing it. It can't hurt to give it a shot and see what happens." We disagree.

Few students can take, and fail, their bar exams without having their "failure" become a significant hurdle to eventually passing. The biggest risk you take by sitting for an exam unprepared is becoming a "repeater." Once you shift from first-timer to repeater status, your statistical likelihood of passing a bar exam drops dramatically as demonstrated by the statistics in table 18-1.[1] Failing a bar exam is thus a risk factor when taking a subsequent exam.

---

1. See National Conference of Bar Examiners, 2004 Statistics, The Bar Examiner 10–12 (May 2005), available at www.ncbex.org/pubs/pdf/740205_2004statistics.pdf.

It's easy to dismiss this data as reflecting a group of students who lack the ability to pass the bar. We disagree, in large part because we each know some very smart people who've never passed a bar exam. Because we believe that everyone who gets into and graduates from law school is smart enough to pass the bar, we believe that the problem with failing the bar is that it creates a psychological barrier to passing.

Table 18-1: Sample Statistics for First-Time Takers and Repeaters[*]

State	First-Time Takers	Repeaters
Alabama	86%	17%
Georgia	87%	29%
Maryland	73%	23%
Michigan	76%	28%

Finally, be aware that some states limit the number of times you may be allowed to sit for a bar exam.[2]

Nonetheless, many students, knowing that they're unprepared, take a bar exam just to have the experience of doing so. If you want to proceed for this reason, there's one more option we suggest: show up at the exam; see the environment, how the exam check-in and logistics operate, and how the experience feels. If, however, once you begin, you feel like you won't be able to perform well enough to pass, withdraw from the exam rather than risk "failing."

In sum, making a "go," "no go" decision after experiencing a life crisis during your bar preparation is a difficult call. Consider the issues discussed in this chapter and the factors listed in exercise 18-1. If you know your focus and preparation have been significantly affected, assess how you'll feel if you proceed anyway and fail. If you feel you've been able to focus and prepare, however, it may be worth giving your exam a shot. Make the decision that's right for you.

---

[*] NCBE, 2004 Statistics, The Bar Examiner 10–12 (May 2005), available at www.ncbex.org/pubs/pdf/740205_2004statistics.pdf.

2. Robert M. Jarvis, An Anecdotal History of the Bar Exam, 9 Geo. J. Legal Ethics 359, 404 (1996) (reporting that twenty-four states have such a limit, ranging from two to five times).

Exercise 18-1: "Go" v. "No Go" Self-Assessment

Once you've experienced some type of crisis during your bar exam preparation, it's difficult to determine whether you should press forward and take the exam anyway or whether you should defer taking the exam. To help you determine what's right for you, consider the checklist below. If you can check off almost all the items listed below, you should be in a fairly good position to proceed with your bar exam plans. If, however, there are several items that you cannot check off, you may be better off deferring the bar exam. It may be helpful to review the list with a third party who can be somewhat objective about your situation. In any event, make a thoughtful decision that's right for you.

❐ I'll still be able to control my anxiety and stress so I'll be able to focus and perform my best while studying and during my exam. *While some anxiety and stress are typical, uncontrollable anxiety and stress have a negative impact on performance. See chapter 3.*

❐ I still believe I can pass my bar exam. *If you believe you can pass the bar, you're more likely to do so. See chapter 3.*

❐ I have the support of significant others in my life. *Social support can increase your chances of passing your exam. See chapter 4.*

❐ I've still been able to attend my bar review course and keep up with reading and studying each subject. *You must have time to review and reinforce the substantive law to be prepared for your bar exam. See chapters 13, 17.*

❐ I didn't have a high level of risk entering into my bar review study period. *If you didn't begin your bar study with many risk factors, you're more likely to be able to pass even if you encounter a crisis. See chapter 9.*

❐ I'm able to recall much of the substantive law I've studied so far. *You need to have a high level of recall of the substantive law to be in passing range for your bar exam. Test yourself in specific areas of substantive law—for example, you can use flashcards for a few sample areas of law, or see to what extent you're able to complete an outline, flowchart, or mind map for several areas of law from memory. See chapter 13.*

❐ I've still been able to fit in at least one set of thirty-four multiple-choice questions per day, five days per week, and I've consistently scored within ten percent of the percent I need to get correct to pass my bar exam. *To be in passing range, your practice MBE scores should be within approximately ten percent of the percent you need to get correct on your bar exam.* See chapter 14.

❐ I've had enough time to work out a system for approaching essay exams and a template for writing essays, and I can consistently write solid essays within the time constraints I'll face on my exam. *To pass your bar exam, you must be able to write solid essays within the time constraints you'll face on your exam. See chapter 15.*

---

* For example, if you need to score at least 65% correct to pass your exam, you need to be getting at least 55% correct in your sets of practice MBE questions.

Exercise 18-1: (continued)

❑   I've still been able to invest a consistent amount of time preparing, at least forty hours per week. *Most students study at least fifty hours per week; thus, if your availability drops below forty hours per week you'll be disadvantaged. See chapters 10, 17.*

❑   If my state's exam includes performance questions: I've had enough time to work out a system for answering performance questions, and I can consistently complete a solid performance answer within the time constraints I'll face on my bar exam. *To pass a performance test, you must be able to write a solid performance test answer within the time constraints you'll face on your exam. See chapter 16.*

❑   I have additional factors weighing in favor of taking the exam now. *Passing your bar exam depends on a combination of individual factors; if there are additional reasons why you believe you will pass your exam, take them into consideration in addition to the factors we listed above.*

Reflection Questions

1. If you've experienced a crisis during your bar preparation, do you think you can still focus enough to study, and will you have time to do so?

2. How will you feel if you take the bar exam and fail?

3. If you've experienced a crisis, is there a reason to push forward rather than waiting until the next exam administration?

4. Is there someone whose opinion you'd trust, who's not in the middle of a crisis or personally affected by your decision, who could help you assess your situation and options?

PART FIVE

TAKING YOUR BAR EXAM
AND MORE

CHAPTER 19

TAKING YOUR BAR EXAM

Introduction

Taking the bar exam is really just another phase of a much larger process of becoming a lawyer that includes deciding to go to law school, taking the LSAT, selecting a law school, attending law school, getting a job, developing expertise as a lawyer, and building a law practice. Like all the other phases, the keys to success with your bar exam include planning and level-headedness.

All students should plan to experience some stress when they take a bar exam. We're not aware of any student who didn't have at least some level of anxiety. Adrenaline surges, anxiety, and "butterflies" are all typical feelings. These feelings are not an issue that'll influence whether you pass the bar—if you know they're coming and have a plan for dealing with them constructively.

The Final Days of Your Bar Exam Process

Below is a list of recommendations for working your way through the final days of your bar exam process. By following the recommendations, you'll be in your best possible frame of mind during your exam.

1. **Take care of yourself.** In the last few days before your exam, it's important to eat healthy food and get plenty of sleep. In simple terms, sleep improves memory.[1] Lack of sleep reduces the levels of neurotransmitters in the brain that control mood and causes depression and increased irritability.[2] Thus, make sure to get plenty of sleep in the days leading up to your bar exam and between the days of your exam.

---

1. See, e.g., Colin Allen, "Sleep Boosts Memory," Psychology Today, Oct. 13, 2004, available at www.cms.psychologytoday.com/articles/pto-3042.html (last visited May 7, 2005).

2. See, e.g., Hugo Rivera & James Villepigue, "The Maladies of Sleep Depravation [sic]," Dolfzine Online Fitness, www.dolfzine.com/page161.htm (last visited May 7, 2005); Farrah Hasen, "Sleep Deprivation: Effects on Safety, Health and the Quality of Life," California State University Fullerton Department of Radio-TV-Film, www.communications.fullerton.edu/facilities/tvfilm _studios/content/safety/sleep.htm (last visited May 7, 2005).

2. **Be optimistic about your exam.** One or two days before you take your exam, complete exercise 19-1, the confidence-boosting exercise at the end of this chapter. Also, continue using the Relaxation Response technique and optimism skills discussed in chapter 3 to help you remain calm, focused, and optimistic. Remind yourself that you have put in a lot of hard work and are prepared to pass.

3. **Pack your car.** Make sure to pack your car the night before your exam with the items you'll need (such as a photo identification, admission ticket, pencils, and pens).[3]

4. **Know your state's exam rules.** Also, make sure that you know your state's rules regarding behavior before and during the exam. For example, exam rules often prohibit examinees from making any notes from memory on scrap pieces of paper before an exam officially begins.[4]

5. **Arrive early and with appropriate clothing.** Plan to arrive at your exam location early, allowing for last-minute hassles with parking, walking to your exam site, and the like. Also, make sure to dress in layers so that you'll be able to adjust to your personal comfort level during the exam. And, if there's rain in the forecast, bring a waterproof coat with a hood because most bar exam rules prohibit bringing umbrellas.

6. **Plan for a wait.** It's helpful to plan in advance what to do while you're waiting to get into your exam and before your exam starts. It's not unusual for the checking-in process and exam administration logistics to consume more than an hour. Thus, plan on having a wait and decide in advance what you'll do while waiting.

    We recommend doing whatever will help you remain calm and focused. The key is to avoid imagining failure and, instead, to stay calm and confident. To do so, try the Relaxation Response technique described in chapter 3 or focus on something unrelated to the bar exam (for example, a relaxing place you enjoy visiting). Or, try to visualize yourself attacking the exam with confidence and succeeding and imagining how great that experience will feel.

7. **Avoid talking about the law or comparing yourself with others.** We discourage talking to any other students about the law or doing any last minute self-testing because these behaviors often result in panic. For example, after overhearing a discussion of a particular legal issue, you may try to remember what the other students are talking about, draw a blank, and then panic.

---

3. See checklists 2-5 and 2-6.

4. See, e.g., Letter from North Carolina Board of Law Examiners to Applicants to the February 2004 Bar Exam (on file with authors). You don't need to worry about making notes, anyway; what you need to know is well stored in your brain and ready for use. Also note that some states have unique requirements, so it's crucial that you've read through your state's rules before your exam. See, e.g., Robert M. Jarvis, An Anecdotal History of the Bar Exam, 9 Geo. J. Legal Ethics 359, 377 (1996) (noting that bar applicants in Kentucky and Virginia are required to wear business attire while taking their exams).

We also discourage you from comparing yourself in any way to other students. Remember, passing your bar exam is not a competition. Your goal is not to have a better score than anyone else or to get an "A." Your goal should be to demonstrate to the bar examiners that you meet the level of competence required to obtain a law license.

8. **Manage your anxiety or stress; stay focused and work steadily.** Likewise, during the exam, ward off negative thoughts. Instead of imagining what you might not know, trust your preparation process and continue to use the Relaxation Response and other stress management techniques. The work you've done has stored the knowledge you need in your long-term memory. Knowledge doesn't just fall out of the brain; if you can stay calm, you can readily access it, and you'll likely remember more than you even thought you knew.

   As you move through your exam, stay focused and work steadily. Make sure to allocate the appropriate amount of time to complete each portion of your exam and stick to that schedule. Also, check from time to time that you're marking all of your answers in the correct spaces.

9. **Have a plan for focusing in the event you get stuck.** Your stress management plan should include plans for what you'll do if you lose focus, get stuck on a question, or panic during your exam. Effective attention-focusing techniques include rereading a question (and answers if you're doing a multiple-choice question), making your best guess about a multiple-choice question and returning to it at the end if you have time, starting an essay with the part with which you feel most comfortable, and using the stress management techniques discussed in chapter 3.

10. **Stay forward-looking, using each new question as an opportunity to succeed.** As you move through your exam, don't let your perception of how well you answered one question or one portion of the exam influence your performance on another portion of the exam. Just as professional athletes force themselves to forget the previous day's game, force yourself to forget your performance on a previous question or section. Time spent evaluating how well you've performed on any question or section of the bar exam that you've completed is a waste of time. The time you spend on this assessment is time you could be spending more productively on the question in front of you or on recharging your mind. Keep your attention forward-looking, and consider each question and each section of the bar exam as new opportunities for improving your overall score.

11. **Use your lunch break and overnight break to refresh.** Before you take your exam, also plan what you'll do during your lunch breaks and between days of your exam. We recommend using your time to relax and refresh. Getting outside, eating, and moving around are all good ways to relax and refresh. For most students, using lunchtime or the evening between exam days to study is overkill. *Remember: what you've learned will not fall out of your brain.* Refreshing yourself should be a higher priority. Also, don't torture yourself by looking up answers to test questions or comparing notes with friends. Instead, keep your attitude positive by remembering that you're well prepared and are giving your exam your best shot.

Exercise 19-1: Confidence-Boosting Exercise[5]

During the week before your bar exam, set aside thirty minutes to do this confidence-boosting exercise. Do this exercise in a location where you'll feel relaxed and where you'll be uninterrupted for the entire time. You can do the exercise alone or with a close friend or study partner. Have this book and a pen handy to use during the exercise. When you're ready to begin, follow the steps listed below:

- Take a few quiet minutes to get yourself comfortable and relaxed. It might help to use the Relaxation Response technique explained in chapter 3. Focus on your breathing for ten minutes to help induce a state of calm.

- When you feel relaxed, think back and recall a person in your past who believed in you, was on your side, and knew you could achieve whatever you set out to do.

- Once you have this person in mind, think about how they demonstrated their confidence and support (what they said to you and how they acted toward you).

- Take a few more minutes to let yourself relax, breathe, and think about their confidence in you.

- Imagine what that person would say to you now, before you sit for the bar exam. Spend five to ten minutes writing about that person and what they would say to you now. If you feel like it, share what you've written with a friend.

5. This exercise is adapted from one led by Professor Ruth McKinney, Director of the Writing and Learning Resources Center, University of North Carolina School of Law, Chapel Hill, North Carolina, during a repeaters' group that she and Professor Riebe facilitated for the February 2001 bar exam.

Exercise 19-2: Final Pre-Exam Checklist

Items to Address	Specific Plans
❒ Plan for sufficient sleep.	
❒ Complete confidence-boosting exercise.	
❒ Check state exam-taking rules.	

❒ Create stress management plans for:
  ○ The last few days before the exam.
  ○ While you're waiting for the exam to start.
  ○ During the exam.
  ○ During breaks.
  ○ If you get stuck.	

❒ Pack extra clothes (*e.g.*, sweater, rain jacket).	
❒ Plan activities for lunch breaks and between days of the bar exam.	

Reflection Questions

1. Why is it so important that you have a detailed stress management plan?

2. Based on what you've learned in this book, why have we included the confidence-boosting exercise in this chapter?

3. Why is it better to refresh yourself than to do additional studying between days or parts of the bar exam?

CHAPTER 20

GETTING LICENSED IN MORE THAN ONE STATE

Taking More Than One State's Bar Exam During the Same Examination Period

Some students are interested in getting licensed in more than one state. Depending on the states' exams and rules, it may be possible to take two states' exams during one exam administration period. For example, assume that state A's and state B's bar exams are on different days, but with the Multistate Bar Exam ("MBE") overlapping on Wednesday. State A's exam is on Tuesday and Wednesday. State B's exam is on Wednesday and Thursday. Students interested in being licensed in both states could take the Tuesday and Wednesday exam in state A, transfer their MBE scores to state B, and then drive or fly to state B Wednesday evening and take the Thursday portion of state B's exam.

If you're interested in taking more than one state's exam during one exam administration period, make sure to check the requirements in each state to ensure you can transfer scores as you need to and that you can take two bars consistent with both states' rules.[1]

Also, think through the logistics and inevitable increase in stress you'll experience to decide whether you're really up for tackling two exams at once. On the one hand, it would be great to get both exams out of the way. On the other hand, however, you'll have to deal with more stress, more materials to study, and a more exhausting exam week. You may also have to deal with conflicting law on certain points. And, worst of all, if you're spread too thin you may risk failing both states' exams.

In sum, taking two bar exams during one administration is do-able for some students. But make sure you understand both states' rules and what you're getting yourself into before deciding what's right for you.

---

1. Make sure to obtain licensing information directly from both states' licensing entities. See appendix B for contact information for state licensing offices.

Taking a Second Bar Exam After
Already Passing Another State's Bar Exam
During a Previous Examination Period

If you've already taken one bar exam and want to get licensed in an additional state, make sure to understand the policies applicable in the second state. First, it's worthwhile to check on the second state's licensing and reciprocity rules to see if there's any way to get admitted without taking a second exam. If you need to take a second exam, check whether you can transfer any portion of your first exam (for example, your MBE score) to the second state. Before deciding to have a score transferred, however, make sure you understand how the second state will score your exam. In fact, we recommend that you consider whether your chances of passing the second state's bar exam would be better if the other state uses your previous MBE score or if you retake the MBE. Once you have all the facts, you'll be in a position to decide how to move forward in a way that'll best meet your needs.

CHAPTER 21

REPEATING A BAR EXAM

Everyone who sits for a bar exam wants to pass, of course, and anyone who fails is devastated at least momentarily.[1] It's like a punch in the stomach. It hurts.[2] But, for most students, the hurt starts to fade away, they regroup, and they are able to move forward. Others, though, might remain down and helpless. If you are unable to get yourself moving forward, it might be helpful to seek professional assistance.[3] The information contained in chapter 3 about Seligman's cognitive approach to promote optimism may also be helpful.

As soon as you discover your results, make sure to review your state's rules about obtaining information about your results, reviewing your exam, and appealing your score. Also find out whether your state has any limits on the number of times you can take your exam.[4] It may, however, be possible to ask for a waiver (for example, by demonstrating there's a compelling reason to believe you'll pass if given another chance).[5]

Most states have specific provisions governing the review of exams and sample answers that attempt to balance their interest in keeping their exams confidential and reusing test questions with students' interests in obtaining information if they fail.[6] In an attempt to balance these competing interests, courts have held that applicants who fail must either be given a right to inspect their exams (at such times and on such conditions as examiners may specify) or the right to take the bar exam as many times as they wish.[7]

Once you get over your initial reaction, take some time to assess your bar exam experience and decide whether you want to take the bar exam again. If you decide to take

---

1. *Cf.* Martin E.P. Seligman, Learned Optimism 45 (2d ed. 1998). *See also* Robert M. Jarvis, *An Anecdotal History of the Bar Exam*, 9 Geo. J. Legal Ethics 359, 387 (1996) (those who fail receive a terrible blow to their self-esteem, often hide the results out of shame, and try to avoid telling their employers for fear they'll be fired).

2. *E.g.*, Jarvis, *supra* note 1, at 387.

3. *See* Seligman, *supra* note 1, at 45. Seligman recommends cognitive therapy targeting explanatory style to move from pessimism to optimism. *Id.* at 89–91. His book contains self-help information and instructions. *Id.* at 207–34. A professional therapist using Seligman's cognitive techniques should also be able to help repeaters regroup and move forward.

4. Many states limit the number of times a student can take the bar exam. Jarvis, *supra* note 1, at 404 (reporting that twenty-four states have such a limit, ranging from two to five times).

5. *Id.*

6. *Id.*

7. *Id.* (citing *Fields v. Kelly*, 986 F.2d 225, 228 (8th Cir. 1993) and *Bowles v. Askew*, 448 S.E.2d 191, 192 (Ga. 1994)).

the bar exam again, take the time to understand what went wrong. Carefully diagnose why you didn't pass your bar exam using the step-by-step checklist in exercise 21-1. Doing the same thing you did during your first review period and exam is unlikely to lead to a different result. Thus, formulate a new plan to meet your individual needs. Make sure to review chapters 9–17 again as you formulate your new plan for success.

Although any failure is hard to accept, there are some facts that may provide some comfort. Failing a bar exam doesn't mean that you won't be successful in the practice of law.[8] Indeed, there have been many applicants who have failed exams initially, then passed and proceeded to have stellar legal careers.[9]

Also remember that, as a repeater, you have some advantages. For example, you know the process, you know what to expect, and you've practiced taking a bar exam. You can use this information to your advantage if you can keep your spirits up.

---

8. *Id.* at 381. *See also* Deborah L. Rhode, *The Future of the Legal Profession: Institutionalizing Ethics*, 44 Case W. Res. L. Rev. 665, 690 (1994).

9. Jarvis, *supra* note 1, at 387.

Exercise 21-1: Bar Exam Failure Diagnostic Checklist

Step 1: Assessment of errors on the exam:

Find out your state's policies for obtaining your scores and reviewing your exam. Follow those policies to get your scores and review your exam. If possible, get another person who can be objective to review your exam with you and take notes on their feedback. Below is a checklist of common deficiencies in students' bar exam performances. Check each that applies to your situation.

Common multiple-choice question errors:

❒ Confusion about or poor knowledge of the law (circle each area of law you didn't know as well as you needed to know it):

        Contracts   Torts
        Real property   Evidence
        Criminal law   Constitutional law

❒ Reading comprehension errors.

❒ Issue spotting errors.

❒ Analysis errors.

❒ Inadequate exam time management.

Common essay exam errors:

❒ Confusion about or poor knowledge of the law (list each area of law you didn't know as well as you needed to know it):

❒ Reading comprehension errors.

❒ Issue spotting errors.

❒ Analysis errors.

❒ Failure(s) to answer the call(s) of the question(s).

❒ Writing issues (see exercise 15-1, essay evaluation checklist).

❒ Inadequate exam time management.

Common performance exam errors:

❒ Failure(s) to answer the call(s) of the question(s).

❒ Reading comprehension errors.

❒ Issue spotting errors.

❒ Analysis errors.

❒ Writing issues (grammar, organization, word choice, etc.).

❒ Inadequate exam time management.

Exercise 21-1: (continued)

Step 2: Assessment of errors in exam preparation:

Think through your review period and what you've learned about the weaknesses in your bar exam performance and identify all errors in your bar preparation.

For example, if you had trouble managing your time, you may have wasted time on the bar exam because your stress management plan was ineffective or you may have been operating on insufficient sleep.

Similarly, if your knowledge of the applicable law was inadequate, your approach to reading the outlines might have been flawed so that you didn't ever really learn the material, your attention-focusing strategies might have been insufficient so you didn't pay adequate attention while studying, your organizational strategies might have been deficient so you didn't recognize how the subjects all related to each other, your study plan might have been insufficient so that you simply did not finish all the studying you needed to do, or your memorization strategies might have been flawed.

Below is a checklist of possible flaws in students' study strategies. Check each that applies to you and add any other issues with your bar preparation in the blank boxes.

❏ Inadequate sleep.	❏ Insufficient time studying.	❏ Insufficient memorization strategies.	❏ Failure to learn from feedback.
❏ Insufficient stress management.	❏ Inadequate approach to subject outlines.	❏ Erroneous self-assessment of preparedness.	❏ Failure to seek feedback.
❏ Failure to address risk factors.	❏ Insufficient attention while studying.	❏ Inadequate study plan.	
❏ Insufficient self-efficacy.	❏ Failure to self-monitor while studying.	❏ Failure to seek help when needed.	
❏ Failure to set mastery-learning goals.	❏ Insufficient organizational strategies.	❏ Not enough practice.	

Exercise 21-1: (continued)

Step 3: Assessment of best practices in prior bar study:

Students who fail their bar exams usually used some effective techniques and strategies and performed well on some aspects of their exams. It's important that you recognize what techniques and strategies worked well for you, and which aspects of your bar exam you performed well on, so that you can expand them to your entire bar study process and exam. In the space below, list the things you did best during your bar preparation and on your bar exam.

The things I did best when studying for and taking my exam were:

1.

2.

3.

4.

5.

6.

7.

8.

9.

10.

FINAL WORDS

We hope this book has given you a realistic overview of the bar review and exam process—and, by doing so, has minimized any fear or anxiety you may have about your bar exam. By understanding the process, you'll also lay the foundation necessary to plan for success.

In addition, in this book we have integrated many skills sets that have been proven to correlate with success: self-management, stress management, planning, learning, studying, and test-taking. For each, we've provided strategies, checklists, exercises, and recommendations to help you maximize your chances of passing the bar exam.

As you go through your bar review and exam, remember that your exam is passable! Students don't just randomly fail. Your success will depend on a combination of factors—including intelligence, skills, preparation, and attitude. Make sure to manage the factors you can control to increase your likelihood of success.

If you take the time to understand the process, assess your risk factors, create your own written plan for success, put in the hard hours of studying, and study wisely, you'll pass the bar!

We wish you the best.

WELCOME TO THE PROFESSION!

APPENDICES

APPENDIX A

NATIONAL CONFERENCE
OF BAR EXAMINERS

Contact Information

National Conference of Bar Examiners ("NCBE")
402 West Wilson St.
Madison, WI 53703-3614
(608) 280-8550
Web site: www.ncbex.org
E-mail: contact@ncbex.org

    The NCBE Web site is worth scanning well in advance of your bar exam because it contains a lot of valuable—and free—information about the NCBE exams, including the:

- Multistate Bar Exam ("MBE");
- Multistate Essay Exam ("MEE");
- Multistate Professional Responsibility Exam ("MPRE"); and
- Multistate Performance Test ("MPT").

    The Web site includes descriptions of the NCBE exams along with free sample questions and answers. It also provides information for purchasing NCBE publications with sample questions and answers. Finally, the Web site contains contact information for the licensing entities in every state as well as maps showing which states use which NCBE exams.

APPENDIX B

STATE LICENSING OFFICES

There are several ways to obtain contact information for the entity that oversees the licensing of attorneys in your state. One of the best sources is the NCBE Web site, www.ncbex.org, under the *Bar Admission Offices* tab. Contact addresses, phone numbers, and Web sites are included. The NCBE updates its information on an ongoing basis, so it's one of the best sources for current contact information.

The American Bar Association ("ABA") Web site also contains a list of state licensing entities. ABA, *Directory of State Bar Admission Offices*, www.abanet.org/legaled/baradmissions/barcont.html.

Below, for your convenience, are Web site addresses for state licensing entities.[1]

Alabama: www.alabar.org.

Alaska: www.alaskabar.org.

Arizona: www.supreme.state.az.us/admis.

Arkansas: www.courts.state.ar.us.

California: www.calbar.ca.gov.

Colorado: www.coloradosupremecourt.com.

Connecticut: www.jud.state.ct.us/cbec.

Delaware: www.courts.state.de.us/bbe.

District of Columbia: www.dcappeals.gov/dccourts/appeals/coa.

Florida: www.floridabarexam.org.

Georgia: www.gabaradmissions.org.

Guam: www.guamsupremecourt.com.

Hawaii: www.state.hi.us.jud.

Idaho: www.state.id.us/isb.

Illinois: www.ibaby.org.

Indiana: www.in.gov/judiciary/ble.

Iowa: www.judicial.state.ia.us.

Kansas: www.kscourts.org/attyadmit.htm.

Kentucky: www.kyoba.org.

Louisiana: www.lascba.org.

---

1. NCBE, *Bar Admissions Offices*, www.ncbex.org/offices.htm (last visited May 7, 2005).

Maine: www.mainebarexaminers.org.

Maryland: www.courts.state.md.us.

Massachusetts: www.mas.gov/bbe.

Michigan: www.courts.Michigan.gov/supremecourt/BdofLawExaminers.

Minnesota: www.ble.state.mn.us.

Mississippi: www.mssc.state.ms.us.

Missouri: www.osca.state.mo.us/SUP/index.nsf.

Montana: www.montanabar.org.

Nebraska: www.nebar.com.

Nevada: www.nvbar.org.

New Hampshire: www.courts.state.nh.us/nhbar.

New Jersey: www.njbarexams.org.

New Mexico: www.nmexam.org.

New York: www.nybarexam.org.

North Carolina: www.ncble.org.

North Dakota: www.ndcourts.com/court.

Northern Mariana Islands: www.justice.gov.mp.

Ohio: www.sconnet.state.oh.us.

Oklahoma: www.okbbe.com.

Oregon: www.osbar.org.

Palau: No known Web site. Phone: 680-488-2607.

Pennsylvania: www.pabarexam.org.

Puerto Rico: www.tribunalpr.org.

Rhode Island: www.courts.state.ri.us/supreme/bar/baradmission.htm.

South Carolina: www.judicial.state.sc.us.

South Dakota: www.sdjudicial.com.

Tennessee: www.state.tn.us/lawexaminers.

Texas: www.ble.state.tx.us.

Utah: www.utahbar.org.

Vermont: www.vermontjudiciary.org.

Virgin Islands: No known Web site. Phone: 340-777-7674.

Virginia: www.vbbe.state.va.us.

Washington: www.wsba.org.

West Virginia: www.state.wv.us/wvsca.

Wisconsin: www.courts.state.wi.us/bbe.

Wyoming: www.wyomingbar.org.

APPENDIX C

MORE BAR PREPARATION RESOURCES

Jeff Adachi, Bar Breaker (1990) (addressing California bar exam).

Suzanne Darrow-Kleinhaus, The Bar Exam in a Nutshell (2003).

Mary Campbell Gallagher, Scoring High on Bar Exam Essays (1991).

Edna Wells Handy, You Can Pass Any Bar Exam (1997).

Loretta Walder, Pass This Bar: A Readiness Guide for Bar Exam Preparation (1982).

Kimm Alayne Walton & Steve Emanuel, Strategies & Tactics for the MBE (2003).

R. Whitman, Preparations for the Bar Exam (1978).

APPENDIX D

ANSWERS TO SAMPLE MBE QUESTIONS

Answers to Table 14-1 Questions

1. The correct answer is A because Able's statement was not an offer, and therefore there could not be a counter-offer. An offer requires a communication of commitment and Able's inquiry about $2,000 was silent as to his commitment to take $2,000.

2. The correct answer is C because the parol evidence rule doesn't apply to agreements made *after* a written agreement.

3. A is the correct answer. As a manufacturer, Sally would be a lost-volume seller because, had Bob not breached, she would have made two sales instead of one. Sellers cannot recover consequential damages under the UCC so B is wrong, and, while Sally can recover for her expenses in readvertising and reselling the TV, her lost profit doesn't measure those losses. D is wrong because *in pari delicto* is an illegality rule and therefore is irrelevant.

4. C is the correct answer. I is not correct because a contract for services for less than one year doesn't need to be in writing. II is correct because the Supreme Court has interpreted specific performance of a services contract to be a violation of the Thirteenth Amendment. III is correct because Carl's services can be readily replaced so damages would be a sufficient remedy.

5. B is the correct answer. While parties may condition their duty to pay on satisfaction, any claim of dissatisfaction must be made in good faith. Because Fred knew all of Paula's work was abstract, he cannot claim dissatisfaction because her portrait of him was abstract.

6. D is the correct answer. The contract is broken into paired performances that are agreed equivalents so it's divisible. Good faith is irrelevant. Estoppel doesn't apply with respect to executory parts of a divisible contract. While *contra proferentem* would justify interpreting ambiguous parts of the contract against Fred, there are no facts suggesting the contract was ambiguous in any respect relevant to this dispute, and therefore this principle is inapplicable.

Answers to Exercise 14-1 Questions

1. B
2. B
3. A

APPENDIX E

ANSWERS TO SAMPLE MPRE QUESTIONS

1. C
2. C
3. D

APPENDIX F

SAMPLE ANSWERS TO ESSAY QUESTIONS

Here are sample answers to the essay questions in exercise 15-5. Make sure to read the essay questions *and take a half hour per essay to write answers*, before looking at or reading the sample answers below. We can't emphasize this approach enough; *you'll only integrate and "own" what you're learning through these examples if you take the time to work through them and write your own answers first.*

After writing your own essay answers, take the time to do a self-evaluation or peer evaluation using exercises 15-1 and 15-3. Then read through the sample answers in this appendix. When you do, pay more attention to the flow of the essays than to the substance. Of course, on your bar exam you'll want to focus on substance. For now, to transition your writing from law school writing to bar exam writing, it's more important to focus on the process of writing. You'll be spending months reviewing and reinforcing the substantive law as a part of your bar review.

Note that we've provided annotations for the first three essay answers (with shaded text). First read the sample answers slowly, reading the annotations along the way. Then read the sample answers again straight through, skipping the annotations, to get a better feel for the overall flow of the essay answers.

After the first three answers, you should be able to annotate the answers yourself. In fact, we recommend that you label the parts of your template, including the parts of the CRAC paradigm, as a way to test and cement your understanding.

Note that the sample answers below are not "perfect" or the only "right" way to answer the sample essay questions. But they are solid essays that touch all the bases you need to cover to write passing essay answers.

Finally, for each sample answer, we have provided a footnote indicating which jurisdiction's law is used in the answer. Realize that the law changes every day as new cases are decided and new laws are passed. Thus, relying on the law stated in these answers would be a mistake. The law used in each essay is the law of the state indicated or is based on multistate rules. Therefore, it may not be the law you'll need to use on your state's bar exam. *Check your bar outlines to ensure that you know what the applicable law is in your jurisdiction.* We recommend writing practice essays reflecting your state's law, then engaging in peer reviews with classmates to check each other's understanding.

Question 1 Sample Answer[2]

Before you read through this answer and the annotations in it, turn to exercise 15-1, "Checklist for Writing Effective Bar Exam Essays." Go through the checklist provided and evaluate your own answer.

The annotations will walk you through the recommended process for answering essay questions in chapter 15. Lower case letters will be used in the annotations that match the steps recommended in chapter 15 (so that, if you want more information about any step, you may refer to the corresponding text).

a. Before reading the question, allot time by writing down when thirty minutes expires on a scrap piece of paper.

b. Don't flip through and look at any of the other questions—doing so is a waste of time and may cause you to feel overwhelmed and to lose your focus. Concentrate only on this single question in front of you.

c. Go to the end of the question and read the call first. The call for this question is a gift; it tells you the cause of action you are to address instead of making you figure it out by yourself. Accordingly, you can put on your torts hat and read the question, looking for facts that would be relevant to an intentional infliction of emotional distress claim. As you read the facts, highlight or circle information that you think is legally significant and that you'll integrate in your answer.

d. After you read the question, take a few moments to outline an answer. For a tort with elements, it will often work best to organize by the elements. Thus, write down the three elements on a scrap piece of paper. Next to each element, write any legal buzzwords and key facts you want to include in your answer. For example, for the intentional/reckless requirement you could write: "R/intent, substantially certain, strong probability ED will result—A/no knowledge/purpose ED would result, intent to close account, no knowledge of susceptibility."

e. Notice how the sample answer is written to look professional: it's neat and organized, includes white space for margins and in between paragraphs, uses indentations to indicate paragraphs, and uses headings to make the essay reader-friendly. In addition, the answer uses transitional phrases which lead a reader through the essay (transitional phrases are italicized in the sample answer below).

f. Also notice that the sample answer uses the same type of legal reasoning used in law school—deductive. The deductive reasoning process is used to organize each element of the essay by using the CRAC paradigm (the CRAC paradigm is shown inside brackets and with shaded information in the sample answer).

g. Finally, notice that the essay is concise and precise. There's no flowery language, the essay isn't overly wordy, and it doesn't ramble. Instead, the essay just states what needs to be said to answer the question, touching all the bases (C, R, A, C) for each element discussed to get full credit.

[Overall conclusion] *No,* Client cannot recover for the intentional infliction of emotional distress ("IIED"). [Umbrella rule] Elements of an IIED claim are: (1) severe emotional distress, (2) caused by reckless or intentional conduct, (3) that is extreme and out-

---

2. This essay is based on Nebraska law.

rageous. Because Client will not be able to show all three elements of the cause of action, he will not be able to recover.

[Notice how the elements of the rule are used to organize the body of the essay answer. You will usually find that, once you outline a rule, you can use the rule's structure as the organizational framework for your answer. Also, notice how headings that match the three elements are used to make the answer reader-friendly. Finally, notice that each element is addressed using a separate CRAC.]

Severity of emotional distress

[Conclusion] *First,* Client will not be able to show that his emotional distress was severe. [Rule] *As a general rule,* liability only arises when distress is so severe that no reasonable person should be expected to endure it. Some degree of distress is inevitable in society and the law will only intervene for an extreme, disabling response. Mere worry, anger, humiliation, and loss of sleep are not enough. *Instead,* a plaintiff needs to prove severe distress with evidence of more than subjective symptoms. *For example,* a medical diagnosis, objective evidence that one's job performance has been adversely affected, or an accompanying bodily injury may establish that distress is severe. Historically, courts have been hesitant to expand liability for emotional distress claims absent clear proof of severe distress in an attempt to limit fictitious claims.

[Application] *Here,* Client cannot show severe distress. The fact that Client was embarrassed, humiliated, angry, and "down" are not sufficient. Client's trouble sleeping and nightmares also are insufficient. And, although Client saw a counselor, he only went twice and never received a diagnosis. *Further,* there is no indication that the days Client took off from work or left early had an adverse effect on his overall job performance. [Conclusion] *Thus,* there is no severe distress.

Intentional or reckless requirement

[Conclusion] *Second,* Client probably cannot meet the intentional or reckless requirement. [Rule] *As a general rule,* the intentional or reckless requirement requires a defendant to: (1) intend to inflict severe emotional distress; (2) be substantially certain severe emotional distress will result; or (3) realize that there is a strong probability that emotional harm will result. It's not enough for a defendant to intend an act; the intent must be to inflict emotional distress.

[Application] *Here,* it will be hard to establish intent or recklessness. There is no indication that the manager's purpose was to inflict emotional distress or that he should have realized that severe distress would follow. Although the manager intended to close Client's account, that goal is unrelated to causing Client emotional distress. The manager's reason for doing so (the effect on customers and bank employees), has no relationship whatsoever to harming Client. There are also no facts indicating that the manager had any basis for believing that closing the account would cause a severe reaction in Client. [Conclusion] *Thus,* absent some additional evidence—for example, knowledge by the manager that Client was specifically susceptible to distress—intent or recklessness would likely not be found.

Extreme and outrageous behavior

[Conclusion] *Third,* extreme and outrageous behavior will also be hard to establish. [Rule] *As a general rule,* liability only occurs where conduct is regarded as atrocious and utterly intolerable in a civilized society. To limit the bounds of distress claims, the extreme and outrageous standard establishes a high bar to recovery. Practically put, the facts of a case must arouse resentment from average members of a community and lead them to exclaim, "Outrageous!"

Mere indignities, annoyances, and petty oppressions that inevitably result from social interactions do not, by themselves, constitute extreme and outrageous behavior. They may, however, rise to the level of extreme and outrageous if a defendant knows of a plaintiff's susceptibility to emotional distress.

Further, when defendants do no more than insist upon their rights in a permissible way, they are not liable even if they know that doing so will result in emotional distress.

[Application] *Here,* there is not enough evidence to establish extreme and outrageous behavior. Although the bank manager was insensitive, his behavior is unlikely to be considered atrocious and utterly intolerable or to prompt an exclamation of "Outrageous!" Because businesses sometimes refuse to provide service to customers and, in general, may do so, the manager's conduct would likely be considered a mere indignity without a showing that the manager knew that Client was particularly susceptible to distress. If, however, it could be shown that the bank closed Client's account in a discriminatory way that exceeded its legal authority, the manager's conduct might arise to the level of extreme and outrageous. [Conclusion] But because there is no indication of severe distress or intent or recklessness, Client still could not recover.

Respondeat superior

[Conclusion) *Finally,* the Bank would be vicariously liable for the actions of its manager. [Rule] *As a general rule,* employers are responsible for the torts of their employees if the employees are acting within the scope of their employment and furthering the interests of the employer.

[Application] *Here,* the manager was acting within the scope of his employment and attempting to avoid disruptions to Bank employees and customers. [Conclusion] *Thus,* the Bank would be liable for the manager's conduct if a tort is established.

[Overall conclusion] *Thus,* because Client cannot show all three elements of an IIED cause of action, he will not be able to prevail.

> h.   Did you have any time left after you finished writing your essay answer? If so, you should have gone back and proofread your essay, making sure to make any revisions as neatly as possible.
>
> i.   Finally, when your thirty minutes were up, did you take a deep breath to clear your mind? Remember to practice doing this so that, on your exam, you'll be prepared to take advantage of the new opportunity to demonstrate what you know that each question presents.

Now that you've read the entire sample answer, go back to exercise 15-1 again. As you look through exercise 15-1's checklist, what do you see that you didn't see before reading the sample answer? Make a list of at least three take-home points to integrate as you write more practice essay answers:*

1.

2.

3.

---

* See the last pages of this appendix for what we believe to be the take-home points from this sample essay. You may have additional ones.

Question 2 Sample Answer[3]

a. Did you allocate your time and write down the time you needed to finish your answer before beginning this essay question?

b. Did you focus solely on the question in front of you, and refrain from flipping around or looking at any other questions?

c. Did you read the call of the question first?

If so, what did you learn by reading the call of the question first?

d. Did you take time to briefly outline the issues, rules, and key facts?

If so, did you notice that it helped you write a more organized and coherent essay answer?

e. Does your essay answer look professional?

If so, what makes it look professional? If not, what do you need to do differently?

f. Go through your essay answer and mark CRAC to ensure that your essay reflects the deductive reasoning process. Then, look at the sample answer below, paying attention to the paradigm.

[Overall conclusion] Yes. Because Sophie is a minor, Sophie's parents probably can have Sophie disaffirm the contract with the car dealership, even though she misrepresented her age. Sophie, however, will have to make restitution to the car dealership for the reasonable value of her use and the depreciation of the car because of the car accident, making her parents success on their claim almost meaningless.

---

3. This essay is based on multistate contracts rules.

Contracts with minors

[Conclusion] Because Sophie is a minor, her parents probably will be able to disaffirm the contract. [Rules] As a general rule, minors do not have the capacity to make binding contracts because they are not considered sufficiently mature to make responsible decisions. However, if a minor makes a contract, the contract will not be automatically void. Instead, a minor's guardians (while she is a minor) and the minor herself (within a reasonable time after she reaches the age of majority) have the option of disaffirming a contract.

[Application] Here, regardless of whether the state age of majority is eighteen or twenty-one, Sophie was only sixteen when she made the contract and therefore was a minor. [Conclusion] Consequently, her parents should succeed in disaffirming the contract.

Effect of misrepresentation

[Conclusion] In most states, Sophie's misrepresentation will not prevent her from disaffirming the contract. [Umbrella rule] The majority rule is that a minor may disaffirm a contract even if the minor misrepresented his or her age. Some states disagree. In such minority rule states, a minor's right to disaffirm a contract is limited. A minor is estopped from disaffirming a contract if: (1) the minor had reached the age of discretion at the time of the contract; (2) the minor made a fraudulent misrepresentation of his or her age; and (3) the other party to the contract justifiably relied on the minor's misrepresentation.

[Conclusion] First, Sophie had reached the age of discretion. [Rule] As a general rule, minors are held responsible for misrepresentations made after they reach the age of discretion. Usually, minors reach the age of discretion between ten- and fourteen- years old. [Application] Because Sophie was sixteen, [Conclusion] she had reached the age of discretion.

[Conclusion] Second, Sophie is unlikely to be found to have made a fraudulent misrepresentation of her age. [Rule] A minor is held to have made a fraudulent misrepresentation when he or she makes an intentional, knowing false representation. Accordingly, if a minor affirmatively states that he or she is eighteen or older, a fraudulent misrepresentation has been made. In contrast, if a minor merely signs a form contract that contains a recital that he or she is eighteen or older, no fraudulent misrepresentation has been made.

[Application] Here, there is no indication that Sophie made an intentional, knowing false representation. Sophie did not state that she was eighteen or older. She merely signed a form contract containing a recital that she was of the age of majority. [Counter-analysis] It appears that Sophie may have intended to deceive the salesman by conducting the transaction with her law school boyfriend present. [Conclusion] However, it is unlikely to be found that Sophie made an intentional misrepresentation.

[Conclusion] Third, it is questionable whether the seller justifiably relied on a misrepresentation. [Rule] Whether reliance is justified is largely a question of fact. Facts considered are a minor's physical appearance, life circumstances known to a seller, whether there is any reason to doubt a minor is eighteen or older, and whether there is an easy means for verifying a minor's age.

[Application] Here, because Sophie was sixteen and accompanied by her twenty-one-year-old boyfriend, there was not necessarily any reason for the salesman to doubt that Sophie was old enough to buy the car. [Counter-analysis] However, there was an easy means available for verifying Sophie's age: the salesman could have easily asked to see Sophie's driver's license. [Conclusion] Thus, the seller probably was not reasonable in assuming that Sophie was of the age of majority.

Limitation on Sophie's right to disaffirm

[Conclusion] While Sophie's action for rescission and restitution is likely to succeed, she is unlikely to recover much. [Rule] To obtain restitution, a minor must pay for the items received under a contract, the reasonable value of their use, and any depreciation in their value.

[Application] Here, Sophie would have to return the car and make restitution reflecting the value of her short-term use of it. She also would have to make restitution for its depreciation. In this case, the car was totaled. [Conclusion] Consequently, in addition to returning the car and paying for her use of it, Sophie would have to make restitution of the full value of the car less any salvage value.

[Overall conclusion] In sum, Sophie will likely be able to disaffirm the contract. Her success on the claim will be almost meaningless, however, because she will have to make restitution to the dealer for the use and depreciation in the value of the car.

    g.   Compare your essay to the sample answer. Is your essay concise and precise (similar to the sample answer)? If not, what do you need to do differently?

    h.   How much time did it take you to do this practice essay?

If you finished in less than thirty minutes, did you go back and proof your answer, making any revisions as neatly as possible?

    i.   Did you remember to take a deep breath and clear your head after you finished your essay answer?

Make a list of at least three take-home points to integrate as you write more practice essay answers:*

    1.

    2.

    3.

---

   * See the last pages of this appendix for what we believe to be the take-home points from this sample essay. You may have additional ones.

Question 3 Sample Answer[4]

a. Did you allocate your time and write down the time you needed to finish your answer before beginning this essay question?

b. Did you focus solely on the question in front of you, and refrain from flipping around or looking at any other questions?

c. Did you read the call of the question first?

   If so, what did you learn by reading the call of the question first?

d. Did you briefly outline the issues, rules, and key facts?

   If so, did you notice that it helped you write a more organized and coherent essay answer?

e. Does your essay answer look professional?

   If so, what makes it look professional? If not, what do you need to do differently?

f. Go through your essay answer and mark CRAC to ensure that your essay reflects the deductive reasoning process. Then, look at the sample answer below, paying attention to the paradigm.

[Overall conclusion] Yes, Lawyer will prevail with a claim for tortious interference with contract so long as he can prove his allegations that Associate undermined him, falsely told partners that he made inappropriate comments about clients, and discussed her desire to have Lawyer terminated. [Umbrella rule] To recover for tortious interference, Lawyer must prove (1) a contract existed, (2) Associate had knowledge of the con-

---

4. This essay is based on North Carolina law.

tract, (3) Associate intentionally induced the firm to terminate the contract, (4) Associate acted without justification, and (5) Associate's conduct caused Lawyer damages. Lawyer can likely prove all of these elements.

A contract existed

[Conclusion] First, Lawyer had a contract with the firm. [Rules] As a general rule, there must be a contract establishing contractual rights for tortious interference to be possible. For employment contracts, both contracts for definite terms and at-will contracts are protected. Even at-will contracts are protected from tortious interference because even when a contract may be terminable by the parties to it, the contract is not terminable at the will of third parties.

[Application] Here, the facts do not indicate whether Lawyer had a written contract or if his position was terminable at will, but either would suffice. [Conclusion] Thus, the contract element is established.

Associate's knowledge of the contract

[Conclusion] Second, Associate had knowledge of the contract. [Rule] As a general rule, the knowledge requirement is met when a defendant knows the facts giving rise to a contract. [Application] Here, as an associate herself, Associate knew of her own contract, knew Lawyer was an associate, and therefore knew of Lawyer's contract with the firm. [Conclusion] Thus, the knowledge requirement is met.

Intentional inducement

[Conclusion] The closest issue is whether Associate intentionally induced the firm to terminate Lawyer. [Rule] As a general rule, conduct is intentional when an actor intends an act (not the consequences of his or her act).

[Application] Here, while Associate admits she wanted Lawyer to leave, her desire, alone, would not be enough if she took no action. Lawyer will need to prove what he has asserted, that Associate either did, in fact, falsely tell partners at the firm that Lawyer made inappropriate remarks about clients' attire, mannerisms, and legal affairs or that Associate discussed her desire to have Lawyer terminated with partners in the firm. Associate's conduct, if proven, was volitional and therefore intentional, whether or not she intended it to result in Lawyer's termination.

[Conclusion] Because Associate would have chosen to undermine Lawyer by false statements and by requests to have him removed, the intentional requirement would also be met.

Absence of justification

[Conclusion] Fourth, Associate acted without justification. [Rule] As a general rule, conduct is justified when it relates to legitimate business interests. For instance, acting within one's scope of authority or to protect one's own contractual rights is conduct relating to legitimate business interests. To show a lack of justification, legal malice must be demonstrated—for example, committing an act that exceeds one's legal right or authority. In contrast, actual malice—personal hatred, ill will, or spite—alone is not sufficient.

[Application] Here, Associate acted without justification. Associate was not a party to the contract, but may have had some legitimate interests in Lawyer's work as a co-associate at the firm—for example, an interest in the reputation and financial well-being of the firm. Her conduct, however, exceeded the scope of that interest.

Associate admitted her dislike for Lawyer and her desire to have him leave the firm. But her actual malice alone is not sufficient to establish legal malice. If Lawyer can prove that Associate falsely told partners at the firm that Lawyer made inappropriate remarks about clients' attire, mannerisms, and legal affairs and that she discussed her desire to have Lawyer terminated with partners in the firm, then Associate acted with legal malice and exceeded the scope of her legitimate business interests.

[Conclusion] Thus, by exceeding the scope of her legitimate business interests, Associate acted without justification.

Resulting damages

[Conclusion] Fifth, Associate's conduct caused Lawyer damages. [Rule] The damages requirement is met when a plaintiff shows that a defendant's conduct resulted in actual damages. [Application] Here, Lawyer lost his employment and the benefit of his employment contract. [Conclusion] Thus, the damages requirement is met.

[Overall Conclusion] In sum, if Lawyer can prove Associate made the statements he claims she made, Lawyer's case satisfies the elements of tortious interference with contract. Thus, he will be able to recover.

g. Compare your essay to the sample answer. Is your essay concise and precise (similar to the sample answer)? If not, what do you need to do differently?

h. How much time did it take you to do this practice essay?

If you finished in less than thirty minutes, did you go back and proofread your answer, making any revisions as neatly as possible?

i. Did you remember to take a deep breath to clear your head after you finished your essay answer?

Make a list of at least three take-home points to integrate as you write more practice essay answers:*

1.

2.

3.

---

* See the last pages of this appendix for what we believe to be the take-home points from this sample essay. You may have additional ones.

Question 4 Sample Answer[5]

a.   What was the first thing you did when you turned to this practice question?

b.   Self-assess your level of attention as you began and worked through this question. How high was your level of attention?

If your attention level was low, what could you do to increase your level of attention?

c.   What part of the question did you read first?

What did you learn by reading the part you read first?

d.   How did you organize your essay?

Why did that work well for this type of question?

e.   Does your essay answer look professional?

If so, what makes it look professional? If not, what do you need to do differently?

f.   Go through your essay answer and mark CRAC to ensure that your essay reflects the deductive reasoning process. Then, look at the sample answer below and label the parts of the paradigm in the sample answer. How similar is your answer to the sample answer below in terms of using the paradigm?

---

5. This essay is based on the federal kidnapping statute and cases construing the statute's requirements.

If there were differences, what did you learn about using the paradigm to write an effective bar exam essay?

Yes, Dave's motion for judgment of acquittal should be granted because there is insufficient evidence to sustain a federal kidnapping conviction.

The applicable standard for a motion for judgment of acquittal

Under the federal rules of criminal procedure, a motion for judgment of acquittal should be granted when there is insufficient evidence to sustain a conviction. Evidence is considered in the light most favorable to the government, and a court must determine whether a rational fact finder could find the essential elements of an offense beyond a reasonable doubt.

Elements of kidnapping

Kidnapping requires the unlawful seizing, holding, and transporting of a victim through interstate commerce. Because all the elements of kidnapping cannot be found beyond a reasonable doubt in this case, Dave's motion should be granted.

Unlawful seizure element

First, there was an unlawful seizure when Dave kidnapped Vicki from her home. As a general rule, an unlawful seizure can be made by seizing, confining, inveigling, decoying, kidnapping, abducting, or carrying away another person. The federal kidnapping statute is broadly worded to encompass every possible method of kidnapping. Because Dave unlawfully entered Vicki's house, threatened her with a knife, and made her leave with him, the unlawful seizure requirement is met in this case.

Unlawful holding element

Dave did not unlawfully hold Vicki. As a general rule, an unlawful holding requires an involuntary restraint for an appreciable period of time with the intent to confine. Involuntary means that the holding must be without a victim's consent. A victim's acts must demonstrate a lack of consent. Not availing oneself of opportunities to escape may demonstrate consent unless a victim has a mental or physical impairment preventing escape.

The holding does not need to be for any particular reason, such as a ransom or reward. The statute is broadly worded to encompass kidnappings for any reason at all because kidnapping is undesirable in and of itself, regardless of motive.

Here, Dave would not be deemed to have held Vicki involuntarily. An involuntary holding must be without a victim's consent. On the one hand, Dave unlawfully seized her using physical threats and refused two requests from Vicki to drive her home, suggesting that her continued presence with Dave was against her will. On the other hand, most of Vicki's actions are inconsistent with an involuntary holding. Vicki could have left Dave at the gas station, but instead she stayed with him, walked hand-in-hand with him on the beach, played in the waves on the shore with him, and rode on his back. All of those acts appear voluntary.

In addition, Vicki had several opportunities to escape, but she did not try to take advantage of them. There is no indication that she attempted to get assistance at the gas station when she went to the bathroom or when they were on the beach and in the presence of other people. There is also no indication that Vicki had any sort of mental or physical impairment that interfered with taking advantage of her opportunities for escape.

There is no indication that Dave asked for a ransom or reward, but that does not matter. The federal kidnapping offense encompasses any taking for any reasons whatsoever. But, in any event, there was no unlawful holding anyway because Vicki's acts displayed consent.

Interstate commerce requirement

Finally, although Dave crossed a state line, it was after Vicki's conduct evidencing consent. Crossing state lines is necessary to establish federal jurisdiction. To satisfy this requirement, the government must merely show that a defendant willfully transported a victim and, in doing so, crossed state lines. A defendant does not need to intend to cross, or even know that he or she is crossing, a state line.

Here, Dave would have to admit that he drove the car across a state line. However, Vicki's conduct, prior to crossing the state line, evidenced general consent to this portion of the trip. Thus, the kidnapping requirements weren't met even though Dave crossed a state line.

In sum, because there is insufficient evidence to sustain a kidnapping offense, the motion for judgment of acquittal should be granted.

    g.   Compare your essay to the sample answer. Is your essay concise and precise (similar to the sample answer)?

        If not, what do you need to do differently?

    h.   How much time did it take you to do this practice essay?

        If you finished in under thirty minutes, did you go back and proof your answer, making any revisions as neatly as possible?

    i.   Did you remember to take a deep breath and clear your head after you finished your essay answer?

Make a list of at least three take-home points to integrate as you write more practice essay answers:*

1.

2.

3.

Question 5 Sample Answer[6]

a.   At what time was your thirty minutes for writing this essay up?

What time did you actually finish writing your essay?

b.   Assess your level of attention as you began and worked through this essay question:

Is there any action you should take to increase your level of attention?

c.   What part of the question did you read first?

What did you learn by reading that part?

d.   How did you organize your essay, and why did you choose that organizational structure?

In retrospect, would you choose the same organizational structure? Why or why not?

e.   Does your essay look professional?

If so, what makes it look professional?

If not, what do you need to do differently?

---

6. This essay is based on Illinois law.

f. Go through your essay answer and mark CRAC to ensure that your essay reflects the deductive reasoning process. Then, look at the sample answer below and label the parts of the paradigm in the sample answer. How similar was your answer to the sample in terms of using the paradigm?

If there were differences, what did you learn about using the paradigm that you can use to write more effective bar exam essays?

No, Hank will not succeed with a motion to vacate the judgment incorporating the marital settlement. A judgment incorporating a settlement agreement may be vacated when the agreement is unconscionable or procured through duress, undue influence, or fraud. All presumptions are in favor of the validity of a settlement. A judgment will only be vacated where necessary to achieve justice, not to give a litigant a second opportunity to do what should have been done earlier.

Unconscionability

Hank is unlikely to prove unconscionability. There are two types of unconscionability: substantive and procedural.[7] An agreement is substantively unconscionable when it is overly one-sided, improvident, or oppressive. But, an agreement is not substantively unconscionable merely because it favors one party over another. Rather, an agreement must "shock the conscience." Substantive unconscionability is judged at the time an agreement is made; subsequent changes in economic circumstances are not considered.

An agreement is procedurally unconscionable when impropriety during the negotiating process deprives a party of a meaningful choice. Gross inequality between parties' respective bargaining power may demonstrate a lack of a meaningful choice. Settlements are generally upheld when they are entered at arm's length with the aid of counsel. Although entering an agreement without the advice of counsel may be a factor in finding procedural unconscionability, it is not determinative—especially when parties have an opportunity to retain counsel. Other factors considered are the amount of time spent negotiating an agreement, whether an agreement contains excessive fine print or legalese, and whether a party used high-pressure techniques. But, there is no *per se* formula for a finding of unconscionability.

Here, Hank cannot establish substantive unconscionability because he received almost fifty percent of the couple's assets; in other words, while Wilma received a better deal, the difference in value between what Hank and Wilma received was less than $30,000 out of total assets valued at $456,800 (Hank received $214,200; Wilma received $242,600). The fact that the value of the stock that Wilma received in the agreement doubled is not a relevant factor because unconscionability is determined as of the date of the agreement, not by subsequent events. Thus, there is no substantive unconscionability.

---

7. In most states, a party claiming unconscionability must prove both of these elements. There is some authority, however, suggesting courts will ignore a weak procedural unconscionability claim if a party has a strong substantive claim.

Similarly, Hank probably would not prevail with a claim of procedural unconscionability, although it is a closer question. Hank had repeated opportunities to retain counsel but chose to proceed *pro se*, a fact that minimizes the significance of his lack of counsel. The time spent negotiating and the timing of the agreement do not render the agreement procedurally unconscionable either. The fact that Hank was depressed, less sophisticated than Wilma, lacked an attorney, reached the agreement with Wilma within a four-day span just before the dissolution hearing, and was pressured by Wilma to resolve the property division all suggest there was a disparity in the parties' bargaining power. But, absent evidence of impropriety, and given Hank's refusal to obtain an attorney in response to Wilma's repeated suggestions that he retain one, this inequality is unlikely to be deemed a gross inequality. Therefore, Hank probably would be unable to prove procedural unconscionability.

In sum, Hank cannot get the agreement vacated on the basis of unconscionability.

Duress

Hank cannot prove he entered the agreement under duress. Duress exists when a party negotiates without the quality of mind necessary to make a contract. Duress includes the imposition, oppression, undue influence, or the taking of undue advantage of another that precludes a party from exercising free will. Here, there was no conduct by Wilma that even slightly constituted a wrongful act or threat; all she did was ask for meetings to discuss the terms of their divorce, suggest Hank hire an attorney, and negotiate a deal that was slightly more favorable to her. Thus, Hank cannot prove he entered the agreement under duress.

Undue influence

Hank is also unlikely to be able to prove undue influence. Undue influence is unfair persuasion in which a person uses a position of trust and confidence to make a contract that is not in the other contracting person's best interests. In several states, undue influence has been extended to include situations when a dominant person who is not in a position of trust and confidence uses unfair and excessive persuasion to influence the other party to make an unfavorable contract. Stress or anxiety alone are not sufficient to show undue influence.

Here, Hank is unlikely to establish undue influence. First, although spouses are deemed to be in a position of trust and confidence, that is unlikely to apply to spouses such as Wilma and Hank, who had been separated for a year before the settlement negotiations at issue took place. Further, Hank would have no reason to think that Wilma was acting to protect his interests because the parties were discussing the terms of their divorce and Wilma twice suggested that he consider hiring his own attorney.

Second, even assuming the parties lived in a state with a broader concept of undue influence, Wilma's initiation of a meeting to discuss the terms of their divorce, and Hank's depression and emotional state during negotiations are not sufficient, by themselves, to establish undue influence.

Further, there is no indication that Wilma or her attorney took advantage of Hank's emotional state. In fact, the agreement they negotiated gave Hank almost fifty percent of the couple's assets. Although the agreement was finalized just an hour or so before the hearing, and Hank says he felt pressure to get the agreement settled, those facts are also unlikely to establish undue influence. This result is particularly likely because Wilma twice encouraged Hank to hire his own attorney and Hank didn't object to the agreement until after he learned that Wilma had a new boyfriend. Thus, Hank will not be able to establish undue influence.

Fraud

The motion to vacate cannot be granted on the basis of fraud. Fraud requires the knowing nondisclosure or misrepresentation of material facts. Here, Hank has said he didn't think there was any failure to disclose relevant information or any misrepresentations made. Thus, the settlement cannot be vacated on the basis of fraud.

In sum, Hank cannot establish fraud, unconscionability, duress, or undue influence, and an agreement cannot be vacated merely because a party has second thoughts. Thus, Hank is unlikely to succeed with a motion to vacate the judgment incorporating his settlement agreement.

g. Compare your essay to the sample. Is your essay concise and precise (similar to the sample answer)? If not, what do you need to do differently?

h. If you finished in under thirty minutes, did you go back and proof your answer, making any revisions as neatly as possible?

i. Did you remember to take a deep breath after you finished your essay?

Make a list of at least three take-home points to integrate as you write more practice essays:*

1.

2.

3.

---

* See the last pages of this appendix for what we believe to be the take-home points from this sample essay. You may have additional ones.

Question 6 Sample Answer[8]

a. At what time was your thirty minutes for writing this essay up?

What time did you actually finish writing your essay?

b. Assess your level of attention as you began and worked through this essay question:

Is there any action you should take to increase your level of attention?

c. What part of the question did you read first?

What did you learn by reading that part?

d. How did you organize your essay, and why did you chose that structure?

In retrospect, would you choose the same organizational structure?

Why or why not?

e. Does your essay look professional?

If so, what makes it look professional? If not, what do you need to do differently?

---

8. This essay is based on the majority and minority rules for alienation of affection claims.

f.   Go through your essay answer and mark CRAC to ensure that your essay reflects the deductive reasoning process. Then, look at the sample answer below and label the parts of the paradigm in the sample. How similar is your
answer to the sample in terms of using the paradigm?

If there were differences, what did you learn about using the paradigm to
write more effective essays?

No, Harry will not succeed with a legal action against Don. An alienation of affections cause of action is not recognized in the majority of jurisdictions. In a small minority of jurisdictions, alienation of affections is recognized as a cause of action. In
those jurisdictions, to recover, a plaintiff must prove three elements: (1) genuine love
and affection existed in a marriage, (2) the affection was alienated by a third party, and
(3) the third party's malicious acts caused the alienation. Even if Harry is in a jurisdiction that recognizes alienation of affections claims, he cannot recover. Although Harry
could probably establish the first two elements, he would not be able to establish the
third.

Genuine love and affection in the marriage

First, Harry could show that love and affection existed in his marriage. As a general
rule, to establish love and affection, a party only needs to prove "some" affection. Testimony from neighbors, friends, and a spouse can provide evidence of love and affection.
A spouse's words and actions can also prove love and affection. Neither a prior separation nor an affair will preclude a finding of love and affection as long as a couple has
reconciled.

Here, neighbors, friends, and Harry will testify that love and affection existed.
Wendy's statement that she loved both Harry and Don, and Harry as the father of Sam,
also proves that love and affection existed. Finally, the couple's prior separation and
Harry's affair do not preclude love and affection from existing because the couple had
reconciled. Thus, Harry could establish the love and affection element.

Alienation of the affection

Second, Harry can establish that Wendy's love and affection were alienated. Alienation of affection can be established by evidence of a separation or that a spouse lost interest in the marriage after interacting with a third-party paramour. Changes in a
spouse's behavior—for example, turning "cold," acting independently, avoiding one's
spouse, avoiding family life, and wearing more fashionable clothing than usual—can
provide evidence that affection was alienated.

Here, the couple's separation provides evidence that Wendy's affection was alienated. The facts that Wendy lost interest in the marriage after interacting with Don, acted
cool toward Harry, withdrew from family life, and started wearing more fashionable
clothing and makeup provide further evidence. Thus, Harry can prove that Wendy's affection was alienated.

Malicious acts destroying affection

Harry cannot prove that Don engaged in malicious acts that destroyed the love and affection in the marriage. To prove this element, a party must show a third party's malicious interference. Courts presume malicious interference where there is evidence of a sexual relationship. Absent a sexual relationship, however, malice must be established with other evidence. A third party must have engaged in active and affirmative conduct that directly interfered with the relationship. Also, the third party's conduct must be a controlling factor in the alienation. Finally, the malicious interference must have occurred before the parties separated.

Here, the facts do not indicate that Don maliciously interfered in the couple's marriage. There are no facts establishing a sexual relationship, so Harry would need to provide other evidence of malicious intent. There is not a record of frequent and open affection between Wendy and Harry. The parties had to interact in their roles as church assistant and committee chair. And Wendy claims that she, not Don, initiated the contact between the two of them and that the relationship started after the parties' separation. Don cannot be said to have acted maliciously simply because he became the object of Wendy's affection.

The note from Don to Wendy also does not establish the required malicious interference. The note is consistent with a platonic relationship between two people who have been working together. The language (for example, "Fondly") does not suggest anything inappropriate was going on at the time it was sent. Wendy's lies, secretive conduct, and "giggling" phone calls may suggest misconduct by Wendy; but, standing alone, they do not establish malice on the part of Don. Finally, because the malicious conduct must occur before a couple separates, the fact that Wendy and Don are now dating does not establish malicious intent on the part of Don. Thus, Harry cannot prove the malicious intent necessary to recover.

In sum, Harry cannot recover in the majority of jurisdictions because most jurisdictions do not recognize alienation of affections as a cause of action. And, even in the small minority of jurisdictions that do, Harry cannot establish all three elements necessary to recover.

g.   Compare your essay to the sample answer. Is your essay concise and precise (similar to the sample answer)? If not, what do you need to do differently?

h.   If you finished in less than thirty minutes, did you go back and proof your essay, making any revisions as neatly as possible?

i.   Did you remember to take a deep breath to clear your head after you finished your essay?

Make a list of at least three take-home points to integrate as you write more practice essay answers:*

    1.

    2.

    3.

---

* See the last pages of this appendix for what we believe to be the take-home points from this sample essay. You may have additional ones.

Question 7 Sample Answer[9]

By now, you should be in the habit of using your template and following the same process for every essay answer you write. Thus, as you move forward and write more practice essays, use an abbreviated checklist (see exercise 15-1) to ensure you're covering the bases you need to cover to write effective essays. For example, check whether you followed the recommended process for this practice essay:

❏ Allotted time, wrote down time by when you needed to finish.

❏ Went in order, focused solely on this essay.

❏ Read the call of the question.

❏ Briefly outlined the issues, rules, and key facts.

❏ Made the essay look professional (headings, white space, paragraph indentations).

❏ Used the CRAC paradigm.

❏ Used transitional phrases.

❏ If time, proofed answer and made neat revisions.

❏ When finished, took a deep breath.

❏ Identified take-home points:[*]

1.

2.

3.

[Note that the essay question centers on the provision of a state statute, and the answer thus focuses on state law construing that statutory provision. Although federal due process issues (*e.g.*, notice and an opportunity to be heard) are often implicated in service cases, those issues are not implicated here because of the focus of the question.]

Yes. Bob should file a motion to quash service and vacate the default judgment because the attempted service was invalid. Jurisdiction over a person can only be acquired if there is proper service. Without proper service, there is no jurisdiction and any judg-

---

9. This essay is based on Illinois' substitute service statute and Illinois cases construing the service statute.

* See the last pages of this appendix for what we believe to be the take-home points from this sample essay. You may have additional ones.

ment entered is void. A sheriff's return of service is *prima facie* evidence that valid service has been made. Clear and convincing evidence is needed to rebut the *prima facie* evidence.

As an alternative to personally serving a defendant, state law provides that substituted service is valid if service is made at a defendant's home with "some person of the family" and a duplicate copy of a summons is mailed to a defendant. "Family" means the collective body of persons living in one house, and may include parents, children, servants, lodgers, and boarders. Although a blood relative may be "some person of the family," a blood relationship is not the test. Rather, a person must be residing at a defendant's home continuously and permanently with the intent of remaining. Facts tending to establish a "family" for the purpose of service include eating meals together, sharing finances, using the same mailing address, and having access to an entire home.

In contrast to persons residing continuously and permanently, temporary guests, even if related by blood, are not considered family for the purpose of the service statute.

The object of the service requirement is to provide notice to a defendant of pending litigation. Thus, substituted service on a family member presupposes a relation of confidence so that the defendant would get the notice.

In addition, substitute service provisions provide a means of serving defendants who may be seeking to evade service. As a matter of policy, the law does not favor those seeking to evade service.

Finally, statutes providing for substituted service are a departure from common law and, thus, are strictly construed. As a matter of policy, defendants should be given their day in court so that they can defend a lawsuit on the merits rather than having a default judgment entered against them.

Here, the attempted service was invalid. Therefore, the court never acquired jurisdiction over Bob, and the default judgment should be vacated. Although the sheriff's return would provide *prima facie* evidence that service was made, clear and convincing evidence rebuts the *prima facie* evidence.

The state's substituted service statute provides an alternative to personal service on an individual by serving "some person of the family" at the defendant's home. Here, service was made at Bob's home, but not on "some person of the family."

Even though Lou is Bob's brother, that fact does not qualify Lou as "some person of the family" for purposes of the statute. Lou does not reside with Bob permanently and continuously. He lives in Pennsylvania during the academic year and had not even seen Bob for a year. Lou only stayed a week at Bob's and then returned to school. Thus, Lou was only a temporary guest. Further, although Lou and Bob ate meals together, and Lou had free access to Bob's entire home, there is no indication that they shared finances or used the same mailing address.

Because Bob never in fact received notice of the lawsuit, holding service valid would undermine the purpose of service requirements. The summons and complaint that were delivered fell behind Bob's cupboard, and there is no indication that Bob received a duplicate copy by mail as required for substitute service.

On the other hand, there's a possibility that Bob left town to evade service based on the fact that he told Lou not to accept any packages for him. If a court finds Bob was attempting to evade service, it might refuse to vacate the default judgment because the law disfavors evading service.

But, a court is likely to find service invalid. Substitute service provisions are contrary to common law and thus strictly construed. This principle weighs in favor of finding service invalid and providing Bob his day in court to defend the suit on the merits.

In sum, the attempted service on Lou is invalid because it did not meet the requirements of the substitute service statute. Thus, service should be quashed and the default judgment vacated.

Question 8 Sample Answer

- ❏ Allotted time, wrote down time by when you needed to finish.
- ❏ Went in order, focused solely on this essay.
- ❏ Read the call of the question.
- ❏ Briefly outlined the issues, rules, and key facts.
- ❏ Made the essay look professional (headings, white space, paragraph indentations).
- ❏ Used the CRAC paradigm.
- ❏ Used transitional phrases.
- ❏ If time, proofed answer and made neat revisions.
- ❏ When finished, took a deep breath.
- ❏ Identified take-home points:*

1.

2.

3.

No, Buyer would not be successful in his complaint for specific performance. To obtain specific performance, a party must show (1) a valid and enforceable contract; (2) breach by the other party to the contract; (3) inadequacy of the remedy at law; and (4) the absence of any basis for the court to exercise its discretionary power to deny the requested equitable relief. Here, there is an enforceable contract, an inadequate remedy at law, and the absence of any basis for a court to deny equitable relief, but the Seller is not in breach. Thus, Buyer cannot obtain specific performance.

Valid and enforceable contract

The contract is valid and enforceable. As a general rule, real estate contracts are valid if they satisfy the statute of frauds. To satisfy the statute of frauds, a contract must be in writing and signed by the party against whom enforcement is sought. Here, the facts state that the contract is in writing but are silent as to whether either party signed. If

---

* See the last pages of this appendix for what we believe to be the take-home points from this sample essay. You may have additional ones.

Seller did not sign, Buyer would be unable to obtain any remedy at all since the contract would be unenforceable. Assuming both signed, the contract is valid and enforceable.

Breach

Seller is not in breach. Because the contract provides for settlement on a date certain and includes a time-is-of-the-essence clause, there are two breach issues: (1) whether timeliness is "essential" (and therefore a condition of the contract) or merely "boilerplate" (and therefore not a condition of the contract); and (2) if timeliness is not essential, whether Seller had a duty to perform.

Breach—effect of the "time-is-of-the-essence" clause

Buyer's failure to tender performance on the extended settlement date excused Seller's duty to perform.

In an ordinary case of a contract for the sale of real estate, where a certain period of time is stipulated for its consummation, equity treats the provisions as formal rather than essential and allows a purchaser who has permitted the period to lapse to make payment after the prescribed date and to compel performance by the seller within a reasonable time notwithstanding the delay.

A specific date may be treated as an essential provision, however, if it appears that time is of the essence based on an express stipulation, inference from the conduct of the parties, the special purpose for which a sale was made, or other circumstances surrounding a sale.

Although recent decisions suggest such clauses are boilerplate and do not make time a condition, the majority of states treat such clauses as establishing timely performance as a condition. Even in jurisdictions inclined to treat these clauses as making timeliness a condition, however, a party can overcome the specific provision by establishing that the parties did not intend to establish an unyielding date of settlement.

Pursuant to the parol evidence rule, no additional terms could be added, and evidence of prior or contemporaneous terms agreed to would be inadmissible, to prove this. Further, in general, an extension fixes a new time by which settlement is to be made, but does not waive the requirement that the settlement must be made by the date fixed.

In this case, the contract included an express time-is-of-the-essence clause. The fact that Seller set sixty days after signing of the contract for closing based upon his best estimate of when his new house would be ready for occupancy is irrelevant; the readiness of the new house was not made a condition to closing. The fact that Buyer's attorney had not completed an examination of title on February 27 is also irrelevant and would not excuse Buyer from tendering payment on or before that date.

Buyer could point to the extension of time granted several days after the initial settlement date had expired as a waiver by Seller of the time-is-of-the-essence clause, or could argue the extension as proof that the closing date was not considered essential by Seller. A waiver requires an intentional relinquishment of a known right. While Buyer may argue that the extension evidenced an intent to waive the timely performance condition, the better argument is that the parties' act of modifying the contract to extend the date of closing actually indicates that the parties still regarded timely performance as crucial. Had the parties believed that a short performance delay would be insignificant, they would not have felt a need to change the settlement date from February 27 to March 11.

Accordingly, timely performance was a condition of the contract and Buyer's failure to perform on March 11 would bar a claim for specific performance.

Breach — effect of Buyer's failure to tender payment

Seller is not in breach because Buyer never tendered payment. In determining the order of performance of a contract, courts defer to any times specified in the parties' contract. By the terms of the contract, Seller was obligated to deliver possession of the property and a deed to Buyer "upon payment" of the balance of the purchase price at settlement. This required Buyer to tender payment and was a condition precedent to performance by Seller. The failure to do so is a default and excuses all subsequently due performances. Here, Buyer never tendered performance. Therefore Seller's performance never became due, and he is not in breach.

Inadequacy of the remedy at law

The remedy at law is inadequate. To obtain specific performance, a party must prove that the remedy at law is inadequate. In the context of a sale of land, each piece of land is presumed unique and therefore irreplaceable, thereby making an award of damages an inadequate remedy because the victim of the breach cannot replace the lost contract performance. Here, because Buyer was acquiring Seller's house, the subject of the contract, land, would be deemed irreplaceable. Thus, Buyer's remedy at law is inadequate.

Discretionary considerations

There is no basis for a court to exercise its discretion to deny relief. Courts have the discretion to deny specific performance if ordering specific performance would place an undue burden on a defendant or a court, if the contract is grossly unfair, or if awarding specific performance would contravene public policy. Here, because a contract for the sale of land requires only a one-time order by the court and performance by the defendant of the very obligation he undertook in the contract, there is no colorable argument for an undue burden on the court or the defendant. Likewise, there are no facts suggesting the contract price is unfair or that the public interest is implicated by this purely private transaction. Accordingly, a court would not exercise its discretion to deny specific performance.

Conclusion

In sum, the contract is valid and enforceable. Seller did not breach the contract; rather, Buyer breached because the contract made time of the essence and he did not perform on March 11. Also, Buyer's performance was due before Seller's, and Buyer never tendered his performance at all. Thus, Buyer cannot obtain specific performance.

Question 9 Sample Answer

- ❏ Allotted time, wrote down time by when you needed to finish.
- ❏ Went in order, focused solely on this essay.
- ❏ Read the call of the question.
- ❏ Briefly outlined the issues, rules, and key facts.
- ❏ Made the essay look professional (headings, white space, paragraph indentations).
- ❏ Used the CRAC paradigm.
- ❏ Used transitional phrases.
- ❏ If time, proofed answer and made neat revisions.
- ❏ When finished, took a deep breath.
- ❏ Identified take-home points:*

1.

2.

3.

1. Eddie's causes of action

Yes, Eddie may bring causes of action against Molly for negligence, battery, and the intentional infliction of emotional distress; against the Town of Beverly for Molly's actions committed under the color of the Town's authority; and against June for negligence and strict liability.

Eddie v. Molly

Eddie would argue that Molly committed the following torts against him: negligence, battery, and the intentional infliction of emotional distress.

First, Molly was negligent. Negligence requires that Eddie prove a duty, breach, causation, and damages. Molly had a general duty to act as a reasonably prudent person would under the same circumstances. Once she assumed the duty to come to the aid of Eddie, she had a duty to act reasonably in doing so. Here, Molly breached her duty of care because she fired a dangerous weapon where people were present without being

---

* See the last pages of this appendix for what we believe to be the take-home points from this sample essay. You may have additional ones.

sure of her target. Molly's failure to act with reasonable care was the direct and proximate cause of Eddie's injuries. Damages can by shown by Eddie's hospitalization. Thus, Molly was negligent.

Second, a battery occurred. A battery is an unpermitted and intentional contact of a person. To be intentional, a party need only intend an act, not the consequences. For intentional torts, a defendant is liable for all consequences, even if they aren't strictly foreseeable. Here, there was an unpermitted and intentional contact caused by Molly (because she chose to fire the gun) when the bullet hit Eddie. Molly may counter that she intended to scare Vichuss. She may be successful if the doctrine of transferred intent cannot be applied between animals and a person. Because it probably can, Eddie will likely prevail with a battery claim.

Eddie may also bring a claim for the intentional infliction of emotional distress ("IIED"). A claim of IIED has four elements: (1) conduct that is intentional or reckless; (2) conduct that is extreme and outrageous; (3) a causal connection between the wrongful conduct and the emotional distress; and (4) severe emotional distress.

Here, Molly acted recklessly by discharging a firearm. There is a question, however, as to whether firing a gun to stop a dog is sufficiently outrageous, especially because Molly was trying to protect Eddie. In addition, although Eddie has suffered insomnia, headaches, and nightmares, such suffering is insufficiently severe. Thus, because Eddie probably cannot meet his burden as to either the outrageous conduct element or the severe distress element, Eddie will not succeed with an intentional infliction of emotional distress claim.

Molly may also argue that she was protected by the privilege of defense of others, which requires a reasonable belief that danger exists and that defensive acts be reasonably necessary under the circumstances. On the one hand, there are no facts suggesting Molly had a reason to believe Vichuss was a dangerous animal. On the other hand, Eddie's reaction and flight arguably indicated that the dog posed some danger. Nevertheless, absent an aggressive act by the dog, Molly lacked a sufficient basis for concluding the dog was dangerous and her act of shooting a gun was excessive absent evident danger to the boys.

In sum, Eddie can prevail with causes of action for negligence and battery, but not the intentional infliction of emotional distress.

Eddie v. Town of Beverly

Eddie may try to sue the Town for Molly's actions because she arguably acted under color of its authority. Since the state has waived sovereign immunity for municipalities for tort suits, the town may be sued for tort claims. Under the doctrine of *respondeat superior*, an employer may be vicariously liable for the actions of its employees acting within the scope of their employment. Here, Molly was on duty checking meters and in uniform. The town would counter that Molly acted outside of the scope of her employment as a meter maid by carrying a weapon and discharging it, and that, therefore, it is not liable. Because Molly used her personal gun, and it wasn't provided as part of her position with the town, she would likely be held to have acted outside the scope of her employment.

Eddie v. June

Eddie may bring causes of action against June for negligence and strict liability.

First, Eddie may argue that June was negligent. Negligence requires that Eddie prove a duty, breach, causation, and damages. Eddie can argue that June was negligent in releasing Vichuss without the muzzle because her actions violated the Town's ordinance and the resulting bite was the type of harm the ordinance sought to avoid. The ordinance is evidence of a duty, and violation of the ordinance would be evidence of a breach. June's actions were also the factual and legal cause of his injury. But for releasing Vichuss, Eddie would not have been bitten. It would probably be deemed foreseeable that Vichuss might bite someone—especially with the existence of the muzzle ordinance, which is based on the expectation that dogs like Vichuss released without muzzles might bite someone. Eddie can also prove damages since he was treated for the bite. June may counter that she used reasonable force to counter the threat which she perceived Molly to be, but Eddie would have the more persuasive argument that June's perception of danger was unreasonable given Molly's meter-maid uniform. Thus, June was negligent.

Second, Eddie may argue that June is strictly liable. Parties are strictly liable for injuries caused by animals if they know that their animals have vicious propensities. Here, the facts are silent as to whether June knew, or with reasonable care should have known, that Vichuss had a propensity to bite. If June knew Vichuss had a propensity to bite, June would be held strictly liable.

Thus, Eddie may bring causes of action against June for negligence and strict liability.

In sum, Eddie may bring causes of action against Molly for negligence, battery, and the intentional infliction of emotional distress; against the Town of Beverly for Molly's actions committed under the color of the Town's authority; and against June for negligence and strict liability.

2. Molly's causes of action

Yes, Molly may bring causes of action against Ward and June for negligence.

Molly v. Ward

Molly may sue Ward for negligence in the operation of his vehicle. A driver is negligent when he breaches the duty to use reasonable care and harms another. Here, as a driver, Ward owed all other drivers and pedestrians the duty to drive safely. It is not unusual for people to be in the middle of residential streets, and Ward should have been using reasonable care under the circumstances. Ward breached his duty by taking his eyes off the road while he changed his CDs, and this breach caused him to run into Molly. Molly suffered damages as a result: broken legs and ribs and a hospital stay. Ward may assert, however, that Molly was contributorily negligent when she was standing in the street. But, Ward had the last clear chance to avoid hitting Molly by being more attentive. Thus, Molly can recover from Ward.

Molly v. June

Molly may also assert a negligence action against June. A party is negligent when he or she has a duty and breaches it, causing damages to others. Here, June violated the ordinance by releasing Vichuss. However, Molly's being hit by a car is not the harm that the ordinance seeks to avoid, and Molly freezing in the street and then being hit by a negligent driver may be too remote to be deemed the proximate cause of Molly's injuries. Thus, June breached her duty to use due care, resulting in damages to Molly. But Molly may not prevail because June's conduct may not be deemed the proximate cause of her injuries. June may assert that she correctly came to the aid of the children and used the minimum force necessary to counter the threat she reasonably perceived Molly to pose, but this will probably fail. Thus, Molly has a negligence claim against June but may not prevail.

Thus, Molly may bring causes of action against Ward and June for negligence.

Question 10 Sample Answer

- ❐ Allotted time, wrote down time by when you needed to finish.
- ❐ Went in order, focused solely on this essay.
- ❐ Read the call of the question.
- ❐ Briefly outlined the issues, rules, and key facts.
- ❐ Made the essay look professional (headings, white space, paragraph indentations).
- ❐ Used the CRAC paradigm.
- ❐ Used transitional phrases.
- ❐ If time, proofed answer and made neat revisions.
- ❐ When finished, took a deep breath.
- ❐ Identified take-home points:*

1.

2.

3.

Yes, there are several bases for disciplinary action against Amanda pursuant to the Rules of Professional Conduct. Specifically, Amanda is subject to disciplinary action for engaging in the unauthorized practice of law, charging an unreasonable fee, representing clients with a conflict of interest, entering a business transaction with a client, failing to communicate with her clients, and failing to provide information upon request to Maryland's disciplinary authorities.

Unauthorized practice of law

First, Amanda has engaged in the unauthorized practice of law by practicing law in Maryland. A state has authority over the practice of law within its border. In general, attorneys must be licensed in a state to engage in the practice of law in the state. However, an out-of-state attorney may handle a corporation's legal business on a limited basis. For example, a corporation's attorney could provide guidance and counseling, but could not appear in court on behalf of a client without *pro hoc vice*. If a person engages

---

* See the last pages of this appendix for what we believe to be the take-home points from this sample essay. You may have additional ones.

in the practice of law without being licensed to do so, he or she has engaged in the unauthorized practice of law.

Here, Amanda is a member of the bar in Delaware, not Maryland. Amanda is subject to the disciplinary authority of Maryland, even though she is not a member of the Maryland Bar, because she provided legal services to Heaven and Universe in Maryland. All of Heaven's business appears to be in Maryland. By preparing documents for Universe, which goes beyond allowable guidance and counseling, Amanda violated the rules regarding the unauthorized practice of law.

Thus, Amanda has engaged in the unauthorized practice of law by practicing law in Maryland without a law license.

Unreasonable fees

Second, Amanda is subject to discipline for charging an unreasonable fee. Under the professional rules, an attorney's fee must be reasonable. To determine if a fee is reasonable, several factors are considered, including the complexity and novelty of a case, the skill and experience of an attorney, the amount customarily charged by others in similar practices, the length of time of representation, and the limitation on accepting other business if conflicts of interest arise.

Here, the facts do not provide sufficient information to address all of these factors; we do not know the standard fee in the industry. However, we do know that Amanda is a recent graduate. It is questionable whether Amanda's fee of $350 per hour, together with the ten percent interest in Universe, is reasonable given her experience level. Thus, Amanda is subject to discipline for charging an unreasonable fee.

Conflict of interest

Third, Amanda is subject to discipline for representing Max and Universe despite a conflict of interest with Heaven.

An attorney must not represent a party if that party's interests are directly adverse to another client or if representing the party would materially limit the duties owed to the other client. It is possible to proceed with representation if a conflict is disclosed to parties and they consent to the representation despite the conflict, but only if representing both parties wouldn't have an adverse impact on either or both parties.

As Heaven's attorney, Amanda had a duty to represent Heaven, not Max or Morley individually, and not a corporation with competing interests. Amanda should not have undertaken either to represent Max individually or to create Universe. When Max asked Amanda what he could do to get out of the business, she was obligated to tell Max she was Heaven's attorney and that Max should hire his own attorney. Although it is sometimes permissible to proceed with representation despite a conflict of interest if the conflict is disclosed and a client consents, here Amanda failed to consult with Heaven and Morley prior to representation of Max and Universe. In any event, because both of these representations were directly adverse to Heaven, and Amanda's representation would be materially limited by her own interests as an owner of Universe and as counsel to both Heaven and Universe, Amanda should not have proceeded with the representation. Thus, Amanda is subject to discipline for representing Max and Universe despite a conflict of interest with Heaven.

Entering into a business transaction with a client

Fourth, Amanda is subject to disciplinary action for entering into a business transaction with a client. An attorney may not enter into a business transaction with a client unless the transaction is fair and reasonable and the client is advised to seek independent counsel and is given a reasonable opportunity to do so.

Here, Amanda failed to comply with the requirements of the professional rules when obtaining an interest in Universe. Amanda could have protected herself by advising Max to have another attorney review the transaction for fairness. Although Amanda may argue that the transaction was only a fee arrangement, it will be seen as a business transaction because, in effect, she is using her fee to purchase an interest in Heaven. Thus, Amanda is subject to disciplinary action for entering into a business transaction with a client.

Failure to communicate with clients

Fifth, Amanda is subject to discipline for failing to communicate with her clients. An attorney has a duty to communicate with his or her clients, including returning phone calls. Here, Amanda has violated her duty to keep the owners of Heaven informed and return Morley's phone calls. Thus, Amanda is subject to discipline for failing to communicate with her clients.

Failure to provide information to the disciplinary authority

Sixth, Amanda is subject to discipline for failing to provide information to Maryland's disciplinary authority. Attorneys have a duty to respond to requests from a state's disciplinary authority. Here, Amanda failed to respond to the commission's requests. Thus, Amanda is subject to discipline for failing to provide information to the disciplinary authority.

In sum, Amanda is subject to disciplinary action under the rules for engaging in the unauthorized practice of law, charging an unreasonable fee, representing clients with a conflict of interest, entering into a business transaction with a client, failing to communicate with clients, and failing to provide information upon request to Maryland's disciplinary authorities.

Question 11 Sample Answer

- ☐ Allotted time, wrote down time by when you needed to finish.
- ☐ Went in order, focused solely on this essay.
- ☐ Read the call of the question.
- ☐ Briefly outlined the issues, rules, and key facts.
- ☐ Made the essay look professional (headings, white space, paragraph indentations).
- ☐ Used the CRAC paradigm.
- ☐ Used transitional phrases.
- ☐ If time, proofed answer and made neat revisions.
- ☐ When finished, took a deep breath.
- ☐ Identified take-home points:*

1.

2.

3.

Absolute divorce

Yes, Al can file for an absolute divorce at this time. Generally, if the grounds for divorce occur outside the State of Maryland, a party cannot apply for a divorce unless one of them has resided in Maryland for one year. There is an exception, however, when the grounds for divorce arise in Maryland; in such circumstances, Maryland has jurisdiction. When the ground for divorce is adultery, no waiting period is required. A plaintiff does need to produce evidence, though, showing opportunity and a disposition to commit adultery.

Here, Al and Brenda were married in Pennsylvania, but that is irrelevant to the question of Maryland's jurisdiction. Although the couple has not resided in Maryland for one year, Maryland has jurisdiction because the grounds for divorce arose in the state. Because Brenda committed adultery, a fault ground for divorce, no waiting period is required. Al will need to show opportunity and a disposition to commit adultery, though.

In sum, Al can file for an absolute divorce at this time.

---

* See the last pages of this appendix for what we believe to be the take-home points from this sample essay. You may have additional ones.

Social Security benefits

No, Al is not entitled to any of Brenda's Social Security benefits. Social Security benefits may not be considered marital property and are not subject to distribution or division in any manner in a divorce case. Social Security income may be a factor considered, however, in the determination of Brenda's entitlement to any monetary award from Al.

Here, Brenda began receiving Social Security disability payments before the couple was married. Brenda's Social Security income will not be considered marital property and is not subject to any sort of division in the couple's divorce case. Brenda's Social Security income could be a factor, however, in the determination of her entitlement to a monetary award from Al.

Thus, Al is not entitled to any of Brenda's Social Security benefits.

Al's assets

Yes, Brenda may have some entitlement to some of Al's assets; specifically, a portion of the increase in the equity in their marital home and the mutual fund acquired from marital earnings.

In general, property acquired before marriage, or property acquired by gift or inheritance to one spouse during a marriage, is separate property. Increases in the value of non-marital property is also separate property. In contrast, property acquired during marriage is generally considered marital, including an increase in the value of marital property.

Here, Al initially acquired the townhouse while the parties were living together but not married. So, initially it was a nonmarital asset. Mortgage payments were satisfied by the rental income so that the increase in equity (by virtue of reduction in the principal balance of the mortgage) was nonmarital property. After the parties married, they moved into the townhouse and used it as their marital residence. From that date forward, if Al made mortgage payments from marital earnings, that portion of the mortgage principal reduction would be marital property. Brenda would therefore be entitled to a share of equity that is marital property.

The 1,000 shares in Turk, Inc., were given to Al by his father and titled in Al's name alone and are nonmarital property. The mutual fund is a marital asset acquired from marital earnings during the marriage and, because it is titled in Al's name, could be a source of a monetary award in Brenda's favor. Finally, the 500 shares received from the Turk stock split is nonmarital property because it was generated from a nonmarital asset.

In sum, Brenda is entitled to a proportionate share of the increase in equity in their marital home and the mutual fund acquired from marital earnings.

Sally's Social Security dependency benefits

Yes, Sally's Social Security dependency benefits may be considered when determining child support.

Under case law, dependency benefits do not result in an automatic credit against a parent's child support obligation. State law does not provide that dependency benefits received by a child are to be a factor for deviating from the support guidelines. A court has discretion, however, when circumstances warrant, to adjust the amount of a parent's child support obligation upon finding that a deviation serves the best interest of a child. Recent legislation provides that the amount of Social Security dependency income paid to a child will be treated as income to the disabled person, but the amount is to be set off against the child support obligation of the parent whose disability generated the payment.

Here, Sally receives Social Security dependency benefits based on Brenda's disability. Under case law, the benefits may be a factor considered in deviating from the support guidelines. Under recent legislation, Sally's benefits will be treated as income to Brenda, and the amount will be set off against Brenda's support obligation because her disability generated the payment.

Thus, Sally's Social Security dependency benefits may be considered when determining child support.

Question 12 Sample Answer

- ❏ Allotted time, wrote down time by when you needed to finish.
- ❏ Went in order, focused solely on this essay.
- ❏ Read the call of the question.
- ❏ Briefly outlined the issues, rules, and key facts.
- ❏ Made the essay look professional (headings, white space, paragraph indentations).
- ❏ Used the CRAC paradigm.
- ❏ Used transitional phrases.
- ❏ If time, proofed answer and made neat revisions.
- ❏ When finished, took a deep breath.
- ❏ Identified take-home points:*

1.

2.

3.

Yes, Mega-Mini can enforce the supply contract; no, Mega-Mini cannot enforce the advertising contract; and yes, Mega-Mini can recover damages for breach of the supply contract, but not the advertising contract.

The supply contract

Mega-Mini can enforce the supply contract. Contracts for sales of moveable items, such as cheese, are sales of goods covered under Article 2 of the UCC. Contracts for sales of goods must be in writing to comply with the UCC's statute of frauds. Provisions of the UCC also govern assignment and delegation of the supply contract. The applicable UCC provision states that a party may perform his duty through a delegate unless otherwise agreed or unless the other party has a substantial interest in having his original promisor perform or control the acts required by the contract. In the absence of a contrary provision, the rights and duties under an executory bilateral contract may be assigned and delegated except when an assignment would materially change the duty of the other party, increase materially the burden or risk imposed on him by the contract, or impair materially his chance of obtaining return performance.

---

* See the last pages of this appendix for what we believe to be the take-home points from this sample essay. You may have additional ones.

Here, the supply contract for cheese is a contract for a sale of goods controlled by the UCC. Because the contract was in writing, it complies with the UCC's statute of frauds. Because there was no provision prohibiting assignment and delegation, Cheeze could assign and delegate its rights and duties under the contract to Mega-Mini. There is nothing that prevents Mega-Mini from performing the provisions of the contract. In fact, there is no difference between the product Pete was to get from Cheeze and that supplied by Mega-Mini. Nor would the assignment to Mega-Mini create a material change in Pete's duties under the supply contract to justify Pete's refusal to accept the assignment and delegation. Therefore, the supply contract is enforceable by Mega-Mini.

The advertising contract

Mega-Mini cannot enforce the advertising contract. A written contract that is to be performed over more than one year satisfies the statute of frauds. Contracts for personal services, as opposed to contracts for the sale of goods, are not covered by the UCC. Rather, general principles of contract law control. Personal service contracts cannot be assigned because a party's skill, judgment, and taste are not transferable.

Here, Mega-Mini's contract is in writing and satisfies the statute of frauds. Because the advertising contract is one for personal services, it is controlled by contract common law rather than by the UCC. Because the advertising agency's contract is based on skill, judgment, and taste unique to that agency, the agency may not delegate its duties under the contract. Thus, Mega-Mini will not be able to enforce the advertising contract.

Damages

Mega-Mini is entitled to damages under the supply contract, but not under the advertising contract. Because the assignment and delegation to Mega-Mini were proper, Mega-Mini can enforce the supply contract and, therefore, can recover damages under the supply contract for breach. Because the delegation to Mega-Mini was improper, however, Mega-Mini cannot enforce the advertising contract and therefore cannot recover damages under it.

The preferred measure of general damages for breach of a contract to buy goods is the contract price less the fair market value of the goods, or the contract price less the amount the seller received in reasonably reselling the goods. If a party is in the business of regularly selling the goods at issue such that it may be deemed a "lost-volume seller," a party may recover its lost profits—the difference between what a party would receive under a contract less what it would have cost to perform. A lost-volume seller is a seller that, absent the buyer's breach, would not only have sold the goods to the buyer but also would have sold goods to a second buyer and enjoyed profits on both sales. There is no basis for punitive damages in a contract action.

Here, Cheeze was a lost-volume seller: it was making multiple sales of cheese to multiple buyers. Consequently, when Mega-Mini took over the business, it became a lost-volume seller. Mega-Mini therefore can recover its lost profits—the difference between its $1,000,000 contract price less what it would have cost Mega-Mini to perform. Mega-Mini would also be entitled to any incidental damages that arose from this breach, including any expenditures made in preparation of, or upon reliance on, the contract or any damages incurred in handling, storing, and reselling cheese that Pete had promised to buy. Mega-Mini could not, however, recover any punitive damages.

Thus, Mega-Mini is entitled to damages under the supply contract, but not under the advertising contract.

In sum, yes, Mega-Mini can enforce the supply contract; no, Mega-Mini cannot enforce the advertising contract; and yes, Mega-Mini can recover damages under the supply contract, but not the advertising contract.

Sample Analyses For Questions 13–15

Questions 13 through 15 are sample MEE questions. The sample analyses below are provided by the NCBE.[10] The NCBE states that its model analyses are illustrative of the discussions that might appear in excellent answers to the questions. Grading of the MEE is the exclusive responsibility of the jurisdiction using the MEE as part of its admissions process.[11] Thus, the model analyses are provided to user jurisdictions for the sole purpose of assisting graders in evaluating exams; they are not an official grading guide. Some states grade the MEE on the basis of state law, and jurisdictions are free to modify the analyses and the weight given to particular points.

You'll see that the model analyses don't follow the paradigm and system we recommend in chapter 15. Nonetheless, we encourage students to use the paradigm and process they've used for all of their other practice essays.

Question 13 Analysis

- ❐ Allotted time, wrote down time by when you needed to finish.
- ❐ Went in order, focused solely on this essay.
- ❐ Read the call of the question.
- ❐ Briefly outlined the issues, rules, and key facts.
- ❐ Made the essay look professional (headings, white space, paragraph indentations).
- ❐ Used the CRAC paradigm.
- ❐ Used transitional phrases.
- ❐ If time, proofed answer and made neat revisions.
- ❐ When finished, took a deep breath.
- ❐ Identified take-home points:

1.

2.

3.

10. Reprinted from the Feb. 1997 MEE exam with permission of the NCBE. Copyright © 1998, all rights reserved.

11. *Id.*

Legal problems

1. Did Husband and Wife die simultaneously, or is the evidence sufficient to establish that Husband survived Wife?

2. Is Son barred from inheriting from his parents because he caused the fire that resulted in their death?

3. If Son is barred from inheriting from his parents because he feloniously and intentionally took the lives of his parents, to whom should the shares that he would have received from their estates pass?

Discussion

The distribution of the estates of Husband and Wife depends on whether each is treated as having survived the other (see point one), on whether Son is barred from inheriting from his parents because he set the fire that killed them (see point two), and depending on the resolution of these issues, on whether the share of a residuary legatee who is disqualified from taking passes to the other residuary legatees (see point three).

Point one: (35–45%)

Under the original Uniform Simultaneous Death Act, Husband and Wife would probably not be treated as having died simultaneously. Instead, Husband would probably be treated as having survived Wife. However, under the revised version of the act and the Uniform Probate Code, Husband would be treated as having predeceased Wife because he did not survive her by 120 hours.

The original version of the Uniform Simultaneous Death Act provides that where the title to property or the devolution thereof depends upon priority of death and there is insufficient evidence that the persons have died other than simultaneously, the property of each person shall be disposed of as if he or she had survived.

The act was revised in 1991 to provide that, even if there is sufficient evidence to establish that a beneficiary named in a will in fact survived the testator, the beneficiary is only treated as having survived the testator if there is clear and convincing evidence that he or she survived the testator by 120 hours. The Uniform Probate Code also treats a beneficiary who does not survive the testator by at least 120 hours as having predeceased the testator.

Under the original act, a jury might conclude that there was sufficient evidence to establish that Husband in fact survived Wife, even though both died in the fire. Evidence supporting that conclusion includes: (1) the fire was started on the second floor of the home; (2) the spouses were apparently in bed when the fire occurred, based upon the time of the fire and the fact that both spouses were in their bedclothes; and (3) Wife was found in the second-floor bedroom while Husband was found on the first floor at the bottom of the stairs, suggesting that both of them attempted to exit the room but that Wife was overcome by smoke before she could reach the stairs. This implies that Wife died before she could get out of the bedroom whereas Husband was able to get out of the bedroom and crawl down to the first floor, as evidenced by the position of, and the marks on, his body.

Of course, if the revised act or the Uniform Probate Code applied, Husband would be treated as having predeceased Wife. Although he may have survived her for some brief period of time, he did not survive her by 120 hours (5 days).

Because Wife did not in fact survive Husband, for purposes of distributing Husband's estate she would not be treated as having survived him under either version of the simultaneous death act. Therefore, Husband's estate passes in equal shares to Son and Daughter, as provided in Husband's will, unless Son is prevented from inheriting (see point two).

If Husband is treated as having survived Wife for purposes of distributing Wife's estate, the estate passes to Husband under her will, and it then passes to the successors of Husband's estate. On the other hand, if Husband is treated as not having survived Wife, Wife's estate passes by intestate succession to her heirs because her will did not provide who would take her estate if Husband predeceased her, and antilapse statutes generally do not save gifts to a spouse who dies before a testator. Wife's heirs would be her children, Daughter and Son, unless, as discussed in point two, Son is barred from inheriting.

Point two: (35–45%)

Whether Son is barred from inheriting from his parents because he caused the fire that resulted in their deaths depends upon whether the probate court would conclude that he feloniously and intentionally took the lives of his parents. If so, he would be barred from inheriting. If not, he would be entitled to claim as an heir or devisee from his parents.

Under the Uniform Probate Code and most modem cases, a person who feloniously and intentionally kills a decedent is barred from claiming a share of the decedent's estate as either an heir or beneficiary under the decedent's will. In a few states only murderers are disqualified, and in a few states all felonious killers are disqualified. Generally, the decedent's estate is then disposed of as if the killer had predeceased the decedent.

For the purposes of probate proceedings, a conviction of felonious and intentional homicide conclusively establishes that the killer feloniously and intentionally killed the decedent. In some states inheritance is barred only if there has been a conviction. In most states, if there has been no conviction, the court having jurisdiction over the decedent's estate must determine whether a preponderance of evidence supports the conclusion that the alleged killer feloniously and intentionally took the life of the decedent. Some states, however, use a clear and convincing standard, rather than a preponderance of the evidence standard.

In some states where there is no slayer statute, courts apply the equitable principle that a wrongdoer cannot profit from his own wrong to prevent the killer from inheriting. In such states, a court is likely to hold that a killer succeeds to the property of a deceased victim, but holds it as a constructive trustee for others. The facts say that there is sufficient evidence to establish by a preponderance of the evidence that Son intentionally set the fire. If the jurisdiction uses this standard of proof, Son would be barred from taking his parents' estates, and they would be distributed as discussed in point three.

If Son is not barred from inheriting from his parents, their estates pass to him and Daughter as described at the end of point one.

Point three: (15–25%)

If Son is barred from inheriting from Wife, her estate passes to her heirs, Granddaughter and Daughter. If Son is barred from inheriting from Husband, his one-half share passes to Granddaughter.

Wife's estate: As noted above, if Husband is treated as having survived Wife, he takes her entire estate under the terms of her last will, and it will be distributed to those entitled to take his estate. If he is treated as having predeceased her, her estate passes to her heirs, Son and Daughter, unless Son is barred from inheriting from Wife. The bequest to Husband is not saved by a lapse statute because those statutes do not apply to bequests to spouses. If Son is barred, he is treated as having predeceased Wife. Under intestate succession statutes, Son's child, Granddaughter, takes by right of representation the one-half share Son would have taken.

Husband's estate: As noted above, if Husband is treated as having survived Wife, his estate passes to the beneficiaries named in his will, Son and Daughter, unless Son is barred from inheriting Husband's estate. If Son is barred, the question arises whether Son's one-half share passes to Granddaughter, Son's child, or to Daughter, the other beneficiary named in Husband's will. As noted above, when a person is barred from inheriting because he feloniously and intentionally killed another, the victim's estate passes as if the killer predeceased the victim.

The argument for Granddaughter is that Husband's will did not expressly condition the gift to Son and Daughter on survivorship and that his will did not provide that the share of either who predeceased him should pass to the survivor. Furthermore, under the typical state antilapse statute, the share of any deceased beneficiary, such as Son, passes to that beneficiary's surviving issue unless the will otherwise provides. Under this analysis, Son's one-half share passes to Granddaughter.

Daughter, however, might argue that Son's one-half share passes to her under the "residue-of-a-residue" rule. Under this rule, a residuary bequest that fails to take effect ordinarily passes to the surviving residuary legatee. If the analysis ends there, Daughter takes all of Husband's estate. However, under the Uniform Probate Code, Granddaughter would take the share that Son would have taken, because the code provides that the antilapse statute prevails over the rule regarding multiple residuary legatees.

Question 14 Analysis

- ❐ Allotted time, wrote down time by when you needed to finish.
- ❐ Went in order, focused solely on this essay.
- ❐ Read the call of the question.
- ❐ Briefly outlined the issues, rules, and key facts.
- ❐ Made the essay look professional (headings, white space, paragraph indentations).
- ❐ Used the CRAC paradigm.
- ❐ Used transitional phrases.
- ❐ If time, proofed answer and made neat revisions.
- ❐ When finished, took a deep breath.
- ❐ Identified take-home points:

1.

2.

3.

Legal problems

1. Did Pres have the real or apparent authority to bind Wareco and, if not, is he personally liable to Able?

2. Did Pres have the real or apparent authority to bind Wareco to Beta and, if so, is he liable to Wareco?

3. Is Wareco liable on the contract with Rancher either because Pres had real or apparent authority or as a result of Sec's erroneous certificate?

Discussion

The facts are clear that Wareco acted promptly to repudiate each of the unauthorized contracts. This eliminates any argument that Wareco had accepted any benefits from the contracts or that Able, Beta, or Rancher had detrimentally relied upon Wareco's execution of the contracts, and that, therefore, the contracts would be binding on Wareco regardless of their unauthorized nature.

Point one: (25–35%)

The January board resolution denied Pres any real authority to enter into the contract with Able. Apparent authority would exist only if a reasonable person in Able's position would believe authority existed. Without real or apparent authority, Pres did not bind Wareco, but did bind himself by breaching his implied warranty of authority.

An agent may bind a principal to a contract if the agent is acting within his real or apparent authority. Real authority may be expressed or implied to the agent by the principal. In this case, no real authority existed because Wareco expressly stated in the board resolution that Pres had no authority to enter into contracts for this amount without prior board approval. Apparent authority exists if the conduct of a principal leads a third party reasonably to believe that the agent has the authority. By electing Pres president, Wareco may have led reasonable third parties to believe that Pres had authority to enter into transactions in the ordinary course of Wareco's business. Even though the nature of the transaction suggests that it was in the ordinary course of business, the number of trucks compared to the size of Wareco's current fleet made the transaction extraordinary. This should have put Able on notice that no authority existed. Thus, Pres had neither real nor apparent authority, and Wareco is not liable to Able.

An agent purporting to act on behalf of a principal, but lacking authority, becomes liable on the contract for breaching his implied warranty of authority. Because Pres had no real or apparent authority, he is personally liable to Able for breach of his implied warranty of authority.

Point two: (25–35%)

The March board resolution denied Pres real authority to enter into the contract with Beta. However, apparent authority existed given the ordinary nature of the transaction, and Wareco is therefore bound. Because Pres bound Wareco when he was directed not to, he is liable to Wareco.

As stated in point one, an agent can bind a principal if operating within his real or apparent authority. Pres lacked real authority to purchase the forklift because the March board resolution instructed him not to enter into this transaction. Apparent authority existed, however, because a reasonable person in Beta's position would believe that the president of Wareco had authority to enter into this ordinary transaction. Thus, Wareco is liable to Beta on the contract.

An agent who injures his principal by acting beyond the principal's manifestation of consent is liable to the principal. In this case, Pres entered into the contract with Beta despite the disapproval of the board of directors of Wareco. Since Wareco became bound on this contract by the act of Pres beyond his real authority, Pres is liable to Wareco.

Point three: (25–35%)

Although Pres had no real authority because the consent resolution was not unanimous and, absent Sec's certificate, had no apparent authority because the transaction was extraordinary, Wareco is bound because Sec had the authority to give the certificate which created apparent authority in Pres.

To be effective, a written consent in lieu of a directors' meeting typically requires signatures of all of the directors. Because the consent resolution in this situation was not signed by all of the directors, it was ineffective. Pres, therefore, had no real authority because the purchase price exceeded the $1,000,000 limitation contained in the January resolution.

In the absence of Sec's certificate, Pres had no apparent authority because the purchase of a $2,000,000 herd of cattle was not ordinary for this corporation. Rancher could not reasonably believe that the president of a commercial warehouse corporation would have the authority to make such a purchase on behalf of a corporation.

However, delivery of Sec's certificate created apparent authority. The secretary of a corporation has the authority to authenticate records of the corporation. Sec erroneously authenticated a resolution approving the execution by Pres of the contract with Rancher. Although this authentication was not accurate, it binds Wareco, and Rancher may rely on the authority of Pres indicated in the authenticated resolution. Therefore, Wareco is liable on the contract with Rancher.

Question 15 Analysis

- ❏ Allotted time, wrote down time by when you needed to finish.
- ❏ Went in order, focused solely on this essay.
- ❏ Read the call of the question.
- ❏ Briefly outlined the issues, rules, and key facts.
- ❏ Made the essay look professional (headings, white space, paragraph indentations).
- ❏ Used the CRAC paradigm.
- ❏ Used transitional phrases.
- ❏ If time, proofed answer and made neat revisions.
- ❏ When finished, took a deep breath.
- ❏ Identified take-home points:

1.

2.

3.

Legal problems

1. What enforcement rights does Collection Agency have on the overdue note?

2. Can Investor raise Bank's failure to make a second loan as a defense to his obligation to pay the note?

3. Can Software raise Bank's failure to make a further loan as a defense to its obligation to pay the note?

Point one: (30–35%)

Collection Agency is the holder of the note and is thus a person entitled to enforce it. Because the note was overdue on its face when Collection Agency acquired it, Collection Agency had notice that it was overdue and is not a holder in due course ("HDC").

Because Collection Agency is in possession of a negotiable instrument (the note) payable to it by virtue of Bank's endorsement, Collection Agency is the holder of the note. As a holder of the note, Collection Agency is a person entitled to enforce the instrument. It is irrelevant that Collection Agency purchased the note for far less than its face amount.

Collection Agency is not, however, a HDC of the note. To be an HDC, Collection Agency must give value for the note in good faith and without notice of claims or defenses to the note. Collection Agency gave value for the instrument; $150,000 is value, even though it is less than the face amount of the note. There is nothing to suggest that Collection Agency did not act in good faith.

However, the note was overdue on its face. Thus, Collection Agency would be deemed to have had notice that the note was overdue at the time it took possession of the note. A person who takes an instrument with notice that the instrument is overdue cannot be a HDC. Thus, Collection Agency is not a HDC and can enforce the note only as a holder and by asserting whatever rights Bank had to enforce the note. As a transferee from Bank, Collection Agency takes any right of the transferor to enforce the instrument.

Point two: (30–35%)

Because Investor's agreement to undertake an obligation on the note was expressly conditioned on Bank's promise to make a further loan to Software and Bank breached that promise, Investor can raise that agreement as a defense to payment and is not obligated to pay the note.

By signing the note as co-maker, Investor became a maker or issuer of the note. An issuer is generally obliged to pay an instrument according to its terms at the time it was issued to a person entitled to enforce the instrument. Thus, Investor has a general obligation to pay the note to Collection Agency, a person entitled to enforce it.

However, because Collection Agency is not a HDC, its right to enforce the obligation of Investor is subject to all of Investor's defenses, including any defenses stated in Article 3. Article 3 includes a defense based on the separate agreement between Bank and Investor. Article 3 provides that the obligation of a party to an instrument to pay the instrument may be modified, supplemented, or nullified by a separate agreement of the obligor and a person entitled to enforce the instrument, if the instrument is issued or the obligation is incurred in reliance on the agreement or as part of the same transaction giving rise to the agreement. To the extent an obligation is modified, supplemented, or nullified by an agreement under this section, the agreement is a defense to the obligation.

Here, Investor incurred an obligation on the note in reliance upon the agreement of Bank (a person entitled to enforce the instrument at the time it was issued) to make a further loan to Software if one became necessary. The case is similar to the situation discussed in a comment to the UCC in which a co-maker on a note signs only on condition that the creditor seek another co-maker. The UCC effectively provides that the separate agreement modifies the terms of the note by stating a condition to the obligation of the Obligor to pay the note. If the condition is not met, the Obligor is not obligated to pay the note to the original creditor or to any subsequent holder who is not a HDC course. Investor undertook the obligation as co-maker only on the condition that Bank would make additional loans up to $250,000 if necessary to complete the project. Bank's failure to do so provides a defense to Investor against Bank and against subsequent holders without due course rights.

The UCC is subject to state law regarding the exclusion of proof of contemporaneous or previous agreements. However, the problem states that applicable state law allows such proof. Thus, Investor has a valid defense against payment of the note.

Point three: (30–35%)

Investor's defense to payment of the note is personal to Investor, and Software may not raise that defense against Collection Agency. Software does not appear to have any other defense and therefore must pay the note.

Investor's defense against payment of the note is not available to Software. Although Software may raise personal defenses, Software may not assert against the person entitled to enforce the instrument a defense of another person. Here, the agreement between Investor and Bank was kept secret from Software until after it obtained the loan. It was not part of the inducement leading to Software's decision to incur the debt. Under the circumstances, any defense provided by that agreement is personal to Investor and cannot be raised by Software against a person entitled to enforce the instrument.

Software might claim that Bank acted in bad faith in refusing to make the separate loan and that Bank's bad faith is a defense that can be raised against Collection Agency, as a non-HDC. Certainly, Bank's refusal to make a second loan after promising that it would do so may be characterized as bad faith. However, any bad faith would be attributable solely to the fact that failure to make the loan was a breach of the agreement with Investor. There is no suggestion that failure to make a further loan was bad faith vis-a-vis Software. Furthermore, there is no hint that Software told Bank a second loan would be necessary or that Software acted in reliance on Bank's stated willingness to make further loans. To the contrary, Software believed that the initial loan was all that was necessary, and Bank apparently agreed with Software. Thus, Software would not appear to have an independent defense to payment of the loan. Because it cannot raise Investor's defense to avoid its own obligation, Software is liable to Collection Agency on the note.

Suggested Take-Home Points For Practice Essays

Question 1

- For a cause of action with elements, start and finish with your overall conclusion. Provide an umbrella rule introducing the elements immediately after your first overall conclusion.

- After stating elements in an umbrella rule, address each element one at a time, using a separate CRAC for each element.

- This question only has one call; an explicit answer to the call is provided at both the beginning and end of the essay.

- Headings are used to break up the answer, element-by-element, to make the answer reader friendly.

Question 2

- This question has only one call; if you have a question with only one call, look for at least two or three issues to discuss.

- The answer is divided with subheadings into three issues to make it reader friendly.

- Students often struggle with where to place counterarguments so that they flow smoothly in their answers. Treat counterarguments as part of the "A" in CRAC; add them after making the arguments they counter in the analysis.

- Within the discussion of a single issue, you also have the option of using sub-CRACs, as in the sample answer for the effect of a misrepresentation.

Question 3

- This question focuses on a tort with elements like question 1. Again, organize these types of questions with an overall conclusion at the beginning and end. Use an umbrella rule setting out the elements directly after the first overall conclusion. Then, use a separate CRAC to address each individual element.

Question 4

- Students often struggle with integrating procedural and substantive information such as that used in this answer. State the procedural standard up front in its own section, and then proceed with the substantive analysis.

- This offense has three requirements; address each requirement with a separate CRAC.

- Sometimes bar exam questions don't provide enough information to answer a question. In that case, use a phrase like "there is no indication that [state missing fact]" to provide a basis for answering the question.

Question 5

- This question asks whether a judgment may be vacated. State the overall conclusion at the beginning, followed immediately by the procedural standard for vacating a judgment. Then, all the substantive bases for vacating a judgment can be stated in an umbrella rule section, and each can be addressed in a separate CRAC.

Question 6

- This is what we would consider a "left-field" question. It is atypical for bar examiners to ask a question for which the majority of jurisdictions don't recognize a cause of action. Note that it would be accurate to simply state: "No, Harry will not succeed with an alienation of affections action because the cause of action is not recognized in the majority of jurisdictions." But, that would not be enough to obtain full credit for the question. Thus, in these types of questions, we recommend addressing another angle as an add-on. Here, the logical add-on is what the analysis would be in the minority of jurisdictions that do recognize the cause of action. You should, however, make it clear what the result would be under the majority rule at both the beginning and end of your essay.

- Organize this answer like the answers to questions 1 and 3: Provide your overall conclusion at the beginning and end, an umbrella rule setting out the three elements immediately after your first overall conclusion, and a separate CRAC for each element.

Question 7

- Again, the overall conclusion is stated at both the beginning and end of the answer.

- This question combines a procedural standard (motion to quash and vacate) with a substantive standard (substituted service under a state statute). As in question 4, state the procedural standard up front, immediately after the first overall conclusion, and then use a CRAC to address the substantive issue.

- Note that there is only one substantive issue—substituted service under the state statute—with no obvious subtopics. So, organize the discussion of the substantive issue with one large CRAC.

Question 8

- This question raises only one legal issue with subtopics: the requirements for obtaining specific performance. Accordingly, start and end the answer with an overall conclusion and address each requirement for specific performance with a separate CRAC.

Question 9

- This question uses two calls; thus, the topics of the two calls are used as headings to organize the essay and make it reader friendly.

- Sometimes you may encounter calls that are imprecise or misleading. If asked whether parties can "bring any causes of action," an accurate answer is simply "yes" (because, of course they could file an action, but that doesn't necessarily mean they'll be able to even proceed with their claims much less prevail). The examiners for this question, however, likely wanted students to explain whether the parties would be able to able to prevail with any causes of action. Accordingly, we encourage you to use common sense when reading calls. For example, for this question we recommend you read the calls as: "Analyze all claims Eddie and Molly might bring, including whether they'll prevail."

- For this type of hypothetical, organize your answer by parties and causes of action.

Question 10

- For this type of question, organize an answer by the different rule violations.

- Some CRACs are short (one paragraph), while others are long (several paragraphs). The length of your CRACs will depend on the specific legal context for your answer.

- An overall conclusion is provided at the beginning and end of the answer.

- The answer points out one missing piece of information that students would need to fully answer the question: the standard attorney fees in the area. Bar examiners expect students to point out such missing information. (Contrast this, however, with adding or changing factual information, which should not be done unless examiners specifically instruct students to do so.).

Question 11

- Question 11 contains four calls; thus use them as the topics for the headings in the answer and use four CRACs.

- Notice how the headings make the answer look professional and make it reader friendly.

Question 12

- Like question 11, question 12 has several calls. So, again, use the topics in each call as headings in the answer.

- An overall conclusion is provided at the beginning and end of the essay answer.

APPENDIX G

MPT POINT SHEET FOR SAMPLE QUESTION[12]

The NCBE provides "point sheets" for its sample MPT questions that describe the factual and legal points encompassed within assigned lawyering tasks. They are provided to user jurisdictions for the sole purpose of assisting graders by identifying issues and suggesting resolutions contemplated by the drafters. The point sheets are not, however, official grading guides or model answers. In fact, examinees can receive a range of passing grades without discussing all the issues on the point sheets. Because grading is the exclusive responsibility of jurisdictions using the MPT, jurisdictions are free to modify the point sheets.[13]

In Re Steven Wallace
Point Sheet

In this performance test item, Steven Wallace, an artist, delivers a painting to Lottie Zelinka, an art dealer, on consignment. Lottie files bankruptcy under Chapter 11 and later converts it to a straight Chapter 7 case. Thereafter, she returns the painting to Steven, and the trustee demands that Steven return the painting to the bankrupt estate. Steven consults Eva Morales, the supervising attorney in this case.

The task for the applicant is to draft a two-part memo in which he or she first analyzes the facts and the law regarding the bankruptcy trustee's claim that the painting is an estate asset and, second, identifies what UCC defenses are available to Steven, explains how the facts currently known support the defenses, and suggests what additional facts might be developed to support the defenses.

---

12. Reprinted from the July 1999 MPT exam with permission from the NCBE. Copyright © 2000, all rights reserved. The point sheet is also available at www.ncbex.org/tests/mpt/pdf/MPT07_1999_Test.pdf (last visited May 7, 2005).

13. *Id.*

The file consists of the assignment memo from Ms. Morales to the applicant, notes of the interview with Steven, and some documents Steven left with Ms. Morales. The library contains excerpts from a basic bankruptcy treatise, section 2-326 of the Franklin Commercial Code (FCC), a section of the Franklin Civil Code, and two cases. All of the materials the applicants need to work their way through the problem are provided.

The following points that might be discussed by an applicant are suggested by the problem. Grades will be assigned depending on the degree of thoroughness, and an applicant can get an excellent grade without covering all of these points.

1. **Based on the facts as they appear in the file, does the bankruptcy trustee have a legitimate claim to the painting?**

The facts make it clear that the painting was redelivered to Steven by Lottie after the bankruptcy proceeding began. Thus, she made a "post-petition transfer" of property that was in the possession of the bankruptcy estate.

Drawing on the excerpts from *Walker on Bankruptcy* and *In re Levy*, the applicants should conclude that the trustee has the right to avoid a transfer of property of the estate that occurs after the commencement of the case. *Walker on Bankruptcy* section 4.08.

The real question then becomes whether the painting was "property of the estate." That calls for an in-depth analysis of the FCC provision on consignments, section 2-326.

The interview notes and the Inventory Receipt show clearly that Steven (consignor) delivered the painting to Lottie (consignee) on a true consignment; i.e., he delivered it to her to see if she could sell it for him, he retained title, she would get a commission if she could sell it, and she could return it without obligation if she couldn't sell it. Thus, it was a "sale or return" transaction under FCC section 2-326.

Unless one or more of the exceptions provided for in section 2-326(3) applies, the FCC makes it clear that "goods held on sale or return are subject to [claims of the consignee's creditors] while in the [consignee's] possession," irrespective of whether the consignor (Steven) retained title. This point is fully discussed in the *First National Bank* and *Levy* cases, and the applicants should have no problem understanding the concept.

Thus, on the face of it, the trustee, standing as he does in the shoes of a lien creditor of Artists' Exchange, has a legitimate claim to the painting.

2. **The defenses and the current and additional facts that might support them.**

Known facts: The applicants should discuss each of the defenses under the section 2-326(3) exceptions and whatever known facts there are to support them; and, if there are no supporting facts, simply say so and move on.

The "sign law" exception (section 2-326(3)(a)) probably doesn't apply on the known facts. Although Steven put a 2" x 3" label on the back of the painting identifying himself as the owner, it is not likely that it was "posted conspicuously" within the meaning of Franklin Civil Code section 3533. See also the discussion in *Levy* as to whether the label was calculated to inform creditors or just possible customers. Whether there was a sign posted by Lottie in the front window (as Steven seems to "think" there was) is not known at this point.

There is no basis, on the facts currently known, to conclude that it was generally known to [Lottie's] creditors that she was substantially engaged in selling goods of others. It is arguable that the very name of the art gallery, "Artists' Exchange," communicates such a notion and that the sign Steven "thinks" he saw in the window (*i.e.*, "All offers will be considered and forwarded to the artists") does too, but there are not enough facts currently known. Thus, the section 2-326(3)(b) exception doesn't help at this stage.

There is no current information that Steven filed a UCC financing statement, so there is no basis for invoking the section 2-326(3)(c) exception.

The strongest defense based on the known facts is that the painting, before Steven delivered it to Lottie, was "used...for personal, family, or household purposes," and that the exception in section 2-326(3)(d) applies.[14] The interview notes are ambiguous on that point. On the one hand, they show that Steven had the painting hanging in his dining room and hadn't thought about selling it until Lottie suggested it. It is also helpful that Steven and his wife had purchased a new rug with colors that complemented the colors in the painting; this is evidence that they intended to keep the painting for personal use. On the other hand, it is clear enough that Steven did regularly sell his paintings. More facts are needed on what their intentions were.

Additional facts, sources, and why the additional facts are important: The notion in this part of the test item is to require applicants to scour materials for facts that are hinted at in the file and library, focusing on facts that would help invoke the protective exceptions listed in section 2-326(3).

Whether Steven filed a UCC financing statement.

Why important: Although it is not probable that he did file a financing statement, it does not appear affirmatively from the facts that Ms. Morales even asked the question. It would help if he had because it would invoke the exception of section 2-326(3)(c) and might get him home free.

Sources: Ask Steven himself or make a search with the Secretary of State's office or other public filing offices.

Whether the painting can persuasively be characterized as goods used for personal, family, or household purposes.

Why important: If that can be shown, it will, without more, invoke the protective exception of section 2-326(3)(d) and establish Steven's right to keep the painting. The footnote in *First National Bank* suggests the inquiry, and it is possible that, as to this painting, Steven might still be a "casual collector." After all, he has only recently retired to go into painting full time.

Sources: Get the facts from Steven and Ella, his wife. The interview notes suggest that, even though Steven regularly sold some of his paintings, perhaps there are some he painted and intended to keep for his own personal use. Check whatever records he maintains because they may help to show that some of his paintings (*e.g.*, the ones he hangs in his home) are intended for "personal, family, or household purposes." Ascertain what discussions they had about keeping the painting when they purchased the rug to complement the colors in the painting. Identify what other paintings, if any, they intended to keep for themselves as opposed to selling.

Whether Lottie dba Artists' Exchange was in fact substantially engaged in selling goods of others.

Why important: The threshold question is whether Lottie's business was in fact predominantly a consignment business. If so, then the applicant can proceed to the inquiry

---

14. The NCBE noted that this exception, found in the library version of 2-326, is not part of the official version of the UCC. It is part of the California UCC and was included by the NCBE because it makes a good test issue. *Id.*

regarding whether the general creditors knew it sufficiently to invoke the protective exception. This inquiry is prompted by Steven's suggestion during the interview that most of the art at Artists' Exchange was on consignment and that most artists he knows of deal with galleries on a consignment basis.

Sources: Lottie herself is probably the best source of this information. The property schedules filed with the court will at least identify the inventory of art and maybe even whether a particular item was on consignment or owned by Lottie. The consignors are also creditors (*see First National Bank*), so they will have to be listed on the bankruptcy schedules as well. The schedules will furnish their names and addresses in case it becomes necessary to contact them directly. The question whether art galleries in general do business predominantly on a consignment basis may be a subject for expert testimony, so a suggestion that an expert be consulted as a source for this information would be in order.

Whether the general creditors of Lottie dba Artists' Exchange knew that the gallery sold predominantly the goods of others.

Why important: Proof of such "general knowledge" is essential to the invocation of the protective exception of section 2-326(3)(b). *See First National Bank* and *Levy*. If it can be shown, it will get Steven home free.

Sources: The bankruptcy schedules will disclose the names and addresses of all the creditors. It may be necessary to contact the bulk of them to find out what they knew when they extended credit. Perceptive applicants might distinguish *First National Bank*. There, the court found that the knowledge of other consignors was irrelevant to the knowledge of "general" creditors. Here, if it can be shown that almost all of Lottie's creditors were consignors, as is suggested in the footnote in *First National Bank*, then their knowledge is relevant to establish general knowledge. Ask Lottie and check correspondence and other records of communication between Lottie and her creditors for the possibility that the extent of her dealing in the goods of others was disclosed to her creditors. Steven said during the interview that he *thinks* there was a sign posted in the front window of the gallery to the effect that, "All offers will be considered and forwarded to the artists." If so, that could be evidence of notice to creditors that Lottie was selling the goods of others. The very name of the gallery, Artists' Exchange, is another source of the knowledge of the creditors. It suggests that Lottie is dealing in the goods of others and that the creditors must therefore have known it. Finally, expert testimony might help establish that creditors of art galleries were on constructive notice because almost all galleries do business on a consignment basis.

Whether there was a sign such as Steven thinks he saw in the front window of the gallery.

Why important: It can serve two purposes: (1) to establish that the general creditors knew that Lottie was dealing predominantly in the goods of others, thus bringing into play section 2-326(3)(b), and (2) as evidence of compliance with the "sign law" (Franklin Civil Code section 3533). Either one will get Steven home free.

Sources: Perhaps a visit to the gallery will show that the sign is still there. Lottie herself can be asked about it. Inquiry can be made of the "general" creditors, including other consignors whose names and addresses can be obtained from the bankruptcy schedules. Photographs, if any, of the front of the gallery might be a source. If the sign was purchased by Lottie, perhaps the vendor can be ascertained and asked about it.

Whether other consignors of art filed UCC financing statements.

Why important: If any significant number of the other consignors filed financing statements, it could be argued that the public nature of such filings served at least constructive notice of the fact that some substantial portion of Lottie's business was dealing in the goods of others. This, too, would help invoke the protective exception of section 2-326(3)(b).

Sources: The other consignors and secured creditors, whose names and addresses can be obtained from the bankruptcy schedules, can be asked directly or a search can be made of the filings at the Secretary of State's office. This will help establish the breadth of constructive knowledge imputable to other creditors.

Whether any of the other consignors of art complied with the "sign law."

Why important: If enough of them did so effectively, it would be evidence that there was at least a form of public notice that the goods of others were in Lottie's gallery. And, if it were widespread enough, it could be argued that it imparted knowledge to the general creditors. It would, however, have to be shown that the signs were intended to impart knowledge to others than the customers of the gallery. *But see Levy* (small cards kept with the shoes satisfied neither the sign law nor the general knowledge requirements).

Sources: Again, the other consignors would be the best source of this information. Their identities can be obtained from the bankruptcy schedules. Lottie might also be able to provide information on this point.

APPENDIX H

MORE PRACTICE QUESTIONS

More Sample State-Created Essays

State-created essay exams and model answers are often available as samples, and there are several ways to obtain them. You can contact your state's licensing entity (see appendix B for contact information) and ask if past exams and answers are available and, if so, how to obtain them. Law schools also frequently have old essay exams. Check in your law school library or with your school's office of student affairs or academic support. Many states also post old exams on Web sites. Several such Web sites are listed below; also check your state's Web site listed in appendix B. To obtain the most up-to-date Web information, we recommend that you do an Internet search for your state's bar exam to find all information available on the Web.

Web Sites with Bar Exam Questions

The State Bar of California, *Essay Questions and Selected Answers*, *Performance Tests and Selected Answers*, www.calbar.ca.gov/state/calbar/calbar_generic.jsp?cid=10115&id=1010 (California bar exam).

Drake University Law School, *Bar Examination Preparation*, www.law.drake.edu/students/default.aspx?pageID=barExamPreparation#previousBar (exam questions from Minnesota, Arkansas, Delaware, New York, Ohio, Pennsylvania, Texas, and Vermont).

FindLaw, *For Students, The Bar, Sample Bar Exams*, at www.stu.findlaw.com/thebar/samplebar.html (essay questions from Arkansas, Delaware, Maryland, Minnesota, and Texas bar exams).

Florida Board of Bar Examiners, *Study Guide*, www.floridabarexam.org/public/main.nsf/SG0305.PDF/$file/SG0305.PDF (Florida bar exam study guide with sample questions and answers).

George Mason University School of Law, *State Bar Exam Resources*, www.law.gmu.edu/academics/bar-va.html#va (Virginia bar exam).

George Mason University School of Law, *State Bar Exam Resources*, www.law.gmu.edu/academics/bar-va.html#other (bar exam essay questions from thirteen states—Arkansas, California, Delaware, Florida, Georgia, Massachusetts, Maryland, Minnesota, New York, Ohio, Pennsylvania, Texas, and Vermont).

University of Idaho College of Law, Online Bar Essay Questions, www.law.uidaho.edu/baressayquestions (bar exam essay questions from twenty-one states: Alaska, Arkansas, California, Connecticut, Delaware, Florida, Georgia, Kentucky, Maryland, Massachusetts, Minnesota, Missouri, New Jersey, New Mexico, New York, Ohio, Oklahoma, Pennsylvania, Texas, Vermont, and Virginia).

Maryland State Board of Law Examiners, *Exam Questions and Answers*, www.courts.state.md.us/ble/examques&ans.html (Maryland bar exam questions and answers).

University of Miami Law Library, *Bar Exam Preparation*, www.library.law.Miami.edu/barguide.html (Florida bar exam).

New Jersey Board of Bar Examiners, *Recent Results, Sample Bar Exam Questions and Answers*, www.njbarexams.org (New Jersey bar exam).

Vermont Judiciary, *Board of Bar Examiners*, www.dol.state.vt.us/www_root/000000/html/barexams.html (Vermont bar exam).

NCBE Web Site: Study Aids
Available For Free Or For Purchase

Test	Free	Available for Purchase
MBE:[15]	Information Booklet 30 mixed-subject questions	Sample I Feb. 1991 200 questions $15
		Sample II July 1991 200 questions $15
		Sample III July 1998 200 questions $15
		Questions 1992 581 questions from 1978–91 $25

---

15. Note that the MBE exams available for purchase list the subject tested in each question in the answer key section of the exam booklets.

Test	Free	Available for Purchase
MEE:	Information Booklet July 2003 exam 7 questions	Feb. & July 2004 7 questions $15
	July 1997 Exam 7 questions	Feb. & July 2003 7 questions $15
	Feb. 1997 Exam 7 questions	Feb. & July 2002 7 questions $15
	July 1996 Exam 7 questions	Feb. & July 2001 7 questions $15
	Feb. 1996 Exam 7 questions	Feb. & July 2000 7 questions $15
	July 1995 Exam 7 questions	MEE Five Pack 1999–2003 exams $60
	Feb. 1995 Exam 7 questions	

Test	Free	Available for Purchase
MPT:	Information Booklet Summaries of Feb. 2002– Feb. 2004 exam tasks	July and Feb. exams from 2001–04 available for individual purchase, $20 per exam
	July 2000 exam 3 questions	Five Pack Feb. 2002–Feb. 2004 exams $85
	Feb. 2000 exam 3 questions	
	July 1999 exam 3 questions	
	Feb. 1999 exam 3 questions	
	July 1998 exam 3 questions	
	Feb. 1998 exam 3 questions	
	July 1997 exam 3 questions	
	Feb. 1997 exam 3 questions	

Test	Free	Available for Purchase
MPRE:	Information Booklet 25 questions	Sample VI 150 questions $17.50
	Online Practice Exam 25 questions	

Subjects Tested in Free Online Exams

MBE 2005 Information Booklet	
Subjects:	Question numbers:
Constitutional law	4, 7, 10, 15, 20
Criminal law and procedure	8, 14, 21, 24, 27
Contracts (including sales)	5, 12, 13, 19, 23
Real property	3, 6, 16, 18, 29
Torts	1, 11, 17, 22, 26
Evidence	2, 9, 25, 28, 30

MPT Exams			
Exam Date:	Question Number:	Task:	Subject:
Feb. 1997	1	Persuasive pretrial brief	Torts
	2	Office memorandum	Professional responsibility
July 1997	1	Client opinion letter	Sales, UCC
	2	Persuasive trial brief	Evidence (criminal law)
Feb. 1998	1	Persuasive memorandum	Civil procedure
	2	Office memorandum	Constitutional law
July 1998	1	DA recommendation	Criminal procedure (professional responsibility)
	2	Client opinion letter	Corporations
Feb. 1999	1	Inner-office memorandum	Torts, agency
	2	Persuasive litigation memorandum	Wills (insane delusions, undue influence)
	3	Office memorandum	Real property
July 1999	1	Office memorandum	Bankruptcy, UCC
	2	Persuasive settlement letter	Family
	3	Will clauses	Wills

MEE Feb. 1995

Question:	Subject:
1	Commercial paper
2	Family law
3	Federal civil procedure
4	Agency, partnership
5	Decedents' estates
6	Conflicts
7	Sales, secured transactions

MEE July 1995

Question:	Subject:
1	Decedents' estates
2	Commercial paper, secured transactions
3	Conflicts, federal civil procedure
4	Corporations
5	Family law
6	Federal civil procedure
7	Trusts, future interests

MEE Feb. 1996

Question:	Subject:
1	Commercial paper
2	Decedents' estates
3	Family, conflicts
4	Federal civil procedure
5	Agency, partnership
6	Secured transactions
7	Trusts, future interests

MEE July 1996	
Question:	Subject:
1	Commercial paper
2	Agency, partnership
3	Decedents' estates
4	Federal civil procedure
5	Family, trusts, future interests
6	Secured transactions
7	Corporations

MEE Feb. 1997	
Question:	Subject:
1	Decedents' estates
2	Family law
3	Secured transactions
4	Agency, partnerships, corporations
5	Federal civil procedure, conflicts
6	Commercial paper
7	Trusts, future interests, decedents' estates, family law

MEE July 1997	
Question:	Subject:
1	Agency, partnership
2	Trusts
3	Commercial paper, secured transactions
4	Family law
5	Federal civil procedure
6	Corporations
7	Decedents' estates

| MEE July 2003 (from MEE 2005 Information Booklet) ||
Question:	Subject:
1	Corporations
2	Decedents' estates
3	Commercial paper
4	Federal civil procedure
5	Partnership
6	Family law
7	Secured transactions

INDEX